Jane Gunther

Original Copy

by the same author

JOHN DONNE: LIFE, MIND AND ART
THACKERAY: PRODIGAL GENIUS
THE VIOLENT EFFIGY: A STUDY OF DICKENS' IMAGINATION
THE FABER BOOK OF REPORTAGE (ED.)
WILLIAM GOLDING: THE MAN AND HIS BOOKS
A Tribute on his 75th Birthday (ED.)

Original Copy

Selected Reviews and Journalism 1969–1986

JOHN CAREY

faber and faber

LONDON · BOSTON

First published in 1987
by Faber and Faber Limited
3 Queen Square London WC1N 3AU

Typeset by Goodfellow & Egan Cambridge

Printed in Great Britain by
Mackays of Chatham Kent
All rights reserved

British Library Cataloguing in Publication Data

Carey, John
Original copy: selected reviews
and journalism 1969–1986.
1. Literature—History and criticism
I. Title
809   PN523

ISBN 0-571-14879-4

Contents

vi　Contents

Contents

Acknowledgements

For permission to reprint reviews and articles the publishers acknowledge the following with gratitude:

BBC Radio 3 for 'Queenie Leavis and the Common Pursuit'; Chatto and Windus for 'Mr Perry' from *People*; the *Listener* for 'On Leslie Thomas's novels', 'TV Reviews from the *Listener*, 1969–73', 'The Heavenly Hound', 'Socialist and Sahib', 'Messiahs and pigs'; the *New Review* for 'Down with Dons', 'Shall we prance?', 'Seer Sucker', 'Inferior soap'; *New Statesman* for 'Paper Tigers', 'Perish every laggard', 'How the style refines', 'Drunk with lilies', 'Friends of promise', 'What exactly do you mean?'; the *Sunday Times* for 'Vegetable Gardening', 'Keeping up with the Coopers', 'Growing up in Tunbridge Wells', 'Discreet charms of the aristocracy', 'Spotlight on the knee-tremblers', 'The last of Beatrice', 'The wife of Westminster', 'Educating John', 'What the workers had to lose', 'The long life of the happy family', 'The strange death of political language', 'Higher, bigger, madder', 'Pope's fallibility', 'Scott: a giant eclipsed', 'The truculent genius of Thomas Carlyle', 'A writer on the front line', 'How they destroyed Thackeray', 'Loti: a many-splendoured thing', 'Stevenson: the optimistic traveller', 'The man who stood for beer and liberty', 'A Victorian clerk's tale', 'The rhymes of the ancient mariner', 'The Czech who kept bouncing', 'The diseases of Thomas Mann', 'Edwin Muir: one foot in Eden', 'Eric, or Gigantic by Gigantic', 'Passionate contradictions', 'The mouse who made the mousetrap', 'Oxford's beer and baccy brigade', 'Sir Galahad of soppiness', 'East African alibis', 'Richard Aldington's septic psyche', 'A long season in hell', 'The disintegration of Sartre', 'Books, raw and cooked', 'Love and the laureate of death', 'A star looks down', 'Admissible evidence', 'The blackboard jumble', 'The flash of lightning', 'Death and the benefits of ignorance', 'The sport of a mad master', 'Larkin: poet of deprivation', 'The joy of Heaney', 'Bringing it all back home'; the *Tatler* for 'Schools at Oxford'; and the *Times Literary Supplement* for 'Viewpoint from the *TLS*'.

Introduction

One bonus of book reviewing is the mail you get from readers. Even when this is abusive or threatening it has, on balance, a reassuring effect since it tells you that someone is out there taking notice. And mail that expresses deeply infatuated personal attachment is, of course, even more acceptable.

As important as the content of the letters, though, is what they look like. Typed or word-processed items, with immaculate layouts, score lower points, from the angle of the reviewer's self-esteem, than chunkily folded handwritten sheets in ill-fitting envelopes bearing provincial postmarks. These raw packets always set a reviewer's spirits soaring because they allow him to feel (momentarily, at any rate) that he has at last made contact with that legendary creature, the General Reader.

Admittedly, this often turns out to be an illusion. You find, on inspection, that the letters have come from titled ladies, or reproachful authors, or lunatics. Admittedly, too, the hope of getting through to the General Reader is not the only thing that keeps reviewers going. Book reviewing is an addictive drug, and reviewers who try to break the habit experience harrowing withdrawal symptons, ranging from identity crisis to severe loss of income. Still, this addictive power is itself bound up with the appeal of writing for the large, indistinct public which lies beyond the sheltered islands of the scholarly, the professionally bookish and the metropolitan.

All the pieces in this book were written in the belief that there is no point in reviewing unless your reviews arouse interest in people who would not otherwise be interested. As anyone who progresses beyond this Introduction will soon discover, a recurrent theme in the book is the contention that English writing in the twentieth century has persistently catered for minorities and élites to the exclusion of a large potential readership of ordinary, intelligent people who have developed, over the years, a thoroughly understandable dislike of 'culture' and the 'cultured'.

Winning this readership back is an important part of the

reviewer's job, and it naturally entails writing hostile reviews as well as favourable ones, when a suitable target breaks cover. I have included some samples of the hostile in this selection, partly to make it representative, and partly because the indications are that they cheer readers up. 'Good, she needed a poke in the nose,' wrote one jubilant lady after reading my appraisal of Lady Mosley's *Loved Ones*. This zest for public execution may seem a bit gruesome, but it undeniably shows that interest and enthusiasm have been stirred.

The pieces I have chosen fall into four categories. The first batch are, broadly speaking, autobiographical. I have included these because it seems to me that, given the subjective nature of literary judgement, the reader has a right to know what sort of person will be laying down the law in the rest of the book – what his quirks and prejudices are, and what sort of background has formed him. All critical books might with advantage, I think, be prefaced by a section of this kind, just as all books of social commentary should carry up-to-date information about the author's income and property-holdings. This would save the reader a lot of time, since he would know from the start how much of the book's contents he could automatically discount.

After the autobiographical section comes a selection of book reviews which reflect generally on the cultural state of England in our century. Then there is a brief Part Three of clips from what seems, in retrospect, a long slog of monthly TV reviewing for the *Listener*. Finally, in the fourth section, the angle is more literary, and the pieces are arranged in chronological order according to the books or authors dealt with, stretching from Alexander Pope to Craig Raine.

The papers in which these pieces have appeared include the *Listener*, the *New Review*, the *New Statesman* and the *Times Literary Supplement*, and 'Mr Perry' was written for an anthology called *People* which Susan Hill edited in aid of Oxfam. But by far the greater part of the book's contents are from the *Sunday Times*, where I have worked under three literary editors, John Whitley, Claire Tomalin and Penny Perrick. To each of them for their unstinting encouragement and advice, and to Xandra Hardie, who helped me pick the pieces, I should like to express my warm gratitude.

PART ONE
Self

Paper Tigers

The only periodical I have ever read from cover to cover over a considerable period, and venerated even to the extent of making artistic water-colour copies of its more striking illustrations, was called the *The Wide World Magazine*. My father subscribed to it when I was eleven or twelve years old. Published by George Newnes Ltd, it appeared monthly, and everything in it was true. A stern note to contributors on the first page advised them that they should submit their adventures (accompanied by a stamped addressed envelope) only if they were absolutely authentic in every detail. The first page also carried a greyish sketch of the globe (designated 'The Unique "Wide World" Contents Map'), which had labelled arrows stuck into different bits of it so that the reader could see at a glance what far-flung spots the month's narratives issued from.

The range was unfailingly impressive. In the tundra, in the outback, in the Malaysian jungles, along the North-West frontier – wherever, indeed, a straight left could be thrown or a machete wielded – the *Wide World*'s contributors were to be found. They slipped down ravines and precipitated themselves from speeding trains. They were overwhelmed by avalanches and tossed by typhoons. They bounded through forest fires dressed as Canadian Mounted Police; they donned divers' helmets and grappled with octopuses. Their destruction of wildlife was prodigious. Wolves, sea-lions, elephants, polar bears, elks, emus, giant tortoises, and the whole tribe of greater and lesser cats, were subdued, month after month, with implements ranging from the lariat to the machine-gun.

At the time of my acquaintance with the magazine, the Second World War happened to be on, so a sprinkling of Huns and Japs mingled with the more traditional quarry. But they never, as I recollect, counted for much among all the fur and feather. Then there were the natives – a staple ingredient – big black fellows and wily little ones; turbaned, grass-skirted, or carrying luggage on their heads. Their discomfiture when they were rumbled in some petty crime, or found themselves face to face with a man-eater on a jungle track yielded endless laughs; and when they gathered in bands and turned nasty, as they often did, they supplied the resident *Wide World* contributor with an invaluable occasion for coolness and bloodshed. They had, too, their mystic streak. A regular feature in the magazine, entitled 'The Queer Side of Things', comprised accounts of voodoo, witch-doctoring, fatal curses and suchlike foreign devilry, generally culminating in reflections by the narrator upon life's inscrutability.

Each story had about half-a-dozen monochrome pictures, with captions drawn from the tale itself. These portrayed the narrative highspots ('I whipped my right to his jaw with every ounce of strength I possessed', or, more simply, 'I shot him in the chest'). Alternatively they afforded a view of the local population ('Dancing savages were silhouetted against the flames'), or of the fauna ('I saw two enormous crocodiles biting at the pontoon bridge'). But the pictorial glory of the magazine was its front cover, shiny, polychrome, and different each month. There enraged whales splintered open boats; assegai and pith helmet clashed with claw and fang; and landslides slid.

The advertisement pages reflected the *Wide World*'s masculine bias, and provided an enthralling literary experience on their own account. Apart from standard items like shaving-sticks, self-stropping razors and braces ('Sartorial Suspension a Surety'), there were countless expedients for acquiring soundness in wind and limb, such as the Litesome Supporter Belt, which guaranteed 'Commando Fitness' to those it encircled, or, for the academically inclined, the Institute of Breathing Postal Course ('One of our most famous Generals writes: "Your rhythmical breathing revives one physically in the most amazing way" '). Wartime had given literacy a boost, and the adverts invited you to send up for a multiplicity of practical manuals which would renovate your system completely, from the memory to the bladder. I particularly coveted *Constipation and Our Civilization*, but the outlay (5/6d) was prohibitive. As a sort of adjunct to the adverts a column called 'Man and His Needs', written by 'The Captain', gave helpful chats on fishing tackle and other male necessaries ('Devotees of the briar are continually complaining to me about the scarcity and cost of decent pipes . . .'). To the twelve-year-old reader, it seemed the very stuff of adulthood. A correspondingly cordial note was struck by a section called 'The "Wide World" Brotherhood', which offered greetings from Wide Worlders beyond the seas, and a metal badge, obtainable by post.

In the interests of research I recently had some files of the magazine dredged up from the Bodleian stack, and was engulfed, the moment they arrived, in floods of nostalgia. They had been clamped between fat, rhubarb-coloured boards, and the pictorial covers, ripped off, were stuffed together at the back. It was like finding a piece of one's childhood pinned out in a museum. The *Wide World*'s first number, I discovered, appeared in April 1898. Its onslaught on the animal kingdom had commenced straightaway with 'The Romance of Seal Hunting' (by Sir George Baden-Powell) and 'A Battle Royal with a Tiger: A True Story'. The publishers promised 'weird adventures' and 'amazing photos', explaining that the supply was 'practically inexhaustible, thanks to the far-reaching arrangements we have made in both civilized and uncivilized countries'.

The magazine finally packed up in December 1965 – bizarre, really, to think that it hobbled on into the swinging Sixties at all. It must have looked odd on station bookstalls among the nudes, though as its jacket always bore the legend 'The Magazine for Men' I suppose its flagging circulation may have benefited occasionally from the mistakes of baffled porn hunters. The final number carried a pious editorial about the understanding the *Wide World* had fostered among peoples: 'to many youngsters in villages in the heart of Africa it has been an education.' Maybe: but in the days I knew it African youngsters would have met with a decidedly undignified view of themselves in its pages. No doubt I wasted time on it when my more precocious contemporaries were already pegging away at Proust and Dostoevsky. But I can't say I regret it. Proust and Dostoevsky could wait, and they are, anyway, short on tigers. Besides, the *Wide World* taught me that the world was wide, heroic, infinitely diverse, teeming with inexhaustible life, and ruled by the British. I must have been one of the last children lucky enough to believe any of that.

                                                                      1977

Mr Perry

One of the things I have always disliked about William Morris is that he is rude (at the start of *News from Nowhere*) about Hammersmith Bridge. For those unlucky enough not to know it, Hammersmith Bridge is a dignified Victorian structure, crowned with small but ornate pinnacles, which joins Middlesex to Surrey. When I was a child it was a source of intense and unmitigated delight. For one thing, being a suspension bridge it wobbled when buses went across. There you would be, clutching a parental hand high over the Thames, when suddenly the pavement would shiver and dance beneath your feet as a double-decker rumbled by. My parents alleged this made the bridge safer, but that did not detract from the thrill – it only made it more scientific and intriguing. Then there were the gulls. At Hammersmith, of course, the river is still tidal. On a good day you can smell the sea. At the ebb, wide mud-flats appear, and these would be covered, especially in stormy weather, with huge gulls. When you crossed the bridge, gulls would bank and glide under you and back and over your head. If you held a piece of bread over the rail, they would swoop and snatch it from your fingers. This, though, required courage, and was regarded as a health hazard. You didn't know where gulls had been. So a safer idea was to take a bag of crusts and toss them in handfuls over the water. Instantly, you would be the centre of a screaming, fighting white tornado. If you didn't look out, they would come straight at you and tear the bag from your fist.

Crossing the bridge from Hammersmith to Barnes you could glimpse, beyond the riverbank trees and the towing path, the edge of a large reservoir. That was the start of Mr Perry's domain. There were eight reservoirs in all, tucked in under the south rim of the big bend in the river opposite Chiswick. If you turned right just over the bridge, at the Boileau Arms, and walked down Lonsdale Road, the reservoirs, with grassy banks between, would stretch away to your right, behind what must have been nearly a mile of green-painted railings. It was a scene

I became used to, because I was born in a house halfway down
Lonsdale Road, and my bedroom (it was really a small dressing
room leading off my parents' bedroom) had French doors and a
balcony looking straight out across the reservoirs. There were no
buildings – just sheets of water, grass, gulls, and the distant
trees marking the river. Beyond that you could pick out the
tower of Chiswick church. Some of the reservoirs, so my parents
said, were not strictly reservoirs but filter beds. These would be
emptied periodically, leaving an expanse of fine sand at the
bottom, a marine smell, and a good deal of green water-weed,
which men would rake into heaps and cart away.

Mr Perry was the Metropolitan Water Board engineer responsible for the site, and he had a cottage which stood, quite by
itself, at the westernmost tip of the whole complex, opposite
Harrods's playing fields. It had high gables, red bricks, green
window frames (to match the railings), a grass bank in front
with concrete steps up it, a squeaky gate, and a neat flower
garden. Behind, Mr Perry's vegetable garden extended – illimi-
tably, so far as I could tell – in a series of square beds
surrounded by grass paths. On Sunday mornings, after church,
my father and I would visit Mr Perry. For me, the occasion
always had a pleasantly ritualistic feel. Apart from anything
else, there was the anticipation of Sunday dinner, with roast
meat and potatoes, when we got home. Also, I was seldom alone
with my father at any other time, but on this particular trip my
brother and sisters never accompanied us – and my mother,
naturally, was cooking the dinner. We were two men together –
or three, if you counted Mr Perry. It was just after the war, and I
must have been about twelve. The purpose of our visit was to
admire Mr Perry's vegetables. Looking back I can see (though I
never thought about it at the time) that the immaculate rows of
peas and beans and cauliflowers must have had a melancholy
appeal for my father. During the war we had lived in the
country, where we had a big garden, and he grew all the
vegetables the family needed. Now, back in the cramped
suburbs, Mr Perry's patch was as near as he could get to his lost
agricultural dream. That, I suppose, is why we went solemnly,
week by week, in our Sunday suits, to watch the cabbages
hearten up and muse upon the thickness of the leeks.

Mr Perry would always be digging when we arrived, in his
tweed cap and blue Metropolitan Water Board overalls, with a
pipe in his mouth. There would be hand-shakings, and a guided

tour of the vegetables – no mere stroll, but a detailed scrutiny, with regular halts and warm debates. I, of course, said nothing. My father and Mr Perry spoke. Mr Perry had a Worcestershire accent – at least, that's what I was told it was – with hearty, long-drawn-out vowels that I found deeply fascinating. I cannot, as a matter of fact, remember a single thing that Mr Perry ever said. Just listening to the noise he made was enough for me – that, and the feeling that I was part of a select male band. Mr Perry's rolled-up shirtsleeves and weatherbeaten face helped to make the occasion manly and mettlesome. It occurs to me that I never saw him inside a building. We stood out there under the sky, surrounded by vegetables and reservoirs, and it felt like an adventure. Mr Perry was, I knew, different from the people I normally met with – though I could not have explained quite why. Even now I can't work out how it is that he has stayed so clearly just under the surface of my mind for all these years – a kind of reference point, or a personification of something which without him would disintegrate into sun and wind and shining water and tobacco smoke and Worcestershire vowels.

Was it that I had a romantic sense of his intimate contact with the life of plants? I honestly can't believe it. Like most children, I was bored stiff by nature. Appreciating Mr Perry's vegetables was strictly for the adults, so far as I was concerned. I was there to appreciate Mr Perry. I could scarcely, if put to it, have told a Brussels sprout from a French bean. When annoyed with my own children nowadays for their lack of interest in gardening, I find it salutary to switch back to Mr Perry's allotment and visualize again the undifferentiated green blur which vegetation then presented to me. So was it something in the social situation that made Mr Perry's company so gratifying? Did I feel it to be generously condescending in my father and myself to pose, Sunday-suited, beside Mr Perry and his spade? Maybe. But flattering though it is to one's adult cynicism, that explanation too lacks credibility. I know that some children are supposed to be wondrously sharp about class distinctions, but my recollections are quite otherwise. In that respect, as in others, I was an abnormally slow developer. As far as social awareness went I seem, on looking back, to have been permanently asleep – cut off from reality by a fog of self-absorption.

Perhaps, then, it was Mr Perry's gusto and joviality that made him so vivid: they aren't qualities you encounter much in a careful middle-class upbringing. Mr Perry stood out because he seemed blithely at one with his world. He was its centre, and its gulls and waterworks radiated round him. I remember how he would jerk back his head to laugh. Even the laugh had a Worcestershire accent. He was a happy man.

Or was he? I have often wondered since; particularly when I have thought of Mrs Perry, and how I must have seemed as a child to the two of them. For they had no children. Mrs Perry was pretty and elegant, in what I recollect as a vaguely Spanish way. She had black eyes and hair, and usually, I think, a black dress and white apron. She never came out into the garden when my father and I were there. So we would see her only when we stepped briefly into the kitchen to pay our respects. Between house and garden was a wood and glass lean-to porch, which rattled enviably with all its panes when you shut the door, and smelled of tarred twine. Was I, as a child, a reproach to their childlessness? Was that why I sensed a coolness in Mrs Perry? And was it – can it have been – why Mr Perry assumed such a jaunty manner when I was around, and threw himself so heartily into his gardening? Was it to show he didn't care?

I shall never know. But such doubts have helped to cloud my memory of him. So have the things which time has done. I grew up, and went away to do my National Service, then to university. One day on a visit to my parents I passed Mr Perry's cottage, and noticed that it was derelict, with corrugated iron sheets nailed across its windows. Mr Perry, I learned, had retired, and I think it was said to Worcestershire, but perhaps I have imagined that. The reservoirs, it turned out, were to be grassed over – no more gulls. St Paul's School had bought the site, and was going to cover the Hammersmith Bridge end of it with its new buildings. Time passed: my parents died. I no longer had cause to visit Lonsdale Road. But driving up it one day, past Harrods's playing fields, I glanced across to Mr Perry's cottage. It wasn't there: just grass, and a gap of sky. All that complicated life was now only a shadow in my mind. Even the place where it had happened had been laid bare. That, I know, is how life always vanishes. But in the case of Mr Perry and his reservoirs the universal process of transience had been, so it seemed to me, rather abrupt. At least it taught me to expect nothing else.

1983

Schools at Oxford

What I remember most is the heat. It was a blazing June, and the sheets of paper on the desks flared up at you like arc lamps. It seemed risky to touch them, let alone start writing on them. People quickly abandoned their jackets, ties and gowns. Heaps of these littered the floor, along with other trash brought in by candidates – teddy bears, smelling salts, wilting carnations – so that you had to wade through a sort of flea market to get to your place.

Finding the right desk on the first morning was the major trauma. Exams in Oxford are held in a gaunt, echoing pile, resembling in size and decor one of the major London railway stations, its gigantic rooms filled with rows of inky little wooden desks, each with a glued label bearing someone's name. During the half hour or so before an exam starts a mob of candidates, several hundred strong, crushes itself into the entrance hall of this building – a few pathetic stragglers still trying to memorize crumpled fistfuls of notes. Then, at a given signal, the entrance hall's iron gates are flung open, and the crowd surges along the corridors, debouching dazzled and bewildered into the exam rooms, where the search for desks begins. Of course, the names are arranged alphabetically, but at this pitch of nervousness you have forgotten the alphabet, and quite probably your name too. Candidates can be seen darting around among the desks, rebounding from one to the next like demented billiard balls, and emitting little animal noises of panic, until caught and subdued by the invigilators.

Once this hazard was past and the proceedings had got under way, I can't say I recall any great sense of strain. I had been cramming English literature into myself for the past few months, so it was practically spilling out of my ears. The answers more or less wrote themselves. True, there were some distractions, apart from the tropical climate. The invigilators, for instance. Shuffling about between the rows in their academical regalia, they looked immensely ancient, like dressed-up wax-works, so that it was strange to see them sloping off to the back

of the hall for coffee and a smoke – rather as if the British
Museum mummies were taking a break for refreshment. Odd to
think that some of them must have been younger than I am now.

The girl undergraduates were another source of slight disturbance. At Oxford you wear subfusc for exams, which means, for
girls, black stockings, black skirts, white blouses and black ties.
This severe costume, designed, I suppose, to quell all thought of
sex, had, as I recall it, rather the opposite effect. Being surrounded by demure, black-stockinged creatures does not induce
academic calm – or not when you're twenty-three. Admittedly,
subfusc has its advantages. Like any uniform, it makes the
wearer feel braver. And it's fun being photographed by the
American tourists.

The only other distinct memory is of tiredness. Schools are a
marathon – five days, six hours a day. By the end, your writing
hand is almost dropping off. Starting the last question on the
last afternoon is the hardest bit. Why bother? you think – the
bright world is only half an hour away. The evening we finished
the weather broke. Torrential rain caught us in a punt on the
river. We didn't mind, of course. After Schools you don't mind
anything.

                                                    1980

Down With Dons

From the viewpoint of non-dons, probably the most obnoxious thing about dons is their uppishness. Of course, many dons are quite tolerable people. But if you ask a layman to imagine a don the idea will come into his head of something with a loud, affected voice, airing its knowledge, and as anyone who has lived much among dons will testify, this picture has a fair degree of accuracy. The reasons are not far to seek. For one thing, knowledge – and, in the main, useless knowledge – is the don's *raison d'être*. For another, he spends his working life in the company of young people who, though highly gifted, can be counted on to know less than he does. Such conditions might warp the humblest after a while, and dons are seldom humble even in their early years. Overgrown schoolboy professors, they are likely to acquire, from parents and pedagogues, a high opinion of their own abilities. By the time they are fully fledged this sense of their intellectual superiority will have gone very deep and, because of the snob value attached to learning and the older universities, it will almost certainly issue in a sense of social superiority as well. Modern young dons sometimes feel guilty on this score, and break out in jeans, sweat-shirts and other casual wear in the forlorn hope that they will be taken for persons of the working class. However, the very deliberateness of their disguise is an earnest of their real aloofness.

Anyone wishing for a whiff of the more old-world, unashamed brand of donnish uppishness could scarcely do better than thumb through *Maurice Bowra* (Duckworth), a sheaf of tributes which, besides giving a complete anatomical run-down of Sir Maurice from his 'curiously twisted navel' to his private parts (resembling, Francis King bafflingly reports, 'Delphi in microcosm'), casts some telling light on the social assumptions of its contributors and subject. The editor is Hugh Lloyd-Jones, Regius Professor of Greek at Oxford. His is a name that sticks in my mind because of a contribution he made, two or three years back, to some correspondence in *The Times* about dons' pay. It was at a time when the miners or the power-workers or some other vital body were having one of their strikes, and an English tutor at University College called Peter Bayley wrote in suggesting that, by comparison with such people, dons were perhaps paid too much. Professor Lloyd-Jones replied that, if Bayley thought that, he could never have done any worthwhile teaching or research. The discourtesy of this retort was, I suppose, calculated: a reminder of professorial eminence. But what struck me as weird was that Professor Lloyd-Jones should apparently have no inkling that, as against a miner or a power-worker, his own contribution to the community was of uncommonly little consequence, and that what he deemed worthwhile teaching or research would impress most of the people whose taxes went towards paying his salary as a frivolous hobby. Humility, it seemed to me, was the only becoming attitude for academics in the debate about pay, since their avocations, and their maintenance at the public expense are, if they don't happen to be nuclear physicists or doctors, notoriously difficult to justify. How these aspects of the matter could have escaped Professor Lloyd-Jones puzzled me for a goodish while. In the end I attributed it to the insulating effect of donnish uppishness. Years of self-esteem had, as it were, blinded the Professor to his true economic value.

Bumptiousness and insolence are the quite natural outcome of such a condition, and the Bowra volume has some excellent examples of both. When holidaying abroad, we are told, Sir Maurice would size up other tourists and, though they were perfect strangers to him, 'pronounce with shameless clarity on their social origins: "English LMC" '. We learn, too, of his behaviour at a Greek play to which he was taken:

> He drew attention, shortly after the rise of the curtain, to the knees of the Chorus, and engaged those on either side in such brisk conversation that a cold message was delivered to me during the interval to keep him quiet or get out.

Behind such conduct can be detected the unhesitating donnish assumption that the comfort and pleasure of ordinary people are of no account when set against the need to advertise one's superiority.

Don-fanciers love this rudeness, of course, and suck up to those who dole it out. The kind of people who work as secretaries and dogsbodies in the various Faculties, for instance,

can often be heard relating, with many a titter, the latest
offensive outburst of Professor This or Dr That. Dons' children,
too, are likely to admire and imitate their parents' ways, and this
can make them peculiarly detestable. A good many Oxford (and,
I suppose, Cambridge) citizens must have bitter memories that
would bear this out, but an experience of my own will serve as
an illustration of the general truth. For a while I lived opposite a
don's family. The father, a philosopher, was a shambling,
abstracted figure, whom one would glimpse from time to time
perambulating the neighbourhood, leering at the milk bottles
left on doorsteps and talking to himself. If he had any contact
with the outside world, or any control over his numerous
children, it certainly wasn't apparent. To make matters worse,
the mother was a don too, and the house was regularly left in the
children's sole charge. The result was bedlam. The din of
recorded music resounded from the place at all hours, and it
never seemed to occur to anyone to shut a window or moderate
the volume. One summer afternoon, when I was doggedly
trying to mark a batch of A-level papers, my patience gave out,
and I crossed the street to protest. As usual, every gaping
window blared: it was like knocking at the door of a reverber-
ating three-storey transistor set. Not surprisingly I had to pound
away at the knocker for a good while before anyone heard.
Eventually a teenage girl, one of the daughters, answered, and –
with the familiar upsetting mixture of outrage and humiliation
that one feels on such occasions – I asked if she would mind
playing the music a little more quietly. The girl gave a supercilious smile. 'Oh,' she said, 'it's no good your complaining
about that. The whole street got up a petition about us once, but
it didn't have any effect.' And with that she shut the door.

I withdrew, trembling with impotent rage and quite unfit,
needless to say, to mark any more scripts that day, even if the
row across the street had abated – which it didn't. For a while
after that I got into the way of asking after this girl whenever I
was talking to anyone who knew the family, in hopes that I
would hear she had been run over or otherwise incapacitated.
Unfortunately she never was, so far as I know. But it was
through one of these conversations that I came to hear of
another of her escapades. My interlocutor on this occasion was a
Professor of Moral Philosophy, and he explained that the girl
had caused considerable consternation at her school because she
had discovered how to manufacture (using clay, All Bran and

other ingredients) a compound which closely resembled human excrement, and had left quantities of this in little heaps around the classrooms. How they found out it was her I don't know, but apparently they did. My informant was immensely tickled by the affair, and shook with laughter when relating the discomfiture it had caused to the school staff.

In a moral philosopher that might seem a surprising reaction to such foulmindedness. But in fact he was illustrating another common donnish attitude, namely, contempt for authority, particularly the authority of those whom, like schoolteachers or policemen, the don feels to be in a lowly position compared to himself. Dons' children are notoriously arrogant at school, and it's hardly to be wondered at since they find that their elders, like my moral philosopher, greet their misdemeanours with asinine hilarity. The donnish cult of liberty extends further than this, of course. One frequently encounters letters in the press, for instance, with strings of academic signatories, gravely informing some foreign government that the way it deals with its refractory minorities does not tally with donnish notions of freedom. No doubt those who put their names to these documents get a pleasurable feeling of importance, but in fact a don is about as well placed to start clamouring for liberty as a budgerigar. Like the bird, he lives in a highly artificial, protected environment, in which all his wants are catered for. Any appreciable degree of liberty conceded to his fellow beings would quickly put an end to his existence. For it cannot be supposed that the ignorant, philistine majority would go on supporting the universities financially if it had freedom of choice in the matter, since it receives no benefit from these institutions, or none that it could be brought to appreciate, beyond, I suppose, the annual Oxford and Cambridge Boat Race, and even that is less popular than it used to be.

In the Bowra volume much hearty commendation is given to Sir Maurice's lifelong sympathy with those who 'desired to resist authority', and his support for 'all libertarian causes'. In his youth, one gathers, the causes he mostly spoke out in favour of were buggery and masturbation, though he also encouraged:

> open snobbishness, success worship, personal vendettas, unprovoked malice, disloyalty to friends, reading other people's letters (if not lying about, to be sought in unlocked drawers) – the whole bag of tricks of what most people think

and feel and often act on, yet are themselves ashamed of admitting they do and feel and think.

The commentator on human nature here is Anthony Powell. He does not record whether smearing ersatz excrement on school furniture would count as 'unprovoked malice' and therefore as a libertarian cause in the Bowra code. However, it seems much on a par with the rest.

But though Sir Maurice continued, apparently, to decry authority long after youth had passed, he himself represented authority for the greater part of his life. He became a Fellow of Wadham in 1922, Warden in 1938, and Vice-Chancellor of Oxford in 1951, and he was an inveterate university politician, adept at imposing his will on committees and at bulldozing himself and his protégés into positions of power. One need go to no hostile account to discover this domineering side to his nature, for his friends who contribute to the memorial volume are effusive about it. For a man so constituted, supporting 'libertarian causes' would plainly entail constant and self-deluding doublethink. Not that Sir Maurice was, in that respect, an untypical don. Dons are inalienably responsible for the government of the colleges and the university, so when they indulge in anti-authoritarian polemics it always involves a lie.

Regrettably undergraduates cannot be counted on to realize this. In their trusting way, they believe that dons are perfectly sincere when they prate of revolution and liberty. It is a misunderstanding that can lead to painful disappointment, for the young tend to carry their beliefs into action, and they then find that the dons, who had seemed such pals, have suddenly turned nasty. Bowra, it appears, was in his early days one of those dons who curry favour by hobnobbing with the undergraduates, and Anthony Powell tells of an occasion on which the conviviality wore thin.

I remember the unexpectedness of a sudden reminder of his own professional status, sense of what was academically correct, when, after a noisy dinner-party at Wadham, someone (not myself) wandering round Bowra's sitting-room suddenly asked:
'Why, Maurice, what are these?'
Bowra jumped up as if dynamited.
'Put those down at once. They're Schools papers. No, indeed . . .'

A moment later he was locking away in a drawer the candidates' answers to their examination, laughing, but, for a second, he had been angry. The astonishment I felt at the time in this (very justifiable) call to order shows how skilfully Bowra normally handled his parties of young men.

Quite so. And his skill consisted in concealing from them the truth, which was that his comfortable job depended on keeping them under. Young Powell's astonishment was, surely, quite reasonable. For had not the libertarian Bowra positively recommended the reading of other people's private papers?

The chagrin and surprise undergraduates feel when they come up against reality in this way was recently demonstrated, on a larger scale, at the trial of eighteen students before the Oxford University Disciplinary Court. They were accused (and eventually found guilty) of having staged a sit-in at the University Registry. In fact they had been ejected from the building, after a short occupation, by irate Registry staff, who got in through a window. This brush with ordinary, hard-working citizens, who wanted to get on with their jobs, was in itself a disillusioning experience for youngsters intent upon organized idleness, and elicited howls of protest from the undergraduate press. But worse was to follow. Brought to trial, the defendants at first treated the court room as an arena for libertarian high-jinks, volubly aided by their friends who packed the public gallery. The proceedings were adjourned in uproar. But the court was then reconvened in a small room; the revolutionary claque was excluded; and the trial went ahead. Defendants who continued to rant and sermonize and interrupt were first warned, then asked to leave, then, after they had refused, forcibly removed.

As it happened, I was on duty as an usher, so I had a ringside seat. The undergraduates linked arms to form a tight bunch against one wall. The barristers and solicitors, clutching armfuls of papers, huddled against another wall to avoid the mêlée. Eventually a squad of specially conscripted university police, decked out in ill-fitting bowler hats for the occasion, marched in, methodically dragged each offender from his clinging companions, and carried him, kicking and shouting, from the room. There was, I suppose, little violence – much less, say, than you could see on the rugby fields round the university any afternoon of the week. But in the elegantly panelled court room the

panting and scuffling and the bellows of rage from the undergraduates seemed crude and debasing. The defendants who
remained behind were stunned. It had plainly never dawned on
them that the university would actually enforce discipline.
Several wept. I remember particularly a graduate student, who
must have been in his early twenties, and whom no one had laid
a finger on, blubbing tempestuously in the middle of the court
room. Nor could the students be blamed for this reaction. They
had been led astray by their upbringing – by the unquestioning
approval of liberty which modern education encourages from
nursery school on, as well as by the revolutionary attitudinizing
of a few leftist dons who, it should be noted, did not appear
before the court to take any part of the blame, but retained their
lucrative posts after the undergraduates they had beguiled had
been sent down.

Bowra, of course, had died a couple of years before any of this
took place. One can be pretty sure that he would have felt
nothing but regret at the recurrent sit-ins, protest-marches and
other diversions by means of which students who have no
academic motivation try to justify being at university. However,
the support for 'all libertarian causes' celebrated by his obitu-
arists exemplifies, as I have suggested, a widespread donnish
cast of mind which inevitably provokes student indiscipline.
His response to what he saw of undergraduate militancy was
tolerant and lacking in foresight.

> When, in 1968, some undergraduates wanted to have their
> objections to the proctorial system heard by the Privy Coun-
> cil, Bowra was the first to give them public support, and in
> answer to the objection 'Why should they?' answered simply
> 'Because they are entitled to and because they want to.'

To anyone less filled with the notion of the special importance of
Oxford and its doings, it might surely have occurred to enquire
why these already highly privileged youngsters should be
'entitled' to occupy eminent public men with their little upsets,
any more than the pupils at any polytechnic or training college
or kindergarten throughout the land. Bowra's assumption here
partly reflects the Oxford of his youth, adorned with gilded
sprigs from the foremost families who would naturally deem it
their right to be heard before the highest tribunal. But it also
represents a grandiose and typically donnish sense of the
university's place in the scheme of things. This, incidentally, is

something dons share with militant students, who invariably
believe that their grouses are of national importance. In placards
and graffiti around Oxford the disciplinary court was referred to
as a 'show trial', and the defendants were labelled 'The Oxford
Eighteen', as if they were at least on a level with the Tolpuddle
Martyrs.

The relative insignificance of Oxford, and of universities in
general, Bowra, like most dons, did not care to think about.
Anthony Powell tells of how, in his undergraduate days, he once
confessed to Bowra, then a rising star in the Oxford firmament,
his own impatience with the university, how little he liked
being there, and how he longed to get it over and go down.
Bowra was so put out that it took thirty-five years for their
relationship to recover. Jobs within the university, and who got
them, mattered terribly to him. He fought and intrigued, on and
off committees, to get his candidates in. He revelled in the
bickering and gossip that surrounded contested elections to
academic posts: they brought drama to his life, exercised his
quick brain, and gratified his malicious sense of humour. 'To
anyone outside a university,' Lord Annan condoningly remarks,
'the frenzy which elections and appointments produce seems
petty and absurd.' To some inside, too, one would hope. The
kind of scholar who is absorbed enough in learning and
teaching to reckon every hour spent on administration and
committees wasted may, it is true, leave the field clear for the
hardened business-fixers, and is to that extent a liability. Still,
he is and must be the life-blood of any university worth the
name. He will have something larger and more permanent in
view than inter-departmental wrangling or the pursuit of his
career, and will consequently be exempt from the degradations
attendant on ambition. Bowra's craving for honours, on the
other hand, was voracious. When E. R. Dodds, rather than
himself, succeeded Gilbert Murray as Regius Professor of Greek,
he was bitterly disappointed and, it appears, purposely made
things difficult for the new professor. Small-mindedness isn't
something one easily associates with Bowra, but it is hard to see
his reaction here as the outcome of anything else, and the
species of small-mindedness involved is persistently if not
uniquely nurtured by universities.

From the academic angle, of course, the chief danger is that
the don who bothers himself with administration will get so
tied up in it that he will have no time for the subject he's

supposed to be studying. The disastrous improvement in
modern techniques of photo-copying and duplication has
greatly added to this peril. Bushels of paper nowadays debouch
from university and college offices every week and, as a result of
the cry for 'participation', even the undergraduates have been
sucked into the papery maelstrom. Some of them sit on committees almost full-time, and the busy-bodies in their ranks are
agitating for sabbatical years, during which they will not have to
study at all, but may devote themselves undistracted to needless
circulars and memoranda. They will then be indistinguishable
from the administrative dons. Even when administration
doesn't oust learning (and it didn't in Bowra's case), there's a
likelihood that the don who becomes attached to the idea of the
university, as distinct from the culture which the university
exists to serve, will apprehend that culture in a form which is
processed and ordered for university consumption. What were
originally great endeavours of the human spirit, the offspring of
passion and inspiration, will decline for him into the material of
lectures and syllabuses, of examinations and career-furthering
books. The flat, pedestrian feel of much of Bowra's writing
about Greek literature, which is rather harped on by contributors to this volume, may be relevant here. So may the awful
donnishness of his jokes on the subject of art and literature.
Traipsing round galleries and churches abroad, he would award
points to the paintings on show. When you had totted up fifty,
you were entitled to a drink. Another game was classing the
poets, as if in the Final Honour School: 'Goethe,' we are told,
'notably failed to get a First: "No: the Higher Bogus", "Maurice,
we've forgotten Eliot." "Aegrotat."' And so on.

If this carries a warning for present-day dons, the social
set-up at Oxford in Bowra's era may seem too remote to have
much relevance. Most undergraduates came from public
schools. Often they had been friends at prep school or Eton or
Winchester before they came up. It was a tiny, ingrown world.
The public-school atmosphere of the memorial volume is appropriately heavy, several contributors debating, as if it were a
matter of genuine concern, whether Bowra's explosive mode of
speech should be traced to Winchester, via New College, or to
his own old school, Cheltenham. As a matter of fact one is
probably over-optimistic if one assumes that all this is a thing of
the past. The public school element in the Oxford and Cambridge intake has never dropped much below a half, and is

bound to increase over the next few years. This is because the
Socialist policy of converting the country's non-fee-paying
grammar schools into massive comprehensives, in which the
clever and the cretinous are jumbled together, means, in effect,
that the non-public-school university entrance candidate will
receive less individual attention from the teaching staff than
formerly. The more crackbrained type of educational theorist
will actually defend this, arguing that teachers should devote
their time to the dullards, whose need is greater. But the result is
that a candidate whose parents haven't the cash to pay public
school fees is no longer able to compete with his intensively
coached public school counterpart. Thus a policy which was, in
concept, egalitarian, is now in the process of turning the older
universities back into public school enclaves, as they were
before the First World War. As the dons are, by and large,
recruited from among the undergraduates, they too will revert to
being exclusively public school before very long. This seems a
pity, because the influx of grammar school dons into Oxford
common rooms over the last twenty years or so has brought a
good deal of sense to the place, and they usually turn out to be
uninfected by the donnish follies and foibles I've been out-
lining. However, the Oxford of the future will not contain them.

Presumably because of the preponderance of public school
boys, there was a fair amount of dandified sodomy around in
Bowra's Oxford, and one gathers that he was a participant. Lord
Annan says that he regarded sex as something 'to be luxuriously
indulged with either boys or girls', and Isaiah Berlin connects
his love of pleasure, 'uninhibited by a Manichean sense of
guilt', with his enthusiasm for Mediterranean culture. But his
homosexuality seems to have been furtive and saddening rather
than blithely Hellenic. He was terrified of blackmail. One of his
friends, Adrian Bishop, had lost his job in an oil company
because of his homosexual escapades, and Bowra dreaded
similar exposure. When Gide came to Oxford to collect his
honorary degree, he refused to put him up in the Warden's
Lodgings for fear of scandal. To commemorate Bishop, he wrote
a homosexual parody of *The Waste Land* entitled *Old Croaker*,
enough of which is printed here to show that he, like Forster,
had only to touch on this topic for his literary sense to desert
him. He wasn't, of course, at all like the popular notion of the
donnish fairy queen. On the contrary, he was robustly masculine, and seems to have coveted a stable heterosexual relation-

ship. He dallied with the idea of marriage more than once. 'Buggers can't be choosers,' he retorted, when someone deplored the plainness of a girl he was wooing. But he never married, and his aloneness was recurrently a misery. When a woman friend referred to him in his hearing as a 'carefree bachelor', he flared up: 'Never, *never*, use that term of me again.' He loved children, and the thought of him having to make do with kindness to other people's is not a happy one.

It seems arguable that his homosexuality did not satisfy the deeper demands of his nature, and maybe it should be regarded as something foisted on him by his education rather than an inherent trait. The Oxford he grew up in was unrelievedly male, so the undergraduates, especially the outgoing and social ones, almost inevitably drifted into flirtations with members of their own sex. In these conditions it was hard to learn how to get on, or off, with girls, and Bowra didn't. He never developed much instinct for what they were thinking or feeling, a friend recalls. His bitterest jokes seem to have been about love and marriage. Given all this, it's rather staggering to consider that, half a century later, most of Oxford's colleges are still single sex, and many dons are determined to keep them that way. Their reasons, when you bother to enquire, never boil down to anything but the obtusest male prejudice. However, they are aided by the fact that the women's colleges also oppose co-education, fearing that mixed colleges, though they would give girls a fairer chance of getting to Oxford, might have an adverse effect on their own class-lists – an ordering of priorities which shows that women, in an emergency, can be just as donnish as men.

Perhaps Bowra's profound interest in eating and drinking was a kind of compensation for the lack of sexual satisfaction in his life. His hospitality was 'gargantuan', we learn, 'his digestion and head ironclad'. The friends who commemorate him plainly regard these as entirely fitting attributes for the successful academic. Indeed *The Times* obituary recorded, as if it were one of his signal achievements, that he had 'greatly raised the standard of hospitality' shown to honorands at Oxford. But to an impartial observer it may perhaps admit of question whether scholarship necessarily entails passing large quantities of rich food and fermented liquor through the gut. True, it is a traditional part of Oxford life. But even Oxford's traditions need reconsideration from time to time, and with Britain rapidly dwindling into a small, unimportant, hungry nation, it seems unlikely that corporate gluttony will flourish in its universities for much longer. Nor need its disappearance be greatly lamented. The spectacle of a bevy of dons reeling away from one of their mammoth tuck-ins is distinctly unappealing, and would be even if there were no such thing as famine in the world. Nevertheless, one may be sure that dons will hotly defend their right to swill and guzzle. Their feelings of social superiority, earlier referred to, unfailingly come into play when this issue is raised, and I have known quite young dons seriously contend that college feasts should not be discontinued because, if they were, they would have nowhere to entertain their grand friends. The question is not a minor one but reflects on the way in which university shapes the personality, and therefore on the justification for having universities at all. If it can be shown that the effect of higher education is to stimulate greed and self-indulgence, the public, whose money keeps universities open, may be excused for feeling that these attributes could be picked up more cheaply elsewhere.

Reading about Bowra and his Oxford teaches you, of course, not only what to avoid but also what to imitate, or try to. His positive qualities were immense. Above all, the breadth of his learning offers a challenge and a reproach to modern dons with their increasingly narrow specializations. He had travelled across Russia as a schoolboy, before the Revolution, and this gave him a lifelong interest in Russian poetry. He also read French, German, Italian, Spanish, Greek and Chinese. World literature to him was not a set of linguistic cupboards, mostly closed, but a warm and welcoming ocean in which he splashed about freely. He spanned time as well as space. From Homer, Pindar and Sophocles his love and knowledge extended to Yeats, Valéry, Rilke, George, Blok, Cavafy, Apollinaire, Mayakovsky and Lorca. Pasternak, Quasimodo, Neruda and Seferis were his personal friends. Set against these riches, the burrowings of the typical modern researcher shrivel into absurdity. The things that pass for education in graduate departments – hunting for subjects sufficiently devoid of interest not to have been researched before, manufacturing unneeded theses on unreadable authors – would have filled Bowra with horror and disbelief. He characterized the graduate student as a dinosaur, sinking into a bog under the weight of his erudition.

Another aspect of his approach to literature which looks

pretty healthy in retrospect was his indifference to the Cambridge emphasis on 'evaluation' which was all the rage in the
thirties. Encouraging youths scarcely out of short trousers to
deliver judgement on the masterpieces of the past was not at all
what he went in for. He made his pupils aware of literature as a
wealth they had still to inherit, rather than as a terrain of fallen
idols and soured hopes into which it would be foolish to
venture. As one contributor here puts it:

> The range of his reading challenged your own provinciality
> and sloth. In the post-war years he was always suggesting
> that one should read poets whom the new orthodoxy had
> dismissed as negligible or harmful – Tennyson, Swinburne
> and Kipling . . . He was a traveller forever suggesting that if
> only you would journey further some new and life-enhancing
> experience was yours for the asking.

He enlarged the imagination of his undergraduates, too, by
becoming a legend long before his death. Like all legends, he
was partly make-believe. People added to him bits and pieces
from their own fancy, so that by the end he was not so much a
man as a joint fictional venture. This is plain enough from the
memorial volume, for we encounter there several different
Bowras, according to the writer. He is variously likened to Yeats,
Hardy, Swift, the *Royal Sovereign*, one of Napoleon's marshals,
and the Heracles of the metope at Olympia. Cyril Connolly's
Bowra 'rode high above academic honours' – quite unlike the
envious careerist other contributors knew. There is dis-
agreement, too, about his eyes. To Connolly they were '*gli occhi
onesti e tardi*, eyes of a platoon commander in the First World
War'. Lord Annan remembers them as 'pig's eyes', while for
Susan Gardiner it was their 'passion and piercing intensity' that
impressed. A passionate pig? Even the story about Bowra and
Gide, which one would have imagined was readily verifiable,
exists in two versions: the second, also printed here, has it that
it was the Vice-Chancellor, not Bowra, who refused to entertain
Gide at Oxford, and that Gide was looked after by Bowra and
Enid Starkie instead. Far from mattering, the contradictions are
proof of Bowra's success. Whatever else may seem obsolete
about him, he inspired others to creativity, which is any
teacher's most important job.

1975

Viewpoint from the *TLS*

The dislodgement of 'evaluation' has been effected with remarkably little fuss. Only ten or twenty years ago it was still widely held that literary criticism could and should issue in firm 'value judgements' and that these could attain general validity – some were 'right', others 'wrong'. Proponents of the belief invoked the very etymology of the word 'critic' to clinch their case, and took a severe line with those who felt that opinions about literary worth merely reflected personal taste. These doubters were accused of dilettantism, impressionism, belles-lettrism, and other deviations from a rational, progressive approach to literature.

Nowadays almost no one believes in the possibility of objective or 'correct' literary judgements any longer. But before the creed dies out entirely it is worth reminding ourselves how strong it was, what the reasons behind it were, and why they were mistaken. The hope that an advance towards certainty in assessment would make criticism more scientific was, of course, misconceived from the start, for science avoids value judgements altogether. The scientist can tell you that water is composed of hydrogen and oxygen, but asked which is the better will pronounce the question meaningless. It was not always so. In the Middle Ages, when the universe was arranged on a graduated scale, a scientist would certainly have known whether hydrogen was better than oxygen, supposing the two gases had been discovered, just as he would have known that an eagle was better than a wren. But scientists have outgrown the medieval era, whereas evaluative critics still reside in it.

Their medievalism comes out clearly in some remarks made by T. S. Eliot in 1931. 'We must assume,' Eliot writes, 'if we are to talk about poetry at all, that there is some absolute poetic hierarchy; we keep at the back of our minds the reminder of some end of the world, some final Judgement Day, on which the poets will be assembled in their ranks and orders. In the long run, there is an ultimate greater and less.' Behind all theories of objective literary value there hovers some version of Eliot's

Judgement Day complex. For the aim of the objective valuer is to see the literary work, in Arnold's words, 'as in itself it really is'. And this aim carries with it the assumption that the work *is* really something, and *one* thing.

Now common experience tells us that different readers respond to, interpret and evaluate particular works in innumerable different ways, as a result of fortuitous but decisive circumstances of age, temperament, class, education, race, politics, width of experience, and so forth. If this were not so, literary discussion, and the publication of literary criticism, would be pointless. So if those who believe in objective valuation are correct, it follows that all these readers, except one (and all their sets of formative personal circumstances, except one) are wrong. With any given piece of writing there will be countless subjective and mistaken responses, and one correct response.

Suppose we were to ask someone who took this view what it is that makes the correct response correct. His only adequate reply, it seems to me, would be that the correct response was God's response; and this, as we have seen, is the position Eliot adumbrates. Of course, to make such a reply you would have to believe in God first, and in a God who takes a keen interest in literature. That is to say, He would have to be a God who was prepared to keep literary and religious considerations apart, otherwise the specifically religious authors on His list would have an unfair advantage. Be that as it may, appeal to a literary critical God is certainly the most satisfactory way of justifying a belief in dependable literary values.

But how can such values retain their credibility in the godless universe which most people now inhabit? Modern man is quite used to the idea that we are the temporary occupants of a cooling solar system; that human life is an accident of chemistry; that all the ages, from the first dawn on earth to its extinction, will amount to no more than a brief parenthesis in the endless night of space; that good and evil and other such ephemera were created by the human mind in its attempt to impose some significance on the amoral flux which constitutes reality. From this perspective, literary evaluation of any kind might seem almost comically irrelevant.

On the other hand, it might be argued that this nihilistic perspective does not eradicate the importance of human life to human beings – indeed, it makes it the only thing that can possibly have any importance – and that consequently the question of whether a given literary work is 'life-enhancing', or more 'life-enhancing' than others, might provide a criterion for objective literary judgements. In general, there are three ways literature may enhance life, according to those who have pursued this line of thought. It can improve the moral character of its readers; or it can make them happier; or, without producing either of these long-term benefits, it can prompt enjoyable aesthetic thrills, sometimes accompanied by physical symptoms, as in the famous case of A. E. Housman, who could recognize genuine poetry because it made his facial hair stand on end while shaving. That literature may have these effects, we need not question. But it is perfectly clear that the same work will minister to the differing moral, psychological and physiological requirements of its readers in a multiplicity of different ways. That a reading of *Paradise Lost*, say, should have precisely the same effect on the morals, happiness and shaving of even half a dozen different people is scarcely conceivable (let alone ascertainable). Consequently the hope that objective value judgements might be grounded upon the life-enhancing effects of literature proves vain. The influence of literary works upon life, far from being a test which allows us to place them on a graded scale, is the opposite: it forces us to concede that all judgements in this area are, like people, infinitely variable.

Faced with the difficulty of isolating any particular aspect of literature which might serve as a criterion of value, champions of value judgements have sometimes pointed to the consistency of received opinion. Whether or not we can say why one work or author is better than another, they argue, the fact remains that there are certain merit awards which no one would dream of questioning. Shakespeare is often cited in this context. Everyone, we are told, agrees that Shakespeare is the world's greatest dramatist, and this proves that value judgements can be absolute. George Watson, who is not only one of the most cogent of English critics, but also a firm believer in objective value judgements, uses a variant of the Shakespeare gambit in his book *The Study of Literature*, substituting Homer for Shakespeare. Opinions about literature may be free, says Watson, 'and yet if anyone were to deny the judgement that the *Iliad* is a great poem, we should all know what to think of the freedom of his opinions'. The sense of corporate superiority invoked here is not, I think, as trustworthy as it sounds. For should we, indeed,

know what to think – except that the defaulter was unlike
ourselves, and unusually honest in speaking his mind? On
questioning him we might, of course, find that he knew little
about literature, compared to us. But what if we found that he
was an authority of even greater eminence than ourselves? Such
an embarrassment does arise when the Shakespeare gambit is
played. For, as is well known, Tolstoy did not think Shakespeare
the world's greatest dramatist. On the contrary, he had a poor
opinion of him, and considered *King Lear* inferior to the primitive chronicle play on which it is based. To retort, according to
George Watson's formula, that we all know what to think of
Tolstoy's opinions, seems now a less happy option than it did
before.

Of course, even if there were consensus about Shakespeare's
pre-eminence, it would not make that pre-eminence a fact. We
have only to think of man's ideas about the structure of the
universe, or of his own anatomy, to realize that opinions which
were unquestioned in past eras are now wholly discounted.
Besides, the argument that our virtual consensus about Shakespeare gives some hope of eventually establishing an agreed
league table of other authors and works will not stand much
scrutiny. For it is apparent that one common reason for liking
particular literary works is precisely the knowledge that other
people do not like them. This takes various forms, ranging from
the crude pleasure in shocking or annoying conventional and
law-abiding folk which animates much modern art, to the
pleased sense of exclusiveness ('we all know what to think of the
freedom of his opinions') which accompanies membership of
the literary cognoscenti. Consensus in value judgements can
hardly be expected when value judgements depend, to some
degree, on lack of consensus.

But, it may be objected, the claim that value judgements are
personal and variable tallies oddly with our endless and bitter
disputes about them. This inconsistency has not escaped the
notice of critics like George Watson, and they naturally pounce
on it as proof that all the talk about subjectivity is mere humbug.
People who claim to think that literary judgements are matters
of personal taste will nevertheless, insists Watson, sit up into
the small hours eagerly contesting the value of novels, plays and
poems in arguments that bear every resemblance to those used
in spheres where rationality, deduction and conclusiveness are
possible. Clearly Watson's observation is correct, but he may, I

would suggest, have misread its implications. The existence of vehement and prolonged controversy is not necessarily an indication that the points at issue can be reduced to ascertainable facts. It may, indeed, indicate the contrary. All that can be safely deduced is that the divergent opinions in such controversies are tenaciously held. Our literary judgements, like all our opinions, help to determine the kind of people we are, but they do so at an unusually profound level because they relate to works which affect us deeply. We are aware that our feelings cannot be justified by appeal to any external authority, and consequently we strive to persuade others to feel as we do, so that we shall be more secure in feeling so ourselves. All literary criticism is ultimately an exercise in persuasion of this kind.

The real usefulness of value judgements, I believe, can emerge only when we have acknowledged that they are subjective. That usefulness lies not in anything they can tell us about works of literature (for they can tell us nothing), but in what they can tell us about the people making the judgements, including ourselves. Debate about differing estimates of the value of a text should prompt us to an exploration of the individual motives and assumptions, the determining configurations of personality, imagination and background, of the debaters. Through this we might come to a clearer knowledge of ourselves, and of the psychological factors which underlie our preferences in art and literature, and perhaps in such similarly disputatious and irrational areas as morals and politics. True, such a programme would subordinate study of literature to study of people. But then, it is for the sake of people that literature exists.

1980

Vegetable Gardening

It's perverse, really, to write about gardening at all. Half the point of gardening is that it repairs that part of your brain which words and thinking are constantly threatening to destroy. That's one thing it has in common with music: it lies beyond the reach of words, and you wouldn't need it if it didn't. Still, you're forced to be articulate about it sometimes, particularly when under attack. The other day one of those acid young women you come across nowadays, who give you the impression that they're on temporary release from an Urban Guerrilla Training Camp, demanded in the course of a chat how I could justify spending time on gardening when, as an academic, I ought to be reading books.

It took some time to sort out the various kinds of rage with which this query filled me. But when I'd done so I realized that it was my puritanism which had taken the worst knock. Whatever other pleasures attach to gardening, they're all based on the assumption that it's a blameless, nay meritorious, occupation. That feeling must go back at least as far as the myth of Eden. And if, as I do, you stick to vegetables and don't grow flowers, your sense of self-approval naturally redoubles.

Quite right too: for you are, after all, producing food, which is one of the few obviously worthwhile human activities. True, someone else would produce it for you, probably more efficiently, if you didn't. But then, you could find someone to perform most of life's functions in your stead if you were sufficiently comatose. By growing what you eat, you keep in touch with economic realities which lie deeper than money. As for the argument about wasting time, it's nonsense. If you're efficient you can keep your family stocked with vegetables by spending about one Saturday in every two gardening. For half the year, from October to March, you have virtually nothing to do but gather the produce – sprouts, leeks, carrots, kale, broccoli, winter cabbages – all of which will stand out in the snow and ice obediently fattening themselves for your consumption.

But these practical considerations, though sound, are by no

means the whole story. Like most puritan pleasures, vegetable gardening contains a strong element of submerged sensuousness. By that I don't mean simply that home-grown stuff tastes better than the plastic-shrouded organisms which pass themselves off as vegetables in supermarkets, alongside the disinfectants and washing-up liquids. Garden produce undeniably does have more intense and varied flavours than anything you can buy, but gardeners are austere people, and it would strike them as indecent to set too much store by the pleasures of the table. The sensuous gains they look for are more remote and devious.

Take parsnips, for instance. With the best will in the world it's difficult to pretend that the parsnip is really eatable, but it's an immense and exacting pleasure to grow. At the start of the season you grub out a row of pits with a trowel, and fill them almost to the brim with finely sieved soil. Then you poke into each soft dell about a dozen of the crisp wafers which are the parsnip's seeds, and pat earth over them. Come the summer, you pull out all but one of the seedlings from each cluster – pale gold pencils, with feathery tops, which it always gives you a pang to throw on to a compost heap, though there's nothing else to be done with them. Then, as the winter approaches, the great spreading leaves of the survivors rot and yellow, and the parsnips withdraw into their subterranean existence until, some time after Christmas, the time comes to crack the frosty crust over them and lug them out gross, whiskered and reeking, from their lairs.

Once you have done that, and have scraped the earth from their sweaty white sides with a sharp knife, the parsnip's capacity for giving pleasure is, in my view, pretty well exhausted. You can, of course, roast or boil them like potatoes, or you can put off the evil hour of trying to get them down your gullet by making them into wine, which takes several months to perfect, and is generally so vile in the end that it has mercifully to be tipped down the sink. However, these posthumous considerations don't affect the satisfactoriness of the parsnip during its lifetime. As a fellow creature, rather than a food, it is truly glorious.

Most of the rich experiences obtainable from the vegetable garden are similarly untainted by any thought of actual consumption. They feed, rather, your other senses in covert and delicate ways. To feel the damp fur inside a broad bean pod, and see how it grips its beans by their little umbilical cords, is a lot better than eating broad beans – good as that is. With onions, nothing that happens on the culinary side is more satisfying than the business of preparing them for winter storage, after they have been uprooted and dried off in the sun. You start with a tattered, mud-caked heap, and one by one you rub the papery outer skins away to reveal row upon row of gleaming amber bellies – the onion equivalent of a riviera beach scene. Then you string the sleek bulbs together by the necks and hang them in dangling swags from the wall of your garden shed, where they will swing and glow through the dark months.

Like all garden jobs, podding beans and storing onions are seasonal – part of a pattern ruled by sky and earth which non-gardeners lose touch with, or apprehend only dimly through vulgarized annual occurrences like power strikes or Easter eggs. But the gardener's annual pattern is also a personal one, giving coherence to his life. At each stage in his year he finds himself rediscovering vivid sensations which have a whole stream of dormant memories trailing behind them. Spend a quarter of an hour, for instance, pinching out the side shoots on a row of tomatoes, and you will find your thumb and forefinger stained a deep and pungent green, so concentratedly that when you put your hand in water the greenness comes off in clouds and fills the bowl. I can still remember my pleased surprise when that first happened to me – or rather, I suppose, I can remember re-remembering it through years of renewal. Agreed, few people would take up vegetable gardening just for the sake of a bowl of green water, but if your nose and eyes are still alive it's a thing you'll find intriguing.

Since the gardener's year is circular, with life always overlapping death, these private annual ceremonies take you into the future as well as the past. Gathering runner-bean seeds, for instance, is a late autumn job with an atmosphere all of its own, compounded of weak sunlight, and that sense of wet collapse which a dying garden exudes. But the bean stems, you find, are dry and brittle, like twigs, and the pods still hanging on them crunch between your fingers into tobacco-coloured flakes, leaving in your palm the chunky beads which will be next year's crop.

As vegetable gardeners aren't primarily concerned with eating they harbour, like librarians, a tidy-minded dislike of anyone who actually wants to use the commodities they're in charge of. To have to uproot cabbages, say, from a row, and hand them over for cooking, is always an annoyance. The gaps look unsightly, like snapped-off teeth. A stalwart, unbroken line of cabbages, on the other hand, with their hearts tight as fists and their purple outer leaves spread to catch the dew, raise your spirit every time you visit them. Among the current cliches I especially deplore is the one which refers to hospital patients kept alive by machines as 'cabbages'. This is both inaccurate and insulting to vegetables. For a cabbage is a sturdy, self-reliant being, and compared with an average specimen of twentieth-century manhood it has, when well grown, a positively athletic air.

That's not to deny that the gardener has his work cut out keeping his vegetables healthy. The only vegetable which no insect seems to attack is the leek. That makes it the easiest of all to grow, which is perhaps why it's favoured by the lyrical and carefree Welsh. All the rest are assailed by ingenious and tireless enemies, with no other purpose in life than to destroy what you have grown. Even your attempts to care for your plants draw down disaster upon them. When you weed out a row of carrots, the smell of crushed leaves brings carrot-flies flocking from far and wide.

In this situation the only adequate response is to thank God for chemical pesticides, and use them liberally. Unfortunately the strongest and most effective ones keep being withdrawn from the market on the grounds that they have been found to damage the environment. So when you hit on a really lethal sort it's a good plan to buy in a large supply, which will allow you to go on using it after it has been outlawed. I did this for several seasons with a splendid product, now alas unobtainable, which wiped out everything from snails to flea beetles. It had no adverse effect on the bird population so far as I could see, though the neighbourhood cats did start to look a bit seedy. That, of course, was an advantage from my point of view, for cats are filthy, insanitary beasts, and a fearful nuisance to the gardener. One of the anomalies of English law is that whereas it would, as I understand it, be an offence to clamber over your neighbour's fence and defecate among his vegetables, you can send a feline accomplice on precisely the same errand with total impunity. It has always amazed me that manufacturers of slug bait, and other such garden aids, should proudly announce on the label that their product is 'harmless to pets'. A pesticide that could guarantee to cause pets irreparable damage would, I'd have thought, sell like hot cakes.

But though gardeners grumble about their battle with pests and marauders, it's really a challenge they wouldn't be without for anything. It gives them a heroic sense of being pitted against the universe, and makes them realize how precariously we maintain life on our planet in competition with the swarming species struggling to shove us off it. It also peps up your aggressive instincts. With a bucket of toxic chemicals you can spread death almost as effectively as you could with a flame thrower, and far more usefully.

A different kind of pest, and just as bothersome, at any rate to the novice, as slugs or vermin, are the people who write the descriptive paragraphs about different varieties of vegetable in seed catalogues. I'm sure they don't mean to mislead, but the fact is that what they omit is far more important than what they say, and it takes years to accustom yourself to deciphering their curiously oblique literary mode. For example, the phrase 'a sure winner on the show bench' actually means 'inedible'. If, unsuspectingly, you grow a runner bean, say, which has this legend attached, you will end up with beans a yard long which have the flavour and consistency of ballpoint pens. Let us suppose that, after this experience, you vow never to grow vegetables which are not specifically recommended for their eating qualities. Next year, accordingly, you choose a strain of lettuce which has sent the catalogue compiler into raptures by its crispness and succulence. Surely now you'll be safe. But no. For the one thing that matters about lettuces is whether or not they bolt in hot weather, and since your author has remained silent on this point it means that you will find your lettuces wagging in the breeze like pagodas after a couple of weeks of sunshine. And so it goes on. Next year you carefully avoid both the show-bench successes and the secret bolters, but you forget to look for the assurance that your selected varieties are resistant to disease. Should this clause be absent, your vegetables, though enthusiastically recommended, and quite hale-looking in the catalogue snap-shots, will prove to be generous hosts to every known virus, and will topple into fungoid ruin long before you have a chance to harvest them.

Not that seed catalogues can't provide their own special pleasures, so long as you don't expect them to be helpful or informative. Learning to outwit the compilers is itself a heartening experience. There's also much amusement to be derived from those fancy catalogues which urge the simple-minded to sow aubergines, soya beans, melons and other ungrowable exotica. It's always good to see fools and their money being parted. A more poetic source of enjoyment are the names of the vegetable varieties that any catalogue contains: Chantenay Red Cored and Musselburgh, Winter Queen and Wheeler's Imperial, Amager Rearguard and Hopkin's Fenlander. They are full of mysterious evocations, like monuments of a lost culture. Who was Ailsa Craig, now immortalized as an onion? Who was Dr Mackintosh, before he became a potato? Who was the Lobjoit of Lobjoit's Green Cos? I imagine Lobjoit as a lean pioneer bent double on some windswept smallholding, surrounded by immature lettuce plants. No doubt research into horticultural history could provide definite answers. But knowledge on such matters would be quite useless, whereas ignorance is a source of inexhaustible fascination.

As with most pursuits, one of the leading pleasures of vegetable gardening is that it makes you feel superior to those who don't pursue it. The degeneracy of the pampered masses, propped half-conscious before their telly screens, becomes, as you toil on your lonely plot, a profoundly satisfying subject of meditation. But here, as in other ways, vegetable growing has an educative, balancing effect – for there is always someone better at it than you. Take a stroll round any village horticultural show, and you will find your self-esteem draining away with horrible rapidity. Onions the size of Christmas puddings, balanced proudly on their little beds of sand; luminous tomatoes, each competitor's group of six standing demurely apart from the rest and as exactly matched as billiard balls; leeks as thick as your arm, with their vast green manes combed and beribboned like show horses; aristocratic carrots, like furled orange umbrellas – how is such grandeur achieved? Naturally you try to console yourself, remembering your experience of seed catalogues, by reflecting that this exhibition stuff is probably useless for anything else. But somehow that thought carries little conviction. For even if it were true, the artistry that goes into these prodigious creations is still daunting and, you are sinkingly aware, far beyond your powers.

This tendency to elate and humble you in quick succession is one of the factors linking vegetable gardening with religion. It is also religious in the devotion it inspires and the elect band it admits you to. Like other religions it instils a set of values combatively out of key with modern trends. The promises dangled before the public by political leaders are likely to strike the vegetable gardener with indifference or dismay. Those rousing forecasts of intensified house-building programmes and greater industrial expansion – what kind of moron, the vegetable gardener wonders, are they supposed to attract? Who wants to see a greater and greater acreage disappearing under concrete and sewage pipes? Isn't it time we realized that, given our bulging populations, vegetables have now become more desirable inhabitants of the earth than people: less destructive, more peaceful, more serviceable for sustaining life? The day I see a row of houses being pulled down to make a vegetable plot, I shall feel that something sane and healthy has happened.

1980

PART TWO
The English Scene

Shall we prance?

This book* is richly stocked with people whom any person of decent instincts will find loathsome. That is partly what makes it fascinating, but also what makes it shaming, because the characters Martin Green describes dominated English cultural life from the end of the First World War until the fifties. These were the dandy aesthetes, the snobs and pansies and 'shrieking little poseurs', as Orwell called them, who, by and large, were in charge of the magazines and the literary columns and conspired to keep one another in the public eye. Most of them were born in the decade 1901–11, and they went to the same few and exclusive prep and public schools, and the same smart Oxford and Cambridge colleges. Mr Green traces the fortunes of the group through two of its central figures, Brian Howard and Harold Acton, and some forty of their friends, including Robert Byron, Cyril Connolly, Claud Cockburn, Peter Quennell, John Lehmann, Evelyn Waugh, Auden, Isherwood and Spender, Cecil Beaton the photographer, John Strachey the politician, and the traitors Guy Burgess and Kim Philby. Many of the clique were protégés of the Sitwells, the dandy impresarios *par excellence*, and they were backed by various other 'uncles' and protectresses like Norman Douglas and Emerald, Lady Cunard, whose daughter Nancy belonged, of course, herself to the dandy set.

Acton and Howard formed the tastes of the group. They were both from arty cosmopolitan families, and they stimulated in their less sophisticated English friends a passion for Pierrot and *commedia dell'arte*, Proust, Diaghilev, rococo, baroque, and other dandy fads. Acton's father was an art-dealer, who devoted his life to filling his Florentine villa with beautiful loot. The money came from Mrs Acton, Harold's mother, whose family were Chicago financiers: her father had founded the Illinois Trust and Savings Bank. The Acton family lived sumptuously. Extravagant

Children of the Sun: A Narrative of 'Decadence' in England after 1918 by Martin Green (Constable).

balls and *tableaux vivants* were part of Harold's boyhood. We hear, for instance, of a ball at the Villa Schiffanoia, which the Actons attended in costumes designed by Paul Poiret from Persian miniatures, and a Florentine pageant, designed by Brunelleschi, for which little William Acton, Harold's brother, was got up in a huge turban and puffed-out satin trousers. Brian Howard's background likewise oozed aestheticism and American cash. His father was a minor painter and fortune-hunter, the son of a Texan woman called Elizabeth Paschal (the name Howard, with its ducal associations, was just a vulgar fraud). He married Brian's mother, Lura née Chess of Louisville, in order to get his hands on the family wealth, which derived from the manufacture of oil and whisky barrels. Lura's sister Mary later started a successful cosmetics firm, Mary Chess Ltd, with a shop on 57th Street in New York, and another in Mayfair. During the Second World War Brian Howard pilfered large quantities of stock from the latter, for his own use, and when in danger of losing an argument would dab some Mary Chess perfume on his opponent and say, 'Now that you smell like a tart, my dear, your arguments carry very little weight.' That accurately conveys his tone and intellect.

At Eton the two were regarded as prodigies of avant-garde culture. They specialized in childishness and affectation. Brian Howard took a toy engine to chapel, for which he was nearly expelled. With Harold Acton he began a literary magazine, the *Eton Candle*, which was reviewed in the *TLS*, and lasted for one issue. It was, Mr Green curiously claims, 'an achievement comparable with those of Cocteau and Diaghilev, granted the difference in scale'. It had a shocking pink cover, enormous margins, and an essay on modern poetry by Brian Howard in which he hailed Edith Sitwell as a 'genius'. She had earlier assured him that he had more talent than anyone else under twenty, except her brother Sacheverell. Not everyone was taken in by Howard, of course. 'I never liked him,' recalls Anthony Powell, 'nor thought, even at Eton, that he had a vestige of real talent in any of the arts.' But this was exceptional. To most of their cronies Howard and Acton seemed to have enormous gifts, and that is how it seemed to the two themselves. 'I HAVE JUST DISCOVERED OUR CATEGORY,' wrote Brian to Harold, after reading Arthur Symons's *The Symbolist Movement in Literature*. 'We are the New Symbolists.' In fact Howard's poems were so bad and so derivative that Orage printed one that had been submitted to the *New Age* on the pastiche page, taking it as a satire on Joyce.

From Eton the two proceeded to Oxford, where they applied themselves to posturing and dissipation. 'One lives an extraordinarily marvellous life here – a sort of passionate party all the time', wrote Brian. The passion was, of course, homosexual. Even as late as 1938 heterosexual affairs were, according to John Betjeman, the mark of 'state-subsidized undergraduates'. Serious study was, likewise, socially degrading. 'I had not', Louis MacNeice records, 'gone to Oxford to study; that was what grammar school boys did.' The dons were largely ignored, though a few of the younger ones maintained flirtatious and deferential relations with the wealthier undergraduates. Among these were, it appears, Maurice Bowra, John Sparrow and Roy Harrod, an ally of the whole dandy set, who got Brian Howard into Christ Church despite his being involved in cheating in the entrance exam. At university Harold's achievement was to invent and popularise 'Oxford bags' – trousers some 26 inches broad at the knee and 24 inches at the ankle, in light, bright shades such as silver, mauve and pink. Brian, on the other hand, cultivated the acquaintance of young peers, slept with as many of them as he could, and helped them smash windows after their Bullingdon dinners. These orgies of broken glass, it's perhaps worth noting, continued in Oxford until quite recently, and could have unpleasant consequences. I recall that when I was a lecturer at Christ Church in the late fifties, one of my pupils who had, it seems, wandered innocently into the celebrations, was blinded in one eye by flying glass. In the best traditions of his type and class, he never bore any grudge nor, so far as I could discover, thought he had any cause for grievance.

But that is by the way. After going down from Oxford in 1925, Brian and Harold invaded London and became leaders of the bright young things. Cocktail parties – invented, it is said, by Alec Waugh in 1924 – were all the rage, as were bottle parties, which Loelia Ponsonby inaugurated in 1926. Michael Arlen took twelve bottles of pink champagne to the first one. The dandies played leapfrog through Selfridges, set the Thames on fire with petrol, and so forth, and their exploits were avidly written up in the gossip columns which papers like the *Weekly Dispatch* and the *Sunday Express* began to carry in the mid-twenties. A photograph of this period, reproduced by Mr Green, shows a party of bright young things, including Cyril Connolly, Cecil

Beaton and Patrick Kinross, 'making contact with the proletariat'. Arrayed as eighteenth-century French aristocrats in
powdered wigs and knee breeches, they have commandeered a
pneumatic drill and are posing with it while the roadworker,
from whom they have taken it, stands by, grimly resigned.

With the thirties and hunger marches, the plight of the
proletariat became a fashionable topic and, in what is certainly
the most ludicrous development in the whole story, the dandies
cast off their foppish attire and disguised themselves as comrades. Corduroy trousers and beards became the vogue. Auden,
we learn, wore a worker's cap, dropped his aitches, and ate his
peas with a knife. Isherwood drank bad tea and ate chocolates to
ruin his gleamingly upper-class teeth. Gabriel Carritt changed
his name to Bill. Michael Roberts in his *New Country* anthology
(1933) demanded a new social system and 'an English Lenin'.
The spuriousness of the whole movement (a spuriousness still,
of course, perfectly observable in English left-wing intellectuals)
is well illustrated by its essentially public school origins –
indeed, public school was the only experience many of the new
comrades had. John Strachey, whose *The Coming Struggle for
Power* (1932) was taken very seriously by the leftward-turning
English intelligentsia, explained that he had become a Communist because he had failed to get into the Eton Cricket XI. Like
others of the new left, he remained an Oxford aesthete, conspicuous when among normal people by reason of his asinine
high-pitched Bloomsbury voice. He was never more than a
thinly-disguised dandy, and when out of temper with Communism in 1939 he sold his Russian bonds and bought General
Motors stock instead with, as Mr Green puts it, 'his usual speed
in switching sides'. The schoolboyishness of the lefties is also
demonstrated by figures like Giles and Esmond Romilly. At
Wellington, Giles's revolutionary activities consisted of stealing,
masturbating and resigning from the OTC. Esmond ran away
from school and published a magazine for rebellious public
school boys called *Out of Bounds*, which sold like hot cakes at
Eton.

Harold Acton, to do him justice, did not go Left. Instead he
decided to make himself an oriental scholar, and went to live in
China in 1932. But Brian Howard became an ardent left-winger,
declaring that Russia was 'the one beacon of progress'. Tem-
peramentally he was still a dandy and a child, of course,
interpreting politics as if they were part of his own childish

experiences – a typical dandy habit. He told his mother that Hitler's voice on the radio reminded him of his father in a rage. To find someone of Howard's character writing for the *New Statesman* and joining the Left Book Club is to realize, as Martin Green insists, that the very institutions of anti-Fascism in England were tainted with unreality. When, in 1940, Howard's social connections secured him a safe job in MI5, he became a close friend of the traitor Burgess – in many ways a similar type. At Eton Burgess had affected Oscar Wildey mannerisms, and the first night that he dined in Hall at Trinity, Cambridge, had invited a rowing blue to sleep with him. He once remarked that he could never travel by train because he would feel obliged to seduce the engine driver. He and Howard, in their new role as leaders of the Left, enjoyed fulminating against *rentiers* and Money Men, though each remained (as Acton, with presumably inadvertent word-play, recalls) 'at bottom a hedonist and a snob'. Once during the war, when Howard was publicly discussing official secrets with Burgess in a loud voice, as he often did, a policeman approached and asked for his name and address, whereupon he replied, 'I am Brian Howard and I live in Mayfair. No doubt *you* come from some dreary suburb.' The English Left in the thirties emerges from Mr Green's account, then, as of a seriousness and importance precisely equivalent to wearing fancy dress or playing leapfrog through Selfridges. It was, essentially, a new way for the dandified and over-privileged to express their resentment at the decent, responsible and hard-working middle-class elements in society, whose existence was a continual reproach to their own foppish incompetence, and a continual threat to their undeserved cultural eminence.

The heroes of Mr Green's story are the Leavises and Orwell. They saw through the dandies early on, and campaigned unremittingly against them in the interests of responsibility and maturity. Already in 1936, reviewing Connolly's novel *The Rock Pool*, Orwell remarked that 'even to want to write about so-called artists who spend on sodomy what they have gained by sponging betrays a kind of spiritual inadequacy'. Mrs Leavis in her essay 'The Background of 20th-Century letters' (1939) portrayed the 'odious little spoilt boys of Mr Connolly's schooldays' going up to university to become 'inane pretentious young men', and then moving into controlling positions in literary life: 'Those who get the jobs are the most fashionable boys in the school, or those with feline charm, or a sensual mouth and long eyelashes' (she is quoting from Connolly's description of Brian Howard). If it is possible, nowadays, to find *Scrutiny's* views joyless and narrow, it is because we no longer see them against the background of the menagerie of limp-wristed exquisites who provoked them, and whom Martin Green has here depicted in such absorbing and repellent detail.

His triumph, apart from the richness and density of the historical material he accumulates, is the sympathy with the dandies which, by a deliberate exercise of the will, he manages to display. Written from a hostile viewpoint, the book would have less impact, because it could more easily be shrugged off as prejudice. But Mr Green does all he can to explain and excuse the dandy phenomenon. The decision of a generation of English intellectuals to behave like effeminate children was largely, he argues, an effect of the Great War. The dandies rebelled against the masculine *Blackwood's Magazine* world of their fathers, with its premium on courage and enterprise, because as they saw it the natural fruit of that world had been the massacres on the Western Front. Beneath their posturings lay horror, and a sense of inferiority. They could never match the heroism of that titanic conflict, and so could never attain full manhood in their own eyes. Besides, England was, after the Great War, economically emasculated, hopelessly in debt to America, and with major industries – like the cotton industry – crippled. Unemployement soared. The dream of Empire and enterprise had collapsed, and the young, powerless to stem the tide of history, viewed the spectacle with giggling ineptitude. The sack of England by America had also begun, with great paintings and libraries crossing the Atlantic, and historic English houses being taken down stone by stone and reassembled in the States. Even in sport, the major masculine roles were being pre-empted by America. In the post-war years, as Mr Green points out, Americans took the world championships in tennis, boxing, golf, yachting, and athletics away from England. In the face of such humiliations there seemed nothing left for the young male in England but to adopt an effete and dandyish style – it was, indeed, a kind of defiance. Mr Green has written a brilliant book – but, more than that, it is one that helps us to understand how we have come about, and to appreciate the forces and falsities that have shaped and shattered our culture.

1977

Keeping up with the Coopers

This book* is not half so awful as you might expect, given the miasma of stale gossip and snobbism that hangs around its subject. For one thing, it is very well written. For another, its heroine, though a walking affront to one's instincts of social justice, displays such dauntless trust in the supremacy of herself and her class that it commands, in the end, grudging respect. Daughter of the Duke and Duchess of Rutland (or, as was commonly supposed, of the Duchess and the dashing belletrist Harry Cust), she grew up amid feudal splendour and became the darling of the Edwardian bloods, who extolled her nigh-divine beauty.

Tastes have changed, and the old photos show a blank, helpless sort of face, rather like a rose just before you drench it with DDT. This expression was, we learn, largely due to short sight, which also enhanced her reputation for cruel disdain, as she would sail past acquaintances without a glimmer. At all events, men of every age flocked round her like gulls round a council tip, and abandoned all restraint once in her presence. Maurice Baring, seated next to her at dinner, set light to his hair; the King of Spain put his hand up her skirt; Lord Wimborne, Viceroy of Ireland, had to be chased from her bedroom; and even the mountainous Ernest Bevin leaned libidinously against her in a lift.

The physical side of love, Mr Ziegler tells us, attracted her little, but she liked money, and all it could buy, very much indeed. Accordingly she accepted tributes from her lovers – mink, ermine, diamonds – but resorted to unarmed combat and cries for help when the deluded males tried to cash in on their investment. Women of lower market value naturally found this conduct outrageous, but the men never seem to have given up trying. Even after her marriage to Duff Cooper her sugar daddies outbid one another with promises of rent-free housing, and the American George Gordon Moore offered the couple

Diana Cooper by Philip Ziegler (Hamish Hamilton).

£6,000 a year for life. Rich admirers like Lord Beaverbrook supplied the champagne, salmon and game for the Duff Coopers' lavish parties, while the endless holidays abroad were also generally funded from an outside source.

Though amply provided for, she retained a talent for scavenging that would have done credit to a coyote. Once, after staying with Lord Rosebery, she begged for a loan of his Rolls-Royce to take her to the station and, on her way down to the car, stole the breakfast kipper from the tray outside his bedroom door, to eat on the train. Scruples about such lapses, as about her sexual freedoms, would have been dismissed as 'common' or 'bourgeois'. Lawrence, who put her into *Aaron's Rod* as Lady Artemis Hooper, described her admiringly as a 'social freebooter'. She had no use for morals, and always omitted 'Lead us not into temptation' when reciting the Lord's Prayer. 'It's no business of His,' she proclaimed.

Her toughness came partly from the ordeal of the First World War. The golden lads who had worshipped her almost all perished, often horribly. One, Basil Hallam the music-hall star, had joined the Balloon Corps and was shot down by a German fighter at 6,000 feet. 'He came to earth', noted Raymond Asquith, 'half a mile from where I stood, shockingly foreshortened, but recognizable by his cigarette case.' Within months Raymond himself, the one man whom she wholly loved, was killed. She volunteered as a nurse and helped tend casualties at Guy's – emptying bedpans and dressing wounds, to the dismay of the Duchess who had envisaged nursing as more serene. In the Second World War she ran a small-holding at her cottage near Bognor, bustling about cheerfully among the muck-heaps and butter churns. When some ARP workers who were sleeping in the outbuildings protested at the smell of the goat, she replied with typical aplomb that the goat had, only that morning, made the same complaint about the ARP workers.

Her cultural efforts were less impressive. Mr Ziegler contends bravely that 'she did much to make Mah Jong fashionable in Britain', and her salon at the British embassy in Paris, when Duff was ambassador after the War, attracted a flutter of minor arty talents – some of them with doubtful war records, so that the embassy became known as a haunt of collaborators. But unless writers or artists were 'fun' and could make a party go, she had little use for them. The only two undoubtedly world-class figures who strayed into her orbit, Hemingway and T. S.

Eliot, were both pronounced boring. Her capacity for abstract thought seems to have been roughly that of a strawberry mousse, and since like most girls of her class and period she had received little formal education, her practical ideas were unlikely to be helpful either. When the Blitz began she contacted the War Office, suggesting that large magnets should be placed in London's parks to attract the bombs.

On the other hand she had splinter-keen gifts of observation, and an exuberant style. Her letters, which form Mr Ziegler's main source, catch voice and gesture mercilessly – as in her account of Edward VIII and Mrs Simpson aboard the *Nahlin* in 1936, with the boyish king kneeling and cringing before his critical lady. It was as actress, not writer, that she made her biggest hit, though. Improbably cast as a statue of the Virgin Mary in Reinhardt's *The Miracle*, she toured the USA and Europe to world acclaim in the twenties. Since the part entailed standing mute in a stone niche, it did not test her to the full, but devotees agreed that her aristocratic poise distinguished her gratifyingly from the mere professionals.

The proceeds of her acting went to launch her husband on his political career. From what we learn here, Duff was no great catch. A noted lecher, he began seeking extra-marital diversions even during their honeymoon, and procuring suitable partners for him became one of his wife's occupations. Of the excessive amount of alcohol that sloshes around in these pages, a high proportion found its way into Duff. He also gambled excessively, bilked tradesmen, and had, for a politician, a fatal knack of being around when failure occurred. Still, it's instructive to discover the human reality behind his pompous autobiography *Old Men Forget*, and it must be some kind of tribute to his wife that their marriage, despite everything, remained happy. Never short of courage, or averse to publicity, she has, at eighty-nine, sanctioned the publication of this affectionate but by no means uncriticial biography – which, even her sourest critics must admit, is game.

1981

Growing up in Tunbridge Wells

Fear, says Richard Cobb,* does not dominate childhood, as people often suppose. It's not clear where he gets this doubtful idea from, for he seems to have spent about half his own youth terrified out of his wits. Dogs, cricket balls, thunderstorms and the picture of the dying Nelson in his uncle's house all affected him, on a scale ranging from tearful dread to screaming nightmares. More awful still were the lower classes, who poured into Tunbridge Wells at fairtime in August. Half-naked, hairy-chested, tattooed, they would lie on top of one another in couples on the Common locked in fearsome activity, or stagger drunkenly past his window at night while he quaked beneath the sheets, awaiting their ghastly arrival at his bedroom door.

By day, the rough boys of King Charles Choir School presented the chief threat. They would burst from their horrible institution, built of lavatory brick, in a whooping mob, and encounter the young Cobb – or rather, a distant prospect of his fleeing form – at a point in the High Street where two terrible eyes, clad in spectacles, hung over the shop of Mr Bateman the optician. It seems unlikely that these high-spirited lads meant him any harm, but he felt sure they planned to stone him, and a major worry was that his parents' flat lacked a back door, so that there would be no escape when the revolution finally occurred and the whole phantom pack – giant optics, copulating couples, choirboys – came howling through the dark to get him.

Endowed with timidity of this order, Cobb early felt the historian's preference for the dead, as being quieter and more predictable than the living. He liked stuffed animals, and was an eager spectator at the showrooms of R. Septimus Gardiner, Taxidermist, on Grove Hill. Graveyards and lines of washing provided favourite subjects for his sketch pad – both of them reassuringly devoid of animation. A friendship with the dispenser at a local hospital enabled him, he explains, 'to replenish my stocks of glass eyes and ether'. What use he found for these

Still Life by Richard Cobb (Chatto and Windus).

found for these supplies remains mysterious, but their mortuary flavour is quite in character.

Tunbridge Wells earned his love because it came as close as a town could to being a group autopsy. Quite a few of the inhabitants could not move at all (one stationary female geriatric dating from Tsarist Russia was an 'adored' Cobb familiar), and for those who could, dragging themselves a few yards in the weak sunshine was often the limit of endurance. Even the relatively mobile tended to be museum pieces – the Crimean War general who wore his medals at dinner; the heavily enamelled lady who toured the town daily in her de Dion Bouton, behind two ramrod chauffeurs. Over all lay a snug shroud of snobbery, an entanglement of class relations within which a scared child could feel secure.

Or almost: for young Cobb still needed a panoply of talismans and rituals to get him through the day without actually collapsing from panic. Various town landmarks – two garden gnomes coated in shells, a stone swan – became in his eyes magical sentinels against the envious hordes who wished to bring down Tunbridge Wells's tone. Another potent charm was the outline of a man discernible among the cracks on the lavatory door at home. Cobb would sit facing him gratefully each morning, and feel like waving, to acknowledge the little totem's protective efforts. Reading these confessions from a major historian, you begin to suspect that the writing of history may itself be a kind of hopeful magic – a voluminous spell on the lavatory doors of time, which reduces all the world's disasters to safe, academic proportions.

The historian's hunger for detail, which can alone allay his fear of the unknown, took up a lot of Cobb's time. He seems to have memorized the daily itineraries of practically all Tunbridge Wellers of any standing in the period circa 1923–35: what time they called in at Durrant's for dog food, what time they paused at the bandstand. Years later, revisiting the town in the fifties, he spotted a survivor from his childhood still tottering into the grocer's, dead on schedule, to purchase water biscuits, and this evidence of an entire existence wasted in trivial routine greatly cheered him, because it satisfied his mania for continuity.

His mother's bedroom drawers were another sphere of research, almost archaeological in its rigour, for he concentrated, as he rummaged through her privacies, on identifying relics from different strata of her life – the green silk parasol from a girlhood summer, the beaded reticules of pre-1914 vintage. The drawers were a seraglio as well as an archive, the feminine feel of their folded silks arousing vague excitement. But their main role remained scholarly: the lower layers, containing more intimate garments, he left unravaged. Most children, probably, have carried out similar searches, lured by their parents' unknowable antiquity, but a singular feature of Cobb's raids was that his mother was quite aware of them, and would scatter halfcrowns among her things as surreptitious pocket money. This unspoken complicity continued until he was well into his thirties. He took his first salaried job at thirty-eight, and prior to that regularly obtained his drink money via his mother's stored clothing.

Perhaps the awkwardness of their relationship, coupled with his intense love, was one explanation of his almost pathological insecurity. But it had social origins too. He realized they were not well off. They occupied a series of poky furnished lodgings, and his father, a shadowy figure in oatmeal plus-fours, caused him agonies of shame by his familiarities with grander folk. When Cobb went to Shrewsbury (a wretched, lively place, where he pined for Tunbridge) a rich classmate's mother added to his humiliations by kindly transporting him to and fro each term in her majestic beige Daimler.

Insecurity made him watchful and secretive, turning him into a writer, not just a historian. He prefers the shabby angles of things: the backs of smart terraces, pock-marked with blinds; low pubs; gypsy greengrocers. He is never censorious. The disgracefully wealthy Limbury-Buses (maternal cousins of his) whose sole avocations were eating huge meals and lying in bed till noon, raise no spark of indignation in him. He documents them appreciatively, as natural curiosities, along with the chars, village idiots and businessmen who populated the fringes of his boyhood.

Only change enraged him, because it touched the quick of his fear. When some new houses went up nearby he took his airgun to the building site and shot out all the windows. A foreman caught him at it and, under threat of reporting him to his father, demanded £4 damages, which Cobb raised by covertly selling a gold Kruger sovereign his parents had given him. Later the coin was missed, a housemaid fell under suspicion, and had to leave. Cobb kept mum. But what, as he says, could he do? Those who retort that he could have spoken up and saved the girl's name

have forgotten what it is to be a terrified child. Cobb remembers, and that, as well as his redeeming freedom from all
conventional standards of dignity and relevance, is what makes
this offbeat, capricious book a rare treasure.

1983

On Leslie Thomas's novels

In 1947 Leslie Thomas got a letter from C. E. T. Field, of the *Daily Mirror* Features Department, rejecting a story he had sent in and suggesting that he might 'have a shot at some of the publications for boys'. Since then seven critically accclaimed Leslie Thomas novels have burst upon the bookstalls, and *The Virgin Soldiers* ('scenes rivalling the best of D. H. Lawrence' – *Daily Telegraph*) has alone sold two million copies. For all that, it seems to me that C. E. T. Field had genuine insight. Boyishness is deeply ingrained in Leslie Thomas's fiction. His comedy is boyish, physical, good-hearted. Characters lope, claw, flail, lose their trousers or, retaining them, project fly-buttons 'like bullets' with the power of their erections. Army sergeants play 'schoolboy tricks' on each other, and fight 'like clowns, red and funny', amid wild laughter. The exotic locales which Mr Thomas evokes are the time-honoured settings for lads' adventure yarns – the South Sea Islands, and outposts of Empire in the steamy Orient, where beleaguered Britons blunder on, outnumbered yet full of grit.

'How many British in history have died like this, hands smartly at their sides?' wonders a character in *The Love Beach*. The thrills of battle, as the novels transmit them, are constantly related to boyhood experiences. Warring natives gesticulate 'like schoolboy footballers', and in *Onward Virgin Soldiers* an NCO has his legs blown off by a mine while actually playing football. In another novel a depth-charge flies 'high and wide, like something thrown by a boy', and nearly all the battle-pieces contain juvenile images to domesticate the carnage: a pilot wipes down his helicopter 'like a patient mother tending a snotty child'.

The sex scenes cultivate childlike freshness by similar means. Brigg, in *The Virgin Soldiers*, slips his hand inside a prostitute's panties, 'like a boy wriggling beneath a wire fence'. In the ethical sphere, a boyish admiration for husky males predominates. Bad people are easily spotted, being ugly or physically handicapped. The villain of this new book is a fat man with a grotesquely small head, employed by a mute woman in a wheelchair. Herbie, on the other hand, 'funny, friendly, childish', and covered in hair and muscle, is the hero's best pal.

A confident superiority to religion is another aspect of Mr Thomas's healthy, boyish viewpoint. Religious people in the novels reguarly turn out to be frauds, and often vicious as well, like Parsons, the unarmed-combat instructor in *Onward Virgin Soldiers* or the bloodthirsty islanders of St Paul's in *The Love Beach*, sold on 'all that junk from the Bible'. *The Man with the Power** is about a farcical crusade across the USA from New York to Las Vegas, led by the Rev. John Properjohn, a fake evangelist and overgrown boy, avid for candyfloss, toffee-apples and comic papers. The other crusaders are either cranks or mercenaries, like the hero, Willy Turpin, who has the job of impersonating Christ with the aid of a giant balsa-wood cross. Despite his disbelief in the venture, Willy finds himself developing 'a special friendship, a comradeship' with his fellow marchers. Team-spirity urges of this sort rank high among Mr Thomas's boyish enthusiasms: he always gets warm and serious when he writes about them. Davies, in *The Love Beach*, finds he has a lump in his throat when he helps some men haul up an old barge, and William Herbert, in *His Lordship*, even chums up with the detective-sergeant who is interrogating him. They converse throughout the novel in small-boy language ('fib', 'belly-button').

When it comes to sexual intercourse (which it does about every twenty-five pages), the impulse to keep things juvenile takes over completely. Practically all Mr Thomas's leading men are middle-aged and have broken marriages behind them, but they all contrive to strike up joyous physical relationships with preternaturally available teenage girls. 'He thought how much like a child she was' is the hero's standard reaction, and not uncommonly he starts by teaching the girl nursery rhymes. Her miniature physique receives much stress. She always has 'tiny buttocks', 'a small flat stomach', and other parts to match. 'You split me, Christopher,' complains Shoshana in *Come to the War*. Though Shoshana is supposed to be an Israeli girl-soldier fighting the Arabs, she is given an elaborately babyish flavour, and retires at night to a nursery with Donald Duck on the door and shelves full of dolls. The teenage twins, 'white and small',

*The Man with the Power by Leslie Thomas (Eyre Methuen).

who share Brigg's bed in *Onward Virgin Soldiers* are likewise notable for their Mickey Mouse alarm clock and their habit of tugging at Brigg's private parts 'impatient as a child with a disappointing toy'. In return, Brigg cradles them in his arms 'like a large father'. His earlier love, 'infant, happy' Lucy in *The Virgin Soldiers*, had very similar tastes, and shared her room with a large golliwog. William Herbert, in *His Lordship*, even more fortunate than Brigg, secures employment as a tennis coach at a girls' boarding school and watches his pupils undressing through a hole in their dormitory wall, entranced by their 'baby legs' and other infant fitments ('highly entertaining' – *Sunday Mirror*). He eventually enjoys sexual relations with a large cross-section of them – though the book prudently reveals at the end that some of these encounters may have been William's wishful thinking.

Mr Thomas's new work belongs to the same tradition. Willy Turpin comes upon (or rather peers through a crack in the wall at) Ambrosia Properjohn, the Rev's teenage daughter, masturbating herself with a china leg broken off her doll. 'Would you like to have a look at my whatsits?' Ambrosia artlessly enquires, 'like a child wanting to share a top', and soon Willy is filling in for the china leg. 'You really are a good sport,' declares Ambrosia, after the customary 'volcanic' orgasm.

Sorting out what makes readers go for this particular kind of fantasy is apt to look heavy footed, and best left to psychologists. But a puritanical sense that adult sexuality is shameful or sullied arguably lies behind the recurrent need for child's play. The toys and prattle of Mr Thomas's mini-bedmates are designed to suggest pristine innocence (an innocence which combines, as it cannot in life, with sexual expertise). *The Love Beach*, for instance, has a would-be Edenic scene in which some eleven-year-old girls perform an erotic dance, 'laughing the laughter of innocence and childishness', and watched by the gloating hero. A muddled desire to restore innocence may explain, too, the primness with which sexual deviations are treated in the novels, once they have been amply catered for. In *The Man with the Power* a prostitute gives Willy a stirring account of a whipping she has received from a client. Afterwards Willy has a deep sense of shame at his 'horrible, sick' feelings, and it transpires that the woman made up the whole story, simulating the weals with cosmetics. So the novel cleanses itself, as it were, of the pollution it has fostered. The underlying guilt and shame plainly connect with the prevalent boyishness elsewhere. The underlying fear, too. What the novels shrink from is the idea of having sex with a woman who is the man's equal (or superior) in maturity and intellect.

1973

Discreet charms of the aristocracy

Lady Mosley's eight Loved Ones* tend to be wealthy or arrogant or, like her husband Sir Oswald, both. Most of them have already featured in her autobiography *A Life of Contrasts* (1977), accompanied by the same stories: how Dora Carrington cooked a rabbit which made Lady Mosley ill, how Lord Berners burnt his hands taking a lobster thermidor from the oven. Neither author nor publishers make it clear why these events should require chronicling again so soon.

By far the least engaging Loved One is Professor Derek Jackson, millionaire physicist and husband of Lady Mosley's sister Pamela, whom he 'smothered in diamonds from Cartier'. Jackson seems to have regarded his riches as a licence for boorishness. When riding at steeplechase meetings he regularly incurred fines for impertinence to the stewards, and would proffer a £100 note, demanding change. On trains he made a habit of pulling the communication cord as a way of asserting himself. Once at Victoria when the boat-train had only Pullman coaches, he insisted that, since he had a first-class ticket, a first-class carriage must be found and coupled up, irrespective of the delay to other passengers. He had a twin brother, Vivian, of similar pigheadedness, who bullied a German sleigh-driver at St Moritz into letting him take the reins. By a rare stroke of poetic justice, Vivian turned the vehicle over and broke his neck.

Lady Mosley extols Jackson's 'irresistible wit and brilliance', but the specimens she chooses hardly support the claim. 'Oh you mean Kelly and Sheets', he would quip, whenever English poetry was mentioned. Perhaps Lady Mosley's admiration for such sallies explains why, unlike other commentators, she found Hitler a humorous companion, as well as 'exceptionally charming'.

Compared with Jackson, almost anyone would seem tolerable, and Lady Mosley's other friends benefit from appearing in the

Loved Ones: Pen Portraits by Diana Mosley (Sidgwick and Jackson).

same pages. Not that their appeal is always easy to spot. The chief recommendation of Mrs Violet Hammersley, a banker's widow, seems to have been her exorbitant gloom. She had a hollow laugh, 'resembling a groan', and her letters, filled with complaints about ill health, angle shamelessly for the recipient's pity. 'I still sit, cramped in my chair, staring at the snow and the dying birds', she once pluckily volunteered.

Another relic from the age of elegance is Prince Alfons Clary-Aldringen, an Austrian nobleman who slipped through the Russians' clutches at the end of the war and escaped to the ancestral palazzo in Venice, bearing his wife's jewels in a brown paper parcel. On the question of inherited wealth Lady Mosley seems to diverge from her husband's political beliefs, though she gives no sign that she is aware of any split. In his *Fascism* (1936), Mosley proclaimed that hereditary wealth would not be permitted in his fascist state unless 'public service' was given in return. By means of this reform, fascism would eliminate 'the parasite who creates the barrier of social class'.

That seems an accurate description of several Loved Ones – most notably of Gerald, Lord Berners, who complained on leaving Eton that it would be grossly unfair if he were expected to earn his living, since all his relatives lived in idle luxury. He evidently won his point, and became an amateur painter and composer, writing ballet scores and surrounding himself with exquisiteness at his Faringdon mansion, where the fantail pigeons were dyed crimson, yellow and turquoise. It seems doubtful whether this could count as public service even in Mosleyite terms, and in fact Lord Berners showed little patience with the public when its interests crossed his own. He built a Gothic tower on a hill overlooking Faringdon, despite protests in local papers and the rejection of the plans by the council. Lady Mosley applauds his firm stand: Berners's folly is, in her view, admirably 'non-utilitarian' and much more worthwhile than 'ugly council houses'.

The two sections most readers will turn to, on Lytton Strachey and Evelyn Waugh, are the thinnest. Lady Mosley met Strachey towards the end of his life, when she was nineteen, and understandably she can recollect almost nothing he said, though she retains a misty impression that he 'enthralled us all by being so wonderfully, so exactly what we had imagined him to be'. Her memory of Waugh is less vacuous, though their friendship was similarly brief because Waugh became disenchanted with

the Bright Young People and their endless parties. In his diary
for 16 June 1930 he records snappily: 'Tuesday was Diana's
birthday and I gave her an umbrella from Brigg which she broke
next day'. Lady Mosley protests that, on the contrary, she
treasured it for years, and one can see that Waugh would be
much too taken with the flourish of that sentence to worry about
its truth.

The memoir of Sir Oswald (d. 1980) which forms the book's
climax, is staunchly loyal. He was, it appears, right on every
issue. Had his warnings been heeded, England would not today
be a third-rate country. It would also, of course, be much
emptier, since his recommendations included the deportation of
selected Jews and foreigners and the sterilization of people unfit
to breed. Lady Mosley stresses his lovable side. Even animals
found him irresistible. He had only to go into a wood and make
cat noises for stray pets to come streaking through the undergrowth. A swan once fell in love with him, and waddled around
in his wake till it expired.

This version of Mosley as the St Francis of fascism leaves out
of account, though, the one interesting question, which is why,
given his abilities ('a superb political thinker', A. J. P. Taylor),
he was such a flop at gaining support. As a Labour MP he was a
joke. The spectacle of Mosley, 'with the face of the ruling class
and the gait of Douglas Fairbanks', as one observer recorded,
striding up to socialist platforms, followed by his first wife, Lord
Curzon's daughter, swathed in costly furs, gave the British press
a golden opportunity for mirth. The New Party, which he
formed on leaving Labour, failed dismally in less than a year;
and the British Union of Fascists was never more than a rather
disgusting sideshow.

Why such failure? Lady Mosley offers no answer, and she
bitterly resents the 'unrecognizable caricature' of Sir Oswald in
his son Nicholas Mosley's *Rules of the Game* (1982). Yet Nicholas
Mosley's book, unlike her own, attempts serious analysis. He
believes that Mosley did not ultimately want power; he
wanted to be a legend, to have the star quality that aristocrats
are supposed to posess. However unpalatable to Lady Mosley,
this theory squares quite well with the man she depicts in her
memoir.

Occasionally the reader doubts her grasp of affairs. When she
and Mosley were interned in Holloway prison during the war
the baths, she noticed, had a line painted five inches up the side

to regulate the use of water. 'I never quite understood the point:
we have such a nice rainfall in England, and water is not a
commodity which has to be imported.' Most people, one imagines, would realize that the idea was to save heating-fuel, not
water. Presumably for Lady Mosley bath-water has always been
the servants' job, hence her vagueness about the details. Her
circumstances have allowed her to remain cushioned from large
areas of ordinary reality, which is why her pronouncements on
life and love have only limited interest.

1985

Spotlight on the knee-tremblers

As a response to the rise of the proletariat, Mass-Observation was about as adequate as a stirrup-pump in a fire storm. Makeshift, amateur and profoundly British, it radiates, in retrospect, a period charm like old cigarette cards or Brooklands race track. It was started in 1937 by two amiable eccentrics, Charles Madge, poet and Cambridge drop-out, and Tom Harrisson, self-taught naturalist and anthropologist, who had lived with cannibals in the New Hebrides, and was later sent to Borneo by Special Operations to organize guerrilla warfare against the Japanese.

Harrisson based himself in Bolton ('Worktown' in Mass-Observation code) with a team of observers, mostly unpaid, who mingled with the natives to collect data on local customs such as the aspidistra cult, football pools, dirty jokes, armpit hygiene, and the proportion of males wearing bowler hats in pubs (13 per cent rising to 25 per cent on Saturday nights). Harrisson's pioneer researchers included William Empson, who made a comparative study of sweet-shop windows. Meanwhile in Blackheath Madge organized a 'National Panel' of volunteers whose main task was to send in a detailed account of everything they did on the twelfth of each month, thus affording random chunks of normality for Mass-Observation HQ to ponder.

An element of condescension underlay the whole project. Edward VIII's abdication had revealed the powerful hold which the monarchy still had over the popular imagination, and Mass-Observation's original aim was to subject this 'primitive' allegiance to scientific scrutiny. The aspirant scientists soon found that the masses did not much relish being observed, especially by a bunch of toffee-nosed intellectuals. Humphrey Spender, brother of Stephen, infiltrated a Bolton pub to photograph the clientele, only to be thrown out by the landlord. His self-righteous account, printed here,* puts one instantly on the publican's side.

*Speak for Yourself, ed. Angus Calder and Dorothy Sheridan (Jonathan Cape).

Harrisson had been a keen birdwatcher at Harrow, and his acolytes rather preen themselves on describing their fellow humans as if they were documenting the nesting habits of the lesser shrike. In their write-ups, an impersonal notation is used to pinpoint specimens: 'M45D', for example, means a man of about forty-five who looks or sounds unskilled working class. Consideration for those being observed was not a prime concern, as is shown by the activities of the team investigating extramarital sex in Worktown. In the backstreets researchers would suddenly switch on car headlights so as to count the couples leaning against walls (a practice known locally as 'having a knee-trembler'). They never, it seems, got a brick through the windscreen, presumably because young Worktowners felt inhibited about assaulting social superiors.

This taboo must also have protected the anthropologists when they moved to Blackpool. There, in a bid to plot mating patterns among holidaymakers, they shadowed courting couples, timing the duration of kisses (thirty-three seconds was apparently the record) and monitoring hand positions. When necessary they would pretend to be drunk and fall in heaps on couples found lying on the sand, so as to ascertain exactly what they were up to. These methods, applied night and day over six miles of beach and acres of parkland, established that, though petting was widespread, open-air copulation rarely occurred in Blackpool when Mass-Observers were in attendance. Only four cases were logged, one of them involving a Mass-Observer.

The cool assumption of social privilege that permeates such a report increases its value as a historical document. Acute sensitivity to class is the ruling passion throughout the earlier part of this collection, occupying the national mind much more than art or ideas or religion, which hardly figure at all. A Mass-Observation survey of June 1939 took class as its subject. One woman panel member divided English society into twenty-eight grades, starting with royalty and ending with the 'crude, dirty and irresponsible' who 'live and produce children on the dole'. Her parents, she reported, belonged to this bottom level, but she had managed to climb to Grade 19 by marriage to a member of Grade 10 ('the nicest people of all'). Her husband's family coat-of-arms is, she adds, 'hanging a few feet away as I write this'.

It is hard to imagine anyone nowadays endorsing the class system with such simple pride. What changed things was the

War. Its effect, as panel members' reports show, was to mix the social levels and develop a critical attitude to distinctions that had formerly seemed natural. One woman observer, drafted to a manorial estate in Devon to Dig for Victory, records that her war work includes sweeping the gravel drive when the Colonel is expected home for the weekend. The butler, she wryly notes, has been taught to operate a water-pump in the grounds and reclassified as an engineer, to avoid military service.

Bombing proved the most effective leveller, in every sense. Thousands of tons of high explosive were necessary to persuade the English to talk to one another. Following the big raid on Southampton (4 December 1940) an observer watches a communal exodus – streams of refugees with bedding and prams leaving to spend the night together in the fields. Nearly two years after the last serious raid on London, thousands of Londoners were still going down to the tube stations every night, rather than sleeping in their homes, because they had discovered a new community spirit which freed them from privacy's repressions. Collecting such evidence, Tom Harrisson was already able, in an article of January 1944, to predict the defeat of the Conservatives in the 1945 election.

Apart from war, women were the other good influence. They outnumbered men on the national panel, the special appeal of Mass-Observation for them being, as the editors note, that its insistence on the value of recording mundane detail gave a new status to their daily toil, which still centred, for the majority, on housework and childcare. They made better Mass-Observers than men because they were quicker to observe that the mass did not exist, but was merely an abstract concept concealing the existence of individuals. The most telling and personal reports here are all by women – a WAAF, a NAAFI manageress, an upper-class girl awkwardly explaining to her workmates on leaving a factory job that she had taken it only 'to see how another class of people lives'.

Some Mass-Observation surveys had particular interest for women, like that on family planning (March 1944). It elicited remarkably candid replies, among them an intriguing piece of life-history from the wife of an unnamed literary man (W. H. Davies and Edward Thomas are mentioned as friends). He already had a son by a former marriage and wanted no more children. She recounts, quite without rancour, how this male decision blighted her life. When, despite precautions, she conceived, her husband persuaded her to induce a miscarriage. It happened when they were on holiday in Ireland, and she recalls the primitive village, and the old woman who sprinkled holy water on the bed 'in case there may be life in the poor, wee thing'.

Jabs of actuality like that are the strength of *Speak For Yourself*. Culled from the Mass-Observation archive at Sussex University, it records an England which survived until only yesterday, without – or almost without – central heating, antibiotics, TV, detergents, Biros, supermarkets, convenience foods and package holidays. It cannot have been much fun to live in, but it makes irresistible reading. The only defect of this anthology is that it is not twice as long.

1984

The last of Beatrice

When Beatrice Webb* gets into her stride, you feel like taking cover. Her portraits of friends and relations (among them the luckless Malcolm Muggeridge, her niece's husband) resemble vivisection. 'I do not *like* human beings,' she explains. The question that bothers the reader, though, is not whether she liked them but whether she was one. Put her diary, with its endless mechanical certainties, beside those of contemporaries like Thomas Mann or Virginia Woolf, and you can see at once that for any human quality it contains it could just as well have been composed by an intelligent cockroach. Yet Beatrice Webb was one of the great British Socialists, and devoted her life to the abolition of poverty. Which raises another question: why, if she disliked human beings so much, did she care whether they were poor?

The rather chilling conclusion you come to is that she did not. It was an abstract passion for rightness that drove her. She liked to see people regulated, and shorn of their untidy personal freedoms. As the daughter of a Victorian railway magnate she belonged, she observed, to the class of persons who habitually gave orders, and she did not believe mankind could manage without someone like her in command. Democracy was hopeless, because left to itself the populace voted for blatantly unsuitable candidates, given to alcohol or gambling. There should be a Vocation of Leadership, on the pattern of the learned professions, with entrance tests to eliminate anyone morally or culturally substandard. This improvement, like others Beatrice envisaged, would not, she realized, come about freely. 'What is needed today in Great Britain', she admonished, 'is more discipline, more compulsion.'

Not just in Great Britain: Beatrice's plans were global. In the scientifically organized utopia she foresaw, the surface of the planet would be divided among the various races according to

*The Diary of Beatrice Webb Volume Four, 1924–1943: The Wheel of Life, ed. Norman and Jean Mackenzie (Virago).

their 'relative fitness'. A controlled birthrate would be ensured by introducing 'anaesthesia' for all unwanted infants. Selecting infants to enjoy this facility would presumably (though Beatrice does not specify) be a job for Vocational Leaders. Once a happy balance of population had been secured, genetic experts could, Beatrice hoped, breed a human species that would replace the shamefully haphazard results of free-enterprise love-making.

In the period covered by this last volume of her diaries, it evidently dawned on Beatrice that Britain would not, after all, be the site of her New Jerusalem. The good humour of the British, plus their absurd touchiness about individual liberty, disqualified them as pioneers of the Webb planetary plan. It was a disillusioning time for Socialist visionaries. The advent of Britain's first Labour government, with her husband Sidney as a cabinet minister, gave Beatrice new insights into the weakness of her fellow mortals. The 'unredeemably common' wives of the Labour leaders dismayed her, as did their patent eagerness to be seduced by the glamour of London society.

Beatrice, an intellectual to the bone, despised such frivolities. When Sidney became Lord Passfield in 1929, she refused to kowtow to social caste by adopting a title herself, and was glad when she was dropped from the Buckingham Palace invitation list as punishment. Whatever your views, it is hard to withhold a cheer at this point. Like her enormous appetite for work, Beatrice's contempt for the charade of monarchy bespoke a strength of personal will which, under the kind of totalitarian regime she wished to inaugurate, would almost certainly have earned her a bullet in the base of the skull.

With the fall of Labour in 1931, Beatrice switched her hopes for mankind to Russian communism, and she and Sidney were ushered round the showpieces of the Soviet Union on a two-month guided tour. Their acclaim for Russia has often been ascribed to their gullibility in accepting the statistics ladled out by their guides. But the truth is worse. It is clear from Beatrice's diary that the Webbs knew quite well what was going on in Russia in the 1930s. At first they discounted reports of official terrorism as capitalist propaganda. But soon Beatrice can be found admitting to herself that the realities of Soviet life include the rule of fear, the purging of innocent citizens, and the use of torture to soften up victims in the show trials. Such unpleasantness has to be accepted, she decides, as the teething pangs of a new civilization. 'One just has to shrug one's shoulders.'

This easy resignation to other people's anguish makes you wonder whether Beatrice's problem was not just lack of imagination. But her personality and politics were more mixed up than that. She liked repression because she was repressed. The sexual freedoms of the young in Britain constantly agitate her, whereas she is relieved to note that 'singularly little spooning' occurs in Moscow's Parks of Rest and Culture. Behind her inhibitions lay the stifling of her youthful passion for Joseph Chamberlain, and her choice of mousy Sidney in lieu. She keeps on about the wondrous happiness of their marriage, but there is something gruesome about the childless Webbs chuckling over each new joint-authored tome and referring to it as their 'baby'.

Her ardour for Soviet Communism compensated for the loss of other fulfilments. It was also a case of displaced religious devotion. Like other Victorians, having dismissed God she found the hole left behind hard to fill. She felt drawn to 'mysticism', by which she meant the vague idea that there is a 'righteous spirit' domiciled somewhere in the universe. But what she really hankered for, as she admitted, was a Church, with confession of sins and a rigorous code of conduct. For a disciplinarian like Beatrice the most distressing thing about God's departure was that he had taken the rule-book with him. There were no longer fixed standards for responsible people to browbeat others with.

The doctrine of relativity ('that the thoughts of a man are no more and no less valid than the analogous brain activities of a dog or a bee') seemed to Beatrice simply 'terrible'. Soviet Communism, with its medieval confidence in its own rightness, offered salvation from this modern predicament, and Beatrice took to it like a nun. It would even, she prophesied, solve the problem of death. She dreaded the helplessness of old age, and believed in VWL (Voluntary Withdrawal from Life). But somehow it was hard to choose the right moment, and after Sidney's stroke she felt she must stay alive for him. The Soviet Union, in its future glory, would have the answer to all this. There would rise up 'Temples of Anaesthesia' where, in an environment of communistic charm, and with the permission of their Vocational Leaders, the old and sick could fade painlessly out of life.

The most remarkable page in Beatrice's diary is the last, written a few days before death, when she suddenly goes mad, and believes that she and her electric fire and the earth and sun and moon are all ceasing to exist. God is sweeping them up in painless destruction. 'What an amazing happening, well worth recording in my diary.' But she decides not to tell Sidney, lest it should upset him, and makes a cup of tea instead. It was, after all, no stranger than much else she had believed.

                                                                1985

The wife of Westminster

'I yearn to be alone', sighs Mrs Rae.* To be honest, one would not have thought she would find that a problem, for the personality revealed in these pages is far from magnetic. The most kindly reader could not help noticing that she has an uncanny gift for banality and platitude, and her anecdotes persistently contrast her own virtues with the stupidity or malice of those fate has cast in her path. Once at her school sports day, she typically recalls, she won all the races, whereupon the other girls, instead of revering her, gathered round in a snarling pack, so that she had to beat the ringleader to the ground, bruised and bleeding, before she could secure proper respect.

Similar vexations have dogged her throughout life. As a young master's wife at Harrow School she was handed a note when she first attended chapel informing her that she was sitting in a pew reserved for senior wives, and should move. It was signed by a senior wife. Amazed that such 'pettiness' could prevail in the house of God, Mrs Rae discarded her plans for worship and stormed out before the service began – presumably to show that senior wives had no monopoly of pettiness.

Despite such setbacks, Harrow impressed her deeply. The parental Rolls-Royces, the House dinner parties in 'full evening dress', the senior boys who entertained her and her husband to 'pheasants and venison from their famly shoots', the band from 'one of the smarter Regiments' which played at Speech Day – these glories, carefully chronicled, ensured her warm esteem. That Harrow should be 'a world apart' strikes her as proper and delightful. Its inmates, she takes it for granted, must be groomed to enjoy luxuries that normal people could never expect. Thus she records, with no hint of misgiving, that Sir Bernard and Lady Docker gave the school a fleet of Daimlers so that the boys might learn to drive the kind of car they would ultimately own. On the other hand, she sees no reason why money should be

*A World Apart by Daphne Rae (Lutterworth Press).

squandered on the less well off. She firmly supports the pro-
posal that students should be required to reimburse their
university grants, once in employment, and feels sure this extra
burden would make them work harder.

Social life at Harrow has progressed little, it seems, since
Edwardian times. While the Raes were there the local dustman
was expected to cut their hedge, besides his normal duties, and
Mrs Rae rewarded him each year with one of her husband's
cast-off suits. The grateful menial would instantly don this
enviable perquisite and parade down the road, 'proud as a
peacock', with young patricians milling round. When gas and
electricity bills arrived, Mr Rae would toss them, with lordly
disdain, into the waste-paper basket. The angry artisans who
eventually turned up to cut off the supply would be placated
with a glass of sherry – which just shows that the working
classes can be perfectly reasonable if you know how to handle
them.

Mrs Rae does not possess a sense of humour, but her
stateliness has a comic value all its own. A special gem is her
disclosure that 'To Harrow's great good fortune, Air Chief
Marshal Sir Augustus Walker, GCB, CBE, came to referee
occasional matches for the First XV'. It's the kind of con-
versation-stopper Dickens might have dreamed up for one of
his more formidable *grandes dames*. Another feature of Harrow
life which allures the reader less than Mrs Rae evidently intends
is the school songs. From the selection she admiringly quotes
it's clear these are the most abject trash, hearty and maudlin by
turns. Yet, she recounts, old Harrovians regularly come back to
sing them with the boys, and can be observed weeping and
snivelling in paroxysms of sentimentality.

The retarding effect of public school education charms Mrs
Rae in this instance. Elsewhere she is more critical. Among
masters, she reports, puerility is rife. They will go to any lengths
to curry favour with the pupils. One housemaster she knew (not
at Harrow) would spend evenings boozing with the boys and
then divert them by making lurid telephone calls to women. A
Harrow master smeared Mrs Rae's car with cow dung, to the
accompaniment of sycophantic laughter from his under-age
cronies. Many masters are sexually undeveloped or deviant, and
since some schools select only married men to take charge of
houses, masters, Mrs Rae alleges, will choose marriage partners
on purely platonic terms as career-aids.

It must leave the wives rather at a loose end, and may account for another of Mrs Rae's stories about the young and beautiful wife of a public school master who made it her business to introduce the boys *en masse* to the various pleasures of sexual activity. She would concentrate on a year at a time, amounting to about 100 boys, and Mrs Rae's informant, a peer's son, told her that in his year only three boys declined the favour. Of course, this young man may have been having Mrs Rae on. Being both priggish and apparently agog for such material, she would be a godsend to a hoaxer. But even if you discount the parts of her testimony that depend on hearsay, her celebration of public school life is still a pretty powerful argument for the state system.

The star of the book, however, has nothing to do with education but is Mrs Rae's Uncle Bob, a Cheshire GP with whom, since her mother discarded her virtually at birth, she was obliged to spend her childhood. Mrs Rae says charitably that she would like to find something nice to record about Uncle Bob, but hasn't been able to – and that is certainly true, for he emerges from her account as a conglomerate of moral and physical degeneracy such as you seldom meet even in fantasy fiction. He spat food on the floor, beat Mrs Rae till she bled, and slept with dogs. He did unspeakable things with the house-maids, who seem rather to have liked it, and refused to set his mother-in-law's broken leg until the agonized lady agreed to change her will in his favour.

His misconduct with female patients was notorious. Once Mrs Rae hid in a cupboard under his examination couch to watch evening surgery, and he took advantage of woman after woman, sometimes on the couch above her head, sometimes with the patient astride him in a revolving chair which Uncle Bob, out of some obscure sportive instinct, would whirl round and round during sexual congress. At this point, I confess, my credulity began to waver. If Uncle Bob indeed spent his even-ings in this manner, his virility must have been preternatural. What was his secret? Did it not occur to him to market it?

Can it really be true, too, that Uncle Bob once told the guard on a train to chain Mrs Rae in his van like a dog, and that the man actually obeyed (this, mind, not in the Victorian age but somewhere around 1950)? Whatever the facts, Mrs Rae plainly feels she had a rotten childhood, so it's good she has prospered since. She is at present the wife of the headmaster of Westminster School, and she writes with melancholy grandeur of the isolation which this dizzy eminence entails. Her responsibilities can leave little time for authorship, and she lacks, besides, certain qualities needful for complete success as a writer. But if she takes up her pen again I hope she will give us a fuller account of Uncle Bob.

1983

Educating John

'I wasn't saying whatever they're saying I was saying. I'm sorry I said it really.'* That was John Lennon at a Chicago press conference in 1966, striving to damp down the furore after his remark that the Beatles were more popular than Jesus had shocked the pious heart of America. It sounds, of course, uncannily like William Brown. In just such tones of muddled innocence does William regularly defend himself amidst the ruins of garden fêtes and vicarage teas. Lennon was a keen William fan, and to judge from this reverential biography, he strongly resembles Richmal Crompton's lovable scapegrace in intellect and character.

Like William, he had a deep scorn for traditional culture. 'I hate Shakespeare,' he declared, with a simplicity William would have admired. His school, Quarry Bank High, was a hermetically preserved relic of the William era, with masters in caps and gowns and a fake public school ethos which Lennon quickly found irksome. Idle and disruptive, he terrified the weaker teachers, and despite frequent canings managed to fail all his O-levels before he left. He continued to share William's distrust of formal education. Even after *The Times* had hailed him as an outstanding English composer, he declined to learn to read music.

Like William, he came from a genteel home. Paul McCartney and George Harrison lived in council houses, but Lennon's Aunt Mimi brought him up amid solid middle-class acquisitions. He went to Sunday school and sang in the church choir. When he asked for pink shirts and winklepickers like George's Mimi put her foot down exactly as Mrs Brown would have done. She could never understand why he gave interviews in a vulgar Scouse accent. Had she not taught him to speak nicely? Lennon would explain patiently that he put it on simply for the money: they loved it in Brooklyn. But Mimi remained unimpressed. She

*John Winston Lennon Volume 1, 1940–66 by Ray Coleman (Sidgwick and Jackson).

had always thought John's music a noisy waste of time: when he wanted to practise she packed him off to an outside porch. 'The guitar's all very well, John, but you'll never make a living out of it,' she predicted with epoch-making inaccuracy.

Beneath his rough exterior, Lennon carried a set of perfectly conventional British instincts. He disliked Germans, and enjoyed shouting insults at the 'Krauts' on the Beatles' first Hamburg tour. Luckily he had omitted to learn German, so the audiences remained unmoved. From women, he expected proper feminine subjection. 'You read books like that?' he gasped, on finding some works by de Sade in a girlfriend's apartment, 'It's dirty!' William would have been equally appalled. Cynthia Powell, his first serious girlfriend, was a sweet tweeds-and-twinset maiden from upper class Hoylake, rather on the lines of William's Joan, and as soon as she became pregnant he did the decent thing and married her. Naturally he was a Conservative voter. Socialism was all very well, he would explain, but only the Tories knew how to manage the country.

To hide his shamefully polite background he assumed disguises, differing only in their fashionable incidentals from William's defiantly scruffy rig. Lennon favoured drainpipes, brothel-creepers and teddy-boy drapes which, he confided to Cynthia, made him look tough and hard like Elvis Presley. At Liverpool College of Art (the only place he could find for which total failure in O-level was considered a proper entrance of qualification) he was known for his greasy hair and the smell of deep-fried potato scallops he carried around with him. 'His entire body reeked of scallops,' a fellow student recalls.

During lunchtime sessions at Liverpool's damp underground Cavern Club, the equivalent of the Outlaws' Old Barn, Lennon and the other Beatles revelled in carefree disorder, turning their backs on the audience, pretending to fight, and breaking off in the middle for a smoke and chat. Their principal fans were a bevy of nicely behaved schoolgirls, 'the Beatlettes', who were quite unlike the screaming maenads who later appeared. The Beatles treated them with gentlemanly restraint, delivering them safely home after evening sessions in the group's Commer van.

It was Brian Epstein who put an end to these happy days. A neatly-dressed Jewish homosexual businessman, Epstein was exactly the sort of invader from the adult world that William would have lured into a coal shed or garden pond. Lennon scented danger at once. 'That was where we started to sell out,' he said later, looking back on the Epstein era. Epstein's first impressions were no more favourable. He felt ridiculous in the Cavern among the beehive hairdos and mascara, and saw the Beatles as an unruly bunch of layabouts. But he realized they could be packaged for mass consumption, and determined to do it.

He made them stop larking about on stage, and rebuilt their image from the crêpe soles up. In suits and ties and cute moptop haircuts they were marketed as clean, intelligent boys – and became every sensible mum's answer to the Rolling Stones. Epstein's breakthrough came in 1962 when he got a recording contract for the Beatles with EMI. Three years later they were millionaires. They had met the Queen Mother; Prince Charles had all their records; and 73 million people had watched them on American TV. John Lennon was the world's best-selling author, and Ringo Starr was asked to be President of London University.

Lennon viewed Beatlemania, as William would have done, with horror and disbelief. The squealing mobs, the deluge of dolls and teddy bears bouncing on to the stage, seemed to him insane. He saw clearly that the four of them had been turned into freaks. Waxwork dummies, he said, would have done just as well. You could not hear the singing any more, above the din: often he just stood and made mouth movements – nobody knew. He hated the way the Establishment had clasped him to its heart – the mayors and dowagers, queueing for autographs, the ogling senior citizens. It didn't seem right, he said, to see old people in the audience: they should be at home knitting.

It was all too much: a calamity such as no one had ever had to face in the secure pastoral of William-land. Lennon could find escape only in drugs. 'It's fantastic, it's wonderful,' he burbled, after trying LSD, and in the months that followed Cynthia watched him slip deeper and deeper away from reality. That is where this volume ends, in the middle of the organized childishness of the sixties, with Yoko Ono and oriental wisdom just about to trip on to the stage.

There is a serious book to be written about the Beatles. This is not it. Ray Coleman knew Lennon, and has interviewed many others whose paths he crossed – right down to the toilet attendant at Hamburg's Top Ten Club, who remembers how he would lie on the floor and cry when drunk. But Coleman never

gets beneath the froth of personalities, and he leaks goo over
every available surface like a fractured soap dispenser, recommending Lennon's 'insightful, precious letters', and other
assets. Meanwhile the big questions about the social and
historical phenomenon the Beatles represent remain unasked.
The volume is impressively packaged in black, with 'John
Winston Lennon' in gold lettering, like something you might
stumble over in the grounds of a crematorium. Lennon, and
William, might both have thought it a bit much.

1984

What the workers had to lose

Jeremy Seabrook is the author of an acclaimed study of the Labour movement, *What Went Wrong?*. But his latest book,* it seems to me, has the rare distinction of proving exactly the opposite of what it intends. The question it poses is: are working-class children better off than they were two or three generations ago? Any sane and sensitive observer, with even a vague knowledge of the bad old days, would, you'd suppose, return a confident yes. But not Mr Seabrook. There have, he concedes, been material gains, but these have been offset by spiritual losses. Today's working-class child, showered with possessions from the cradle up, has been cheated, Mr Seabrook argues, of the sense of purpose which the valiant fight against poverty once ensured. The warmth and companionship of working-class life have gone too, and the young wander, like shrunken and bewildered addicts, in the lotus-land of limitless consumerism.

How well this accords with the strapping youngsters you see around is a matter for personal judgement. But what's surprising (and, in its way, honourable) is that having fixed on his thesis Mr Seabrook should include so much evidence that undermines it. For when he questions elderly ex-workers about the conditions of yesteryear, the horror stories that spill out soon put the little worries of consumerism into perspective. Most of his oral historians belong to an era – recent, but already unthinkable to us – when youth and death were gruesomely twinned. They remember TB, meningitis, diphtheria, and the hot, slow deathbeds of siblings. Children who survived faced a working day that could stretch, for a thirteen-year-old, from eight in the morning to eleven at night. 'Many a time I've left the house at seven, faint with hunger,' a woman, now eighty-five, attests. 'I've burnt crumbs of toast, and then poured boiling water on it to make out it was tea.'

Working-Class Childhood: An Oral History by Jeremy Seabrook (Victor Gollancz).

These rigours did not, it seems, ensure spiritual health. Home life was brutal. According to Mr Seabrook's informants, parents regularly set about their children, and each other, with a varied armoury including whips, razor strops and stair rods. Women were ceremonially humbled to puff the male ego. A son recalls how his father, if he didn't like his dinner, would throw the plate at the wall. He also persistently blew his nose on to the grate. The wife never protested, but meekly fetched newspaper and cleaned up. It seems to occur to Mr Seabrook as he records these memories, that they are not as inviting as he intended. He declares that the injustice and lack of love they reveal were not representative of working-class life in the period. But how can he know? To establish that you'd need an extensive survey, and much of the evidence is already in the grave.

As for today's children, they are, on the whole, surprisingly absent from his book, given that its subject is childhood. He chats with a Hell's Angel (one of a splinter group called the Filthy Few), and joins four teenage glue-sniffing truants in a derelict house. About school, where most children spend most of their waking life, he says virtually nothing. Instead he touches contemptuously on the modern juvenile's appetite for Coke, crisps and electronic toys, and on the ludicrous pop 'culture' by which adolescents have allowed themselves to be bamboozled. Such frivolities are admittedly aggravating to the middle-aged. But to imagine they can vie with the real social evils like hunger and disease which still kill seventeen million children a year in the Third World (many of whom would, no doubt, be only too glad of a little consumerism) is to be guilty of the same affluent soft-headedness that Mr Seabrook despises in the young.

He can sustain his case only by political rhetoric which disintegrates immediately on contact with common sense. Thus he maintains that modern parents, by indulging their children in material things, have 'thrown them to the market-place' and 'might as well have thrown them to the wolves'. But surely even Mr Seabrook could distinguish a live child, however degraded by digital watches and potato crisps, from a dead one? And surely even he would prefer the former? Or perhaps not. He doesn't seem to like children much, and his constant insistence that they should have a 'purpose' is obtusely utilitarian. You'd have to be rather strange to ask, when confronted with a child, what the purpose of it was.

On the other hand Mr Seabrook is plainly in love with his own childhood, and recalls it poignantly. It was working-class, and he tells us about the thick green soap, full of grit, with which the kitchen was scrubbed, the foamy arcs it made on the floor, and other details, magical to a child. It's a charming picture, though you can't help wondering about the woman who actually did the scrubbing. Was it such fun for her? She seems to have become a decorative appendage in Mr Seabrook's nostalgia. One part of him, you feel, would like the old working class preserved in a sort of sociological zoo, housing endangered species – the clog-shod labourer swinging over ringing cobbles; the mum with her soapsuds and copper stick; the children playing on whistles resourcefully shaped from natural ash wood.

It was capitalism, Mr Seabrook gloweringly insists, that swept these lovable proletarians away, along with the green soap, and replaced them with their effete modern counterparts. He seems to envisage it as a deliberate plot. Capitalism decided to give working-class children easy and immediate gratification (toys, TV, crisps) so as to sabotage their human potential and stop them developing any critical intelligence, since that might threaten the capitalist system. As a version of history this seems too simple to be interesting – on a par with creeds that ascribe the world's ills to international Jewry or rays from outer space. But Mr Seabrook's need to find a scapegoat in capitalism plainly relates to his own sense of guilt. His strange and querulous book is, among other things, a personal confession.

He tells us how he broke away from his working-class roots, went to Cambridge and indulged, with his clever friends, in 'cruel and shameless exultation' at the 'awfulness' of his parents. Now he feels sorry. Understandably: but it is not a rare case, nor exclusively working-class. Gifted children of ungifted parents must either outgrow them or remain stunted. There's no middle way. As Dr Johnson remarked: 'Nature sets her gifts on the right hand and on the left: as we approach one we recede from another.' It's not capitalism's fault.

So what's left of Mr Seabrook's book? The oral histories themselves, records of long, bruised lives, are fascinating and a tribute to his knack for getting people to talk. He has a Dickensian zest for eccentrics. One man he visits has painted all the interior surfaces of his flat, even the light switches, with a scene of beechwoods – badgers, red squirrels, deer – so that he seems to be living in the middle of a forest. But none of Mr Seabrook's veterans appears to like the young any more than he does, which is a pity, and cannot make them happier. It put me in mind, by contrast, of another oral historian – an old man who figures in Mary Prior's fine history of the Oxford canal people, *Fisher Row* (Oxford). What he remembers is how ugly the children were when he was a boy – deformed, cross-eyed, bandy. 'But now', he says, 'the children are all beautiful.' And he's glad.

1982

The long life of the happy family

'Far from being the basis of good society, the family, with its narrow privacy and tawdry secrets, is the source of all discontents.' Thus spake Sir Edmund Leach, Reith Lecturer in 1968, and his opinion accords with much of what passes for 'advanced' thinking. Our 'nuclear' families, consisting just of parents and children are, we're told, a historical freak, unknown to past ages. Previously people lived in 'extended' families of swarming kinsfolk, or in tribal communes. The ties of affection within the family also, on this view, lack any proper historical precedent. Until recent times parents treated their small children with indifference or worse, and marriages were arranged without reference to the wishes of bride or groom. Romantic sexual love is a bourgeois novelty, it is alleged, linked to the rise of capitalism. According to one version of the myth, favoured by Engels and C. S. Lewis, it was invented by the troubadours of Provence.

Advocates of these beliefs include contemporary historians like Philippe Ariès and Lawrence Stone. But as Ferdinand Mount observes in this heartening and sceptical book,* they can be traced in large part to the muddled theories of Victorian anthropologists, and they are all now under fierce attack from specialists. Mount lays no claim to historical originality himself, taking it as his function to assemble findings from various disciplines and assess the implications. He does, though, acknowledge an overall debt to Peter Laslett, and the Cambridge Group for the History of Population and Social Structure, whose researches provide the statistical underpinning for his argument.

What Laslett has proved is that the nuclear family was always the normal family. It is a universal human grouping, predominating, it seems, in all known societies in world history. Sexual communism has never, so far as can be ascertained, existed

*The Subversive Family: An Alternative History of Love and Marriage by Ferdinand Mount (Jonathan Cape).

anywhere at all. Contrary to popular belief we now see more of our distant kinsfolk than in the past, due partly to improved transport. The idea that marriages were normally 'arranged' for financial gain derives from misdirected study of the property-owning minority, and from the assumption that theirs was the common pattern. The evidence available about ordinary people all points the other way. Peasants, for example, often incurred heavy fines for marrying outside their feudal lord's domain, following what can only have been personal and emotional preferences.

Theories about the historical unnaturalness of romantic sexual attachments have, in recent years, been wholly discredited, along with the old stuff about 'courtly love' and the trouba-dours. Peter Dronke's researches have shown that 'modern' love is at least as old as the second millennium BC, and can be traced in a host of times and places from tenth-century Iceland to the graffiti on the walls of Pompeii. There was never a time, it seems, when falling in love, marrying, and making a home for your children were not the normal human aspirations.

Those who, like the American historian of the family Edward Shorter, claim that motherly feeling is a recent abnormality, and that in 'traditional society' parents did not concern themselves with the development and happiness of their infants, have to contend, as Mount shows, with a considerable body of contrary evidence. St Augustine, in a sermon, remarks how mothers soothe and fondle their little ones at the breast, and look forward to their growing up; Plutarch, comforting his wife on the death of their two-year-old daughter, speaks of the 'wonderful happiness' they experienced at her birth, and of the special kind of poignancy, the 'absolutely pure pleasure', of the love we feel for such small children.

John Evelyn, in the seventeenth century, wrote, on the death of his son Richard, aged five, 'Here ends the joy of my life' – this at a time when, according to Professor Stone, familial emotive ties were weak, and most people found it hard to establish close relations with anyone at all. Nor does the evidence concern only the educated classes. Emmanuel Le Roy Ladurie's famous study of the Pyrenean village of Montaillou, based on contemporary eye-witness reports, shows that there was no great gap between our attitudes to children and those of fourteenth-century peasants.

The historians have blundered partly through misinterpreting past behaviour. The practice of sending infants to wet nurses to be reared has, for instance, been taken to signify parental callousness, when it was in fact widely regarded as a health measure. The thousands of children left in previous centuries, at foundling hospitals, seem to corroborate doubts about maternal fondness, until we remember that, in the prevailing conditions of desperate poverty, a mother might well be forced to choose between her child's starving to death at home and having a chance of survival if she abandoned it. We do not think of Jewish mothers, bound for the gas chambers, who thrust their babies into the arms of strangers, as behaving unfeelingly.

However, academics have misrepresented the evidence not simply, Mount suggests, through incompetence, but wilfully. For the family is the only consistently subversive organism, dividing society and putting private before communal good, and consequently it has always aroused the hostility of intellectuals and nominal subversives – Utopians, feminists, hippies, Jesus, Marx, Lenin, Mao, Hitler – everyone, in fact, who wants to control and change the way people live. 'If any man come to me, and hate not his father and mother, and wife, and children,' Jesus stipulated, 'he cannot be my disciple.' The *Communist Manifesto* displayed a similar disrespect for 'the bourgeois claptrap about the family and education, about the hallowed co-relation of parent and child,' and Hitler, in *Mein Kampf*, warned that marriage and the family should not be ends in themselves but must serve the greater goal of racial purity.

The normal procedure, Mount demonstrates, has been for revolutionary movements to start by trying to destroy the family and, when this fails, to end up appropriating it. Marriage came to be requisitioned as a Christian sacrament; in Stalin's Russia, anti-family theories were found to be the work of 'vile fascist hirelings' like Trotsky, and disowned. But the family-haters linger on, still dreaming, like Plato, Godwin or Germaine Greer, of communes in which no child need know its own parents, or in which (as in the ideal society foreseen by Shulamith Firestone) child-bearing will be taken over by technology and the whole messy business of mother love stamped out altogether.

What such visionaries offer is not love but diluted substitutes – 'brotherhood', 'sisterhood'. For love is necessarily exclusive, so communes can survive only by keeping emotions shallow. That, Mount conjectures, is their attraction for those who find

intimate relations difficult to manage. They turn personal inadequacy into public virtue. Public figures recommend 'community
spirit' because they cannot find fulfilment in anything deeper.
True or not, these speculations of Mount's will concur with what
many people have always suspected about politicians. His book
is a joy, because it vindicates the natural affections, and frees
one from the burden of believing that humankind had, for
centuries, to endure without them.

1982

The strange death of political language

No one could read these publications* without a pang. They look cheery and efficient on the outside, like hospitals. But once you open them you plunge straight into the knacker's yard of language. This is where clichés come to die. It's a pitiable sight. Arthritic old abstractions, bloodless metaphors, superannuated slurs, all dragging themselves along in a grim parody of animation. It seems callous to intrude on their terminal throes. But we should steel ourselves. For words portray their users, and if literary criticism has any public function it ought to help us assess the mental health of the three main parties by comparing their different ways of destroying the English language.

Linguistically the Alliance manifesto is the most woebegone. It exudes well-meaning feebleness, persistently managing to drop its words just off-target. The Alliance will carry out, it promises, 'an extensive decentralization of power from the centre'. You could scarcely decentralize it from anywhere else: the last three words contribute nothing except lameness. A similar lack of confidence appears in the choice of idioms. The Alliance, we're told, 'has faced the question of pay and prices policy head on'. Two figures of speech have got muddled there. You can face something; or you can meet it head on. But you can't face it head on unless you have a face on top of your head. Of course, it's quite clear what the Alliance means. It means to sound as courageous as possible, and it shuffles idioms together in the vague hope they'll do the trick.

A major aim of its programme, it declares, is 'an Incomes Strategy that will stick'. To a normal English speaker, that seems an odd thing to want. Strategies are meant to work, not stick. If they stick, you have to get them unstuck. What the Alliance meant to say was that it would like to reach agreements about pay that everyone would always abide by. But since that would

*SDP/Liberal Alliance, Labour and Conservative political manifestos, 1983.

have sounded idiotically hopeful, it reached for a tough, adhesive metaphor instead, and bungled it.

Alliance language tries to be safe as well as bold. 'Buttressed' is a favourite word. Economic growth will be 'buttressed' by a suitable monetary policy; new legal measures will 'buttress' personal rights; and, in a strange clash of imagery from building and warfare, we're assured that industrial democracy will be 'buttressed by action on two fronts'. The whole point of a buttress, of course, is that it doesn't move, whereas 'action' implies movement. The Alliance's attempt to imagine mobile buttresses suggests painful indecision. But their most poignant moment comes just after the outline of their Home Loan Scheme, when they risk a little self-applause. 'This measure is imaginative and bold,' they explain – just in case you hadn't noticed.

There are worse things than failure of nerve, though, as Labour's manifesto shows. It is appallingly written, and perfectly free from self-doubt. The main question it raises is, of course, why is it so long and boring? One reason is that it says things twice. Some pledges are repeated, almost verbatim, on different pages. Possibly the authors reckoned that readers who had nodded off the first time round might wake up for the replay. But the impression created is of wasteful, self-gratifying officialdom. The solemn enunciation of truisms has the same effect. 'Britain', we're told, 'needs a food and agriculture policy much more in line with our needs.' Clearly we do need what we need, but the circularity of the sentence rather spoils it as an argumentative thrust.

At times the repetitiveness sets up a pleasant rocking motion which, you feel, might go on for ever. 'We intend to protect the rights of individual suspects, while providing the police with sufficient powers to do their job effectively, whilst not infringing the civil rights of individual suspects.' While, of course, providing the police etc. The excess verbiage here results from an effort to sound balanced and see both sides of the question – an unusual exertion for this manifesto, which may be why it brought on a syntactical spasm. Mostly the language opts quite happily for megalomania. Labour will inaugurate 'a massive programme', 'a huge programme', 'a crash programme'. Mr Foot's foreword sets the pattern for this large perspective by accusing Mrs Thatcher of favouring a nuclear arms policy that would 'destroy the universe'. To play down the likely effects of

nuclear war would be criminal lunacy, of course. But surely it's
the inhabited world that's threatened, not the universe. Even
Mrs Thatcher couldn't destroy that, and it would hardly matter
to us if she did. Given that humanity would be obliterated first,
it's difficult to summon up much indignation over the fate of
Betelgeuse or Sirius B.

Mr Foot's concern for astronomy seems undue, but it sorts
well with the manifesto's apocalyptic tone. In the economic
sphere Labour's aim is 'nothing less than to bring about a
fundamental and irreversible shift in the balance of power and
wealth in favour of working people and their families'. This
raises some worrying questions. Who are 'working people'?
Does anyone with a job count? Or do you have to be in some
special kind of job? Probably one should not ask. 'Working
people', in such contexts, is less a precise phrase than an
expression of instinctive feeling, like the hoots and cackles you
hear in woodland at night. 'Irreversible' is worrying too,
though. How could a government with a limited period of office
effect an irreversible shift in favour of one section of the
community – unless, of course, it actually wiped out the other
sections?

Mechanical images have a powerful appeal for the authors of
Labour's manifesto, as buttresses have for the Alliance. Labour
will set up 'machinery' for the trades unions, 'machinery' to
control pollution, and a 'civil service machine' of updated
design. They do not, of course, mean anything as useful as
machinery – just laws and restrictions controlling people's lives.
But the implication of the metaphor is that the closer human
beings can be brought to the regularity and uniformity of
robots, the better. Under Labour, higher education will also be
organized by machines: 'We will establish machinery to plan
and co-ordinate all post-18 education together.' It seems relevant to add here that the difficulty of writing grammatical
sentences is not one Labour's manifesto-writers have overcome.
Maybe their educational machine needs finer tuning before it is
made fully operational.

The education section contains, too, Labour's most daring
modification of the language. 'Private schools', it states, 'are a
major obstacle to a free and fair education system.' 'Free' here
obviously can't refer to freedom of choice, since non-state
schools widen that, if only for those that can afford them. Nor,
plainly, can it mean free from state control. It must mean simply

'free of charge'. Whatever your view of private schools, it's remarkable to find a political party that can use the word 'free' without any connotation of liberty.

The Tory manifesto is easily the best written, and in case that's taken as prejudice I'd better add that it's not at all what I'd hoped to find. Though hackneyed and lustreless like its competitors, it is at least efficient, clear, and uses statistics cleverly – the fact, for instance, that Mrs Thatcher's government did away with 3,600 different types of official form. It's the only manifesto that shows any overt concern for language, apologizing at one point for talking about 'the environment', which it rightly recognizes as an example of the linguistic pollution effected by politicians. Its main fault is the smugness and occasional falsity of its tone. The Tory course is 'sensible', 'reasonable', a return to 'common sense', while Labour sadly continues to display 'vicious' resistance and 'blind prejudice'.

In keeping with this pious mien, Tory rule is presented as perfect freedom: 'It is not for the government to try to dictate how men and women should organize their lives'. It comes as a shock, after so generous a disclaimer, to discover, a couple of pages later, that the Tories plan to step up the construction of court-rooms and build ten new prisons. Evidently some men and women are going to find their lives organized rather more strictly than they had anticipated.

Military glory is used to dignify the Tory case. The Falklands crop up twice. Britain has 'recaptured much of her old pride'. This grand imperial tone slips disastrously in the Technology section, where we are suddenly invited to sample 'the whole new world of tele-shopping and tele-banking'. It's like meeting someone with a light-up bow tie at the regimental dinner. But patriotic splendour quickly returns, and vulgar opportunism is not allowed to poke out again.

One Labour reply to all this might be that style and language don't matter. They are effete, bourgeois concerns. That's an excuse no English Socialist should tolerate. We have magnificent examples of political prose – Swift, Cobbett, Chesterton, Orwell – which show how the language can and should be mobilized to capture minds. The medium of Labour's 1983 manifesto bears as much resemblance to English as sawdust does to a living tree. Socialists should demand, in anger, how this calamity came to be published.

1983

Higher, bigger, madder

The clear message of the 1986 *Guinness Book of Records* is that animals must try harder. Over the last thirty years (i.e. since the GBR started publication), the mile record for humans has come down by 5 per cent, whereas the record for horses shows a meagre 1 per cent improvement. Since last year, humans have toppled 38 per cent of their sports endurance records. The 3,000 one-arm press-up barrier, and the 300-hour non-stop snooker barrier, have both been surmounted, and a new record claim of 354 ft is under investigation for the greatest distance at which a grape thrown from level ground has been caught in the mouth by someone standing on, or just about to fall off, a tall building.

Compared with these achivements, the pages on the animal world make dismal reading. The gestation period of the water opossum, for example, nature's briskest breeder, has remained at 12 days since records began, and the highest speed for a racing pigeon (110 mph, with a strong following wind) has not been bettered for twenty years. Even vegetables can do better than that. A cucumber from Queensland, Australia, has recently turned the scales at 37 lb, to double the world heavyweight cucumber record. True, there has been an equally dramatic breakthrough in the Highest Altitude Achieved By An Animal category, but since this record is now held by some turtles aboard the USSR Zond 5 Spacecraft it is doubtful whether it can be wholly attributed to the competitive keenness of turtles.

The apathy among animals may stem from caution. A quick glance at the *Guinness Book* would assure any reasonably alert animal that breaking records can endanger your health. The Stop Press of the 1986 Book brings the sad news that Poppa of Newport, Gwent, heaviest cat ever recorded in Britain, has munched his last mouthful and gone to the great weighing machine in the sky. The strain of keeping in championship fettle has told on human contestants too. Muscle-man Gary Aprahamian, whose 25-inch biceps outbulged the waist span of many a Miss America, gains an entry in the Stop Press by dying at the age of twenty-three. Roy Fransen, whose speciality was plummeting from a 108-ft platform into 8 ft of water, died performing this feat in July 1985. Fransen, it is fair to add, was seventy at the time – an age by which high-diving must have lost its charm for many.

The publishers of the *Guinness Book* show admirable concern for public welfare, and wise anticipation of possible legal action, by warning would-be competitors about dangers that might otherwise have escaped their notice. Low-altitude free-fall handcuffed parachuting entails, it is pointed out, certain risks, and sword-swallowing has been banned from the *Guinness Book* since the reigning champion injured himself while consuming his thirteenth 23-inch steel blade. Even the humbler ventures can have snags. The record for the world's loudest snore (87.5 decibels) has been captured for Britain by Hampshire's Melvyn Switzer, but his wife Julie is deaf in one ear. The world hiccuping champion, who swept the board with a hiccuping marathon of 20 years' duration, had trouble keeping his false teeth in.

Such cautionary tales have, it seems, little deterrent effect. The current record-holder for the Highest High Wire Act strung his wire between the 1,350-ft twin towers of New York's World Trade Center, and was arrested for criminal damage when he came down. 'Anyone who does this 110 storeys up', a police psychiatrist perceptively urged, 'can't be entirely right.' Some of the best records, though, have been set inadvertently. When Michael Bracey of Newcastle spent a record 58 hours trapped in a lift, it probably never occurred to him that he was competing for a place in the *Guinness Book*; and the survivor of the Halifax munitions explosion in 1917 who flew 1,600 yards through the air, landing in a tree, might have been quite surprised to learn that he had just established a world best in the Human Cannonball class. Getting the good news through to him would have presented difficulties anyway, as he had been deafened by the blast.

For record-breakers, physical deformity is, like disaster, a great help. The sections on the fattest, thinnest, tallest and shortest known humans present a piteous procession of freaks, trapped within their malfunctioning bodies. Most eating and drinking records, the editors advise, are easily surpassed by patients suffering from bulimia (morbid hunger) and polydipsia (pathological thirst). This chastening note does not deter droves of ambitious trenchermen from trying to slurp or gurgle their way into history via measured mounds of meat and veg. Winners in this category do not appear in a winning light. What sort of person wants to eat a kilogram of snails in 3 min 45 sec? All such exertions are eclipsed, anyway, by Michel Lotito of Grenoble, whose unique ability to consume 2 lb of metal a day puzzles doctors. His diet since 1966 has included 10 bicycles, a supermarket trolley, and a cholesterol-free Cessna light aircraft.

The *Guinness Book of Records* was a British idea, conceived in 1951 when Sir Hugh Beaver, managing director of Guinness, was out shooting on the North Slob, Co. Wexford, and missed a golden plover. It struck him that a reference book in which one could check whether golden plovers were Europe's fastest game birds would be of uncommon general usefulness. Ironically, there seems to be nothing about golden plovers in the present book. The fastest bird is given as the white-throated spine-tailed swift, so Sir Hugh would probably have missed that too had he been minded to bombard it.

As an art form the *Guinness Book* is tragi-comic – a typical British compromise which has always annoyed continental critics of our literature. The serious heart of the volume consists of serried statistics about track, team and field events, which are virtually unreadable for anyone over fourteen. But this is offset by domino-toppling, backwards running, underwater violin playing, and occasional human touches which invade the proper sports sections. The most indisciplined football match record, for instance, is held by Tongham Youth and Hawley, Hampshire, at whose local cup clash the referee had to book all twenty-two players (including one who went to hospital) and a linesman. A player described it as 'a good, hard game'.

Politically, the book's bias is, as you would expect, towards capitalist individualism. There are some sour comments about the Soviet Union, whose uncorroborated claims for the longevity of its citizens (especially in the Republic of Georgia, where you can scarcely draw a bead on a golden plover, it seems, without bringing down a centenarian Hero of the USSR) bedevil record-compilers' tasks. Several of the record-breakers included look uncomfortable in this jamboree of free-world enterprise. The silent Indian fakir Mastram Bapu, awarded the Longest Camping Out prize for sitting 22 years on the same spot, had, presumably, purposes undreamed of in record-book philosophy.

But for the West, increasingly baffled and hungry for certainties, however trivial, the *Guinness Book* is just the ticket, and has itself become a record-breaker. Over 50 million copies have been sold – enough, the publishers estimate, to make a pile 631 miles high, reaching out beyond the exosphere. There would probably be someone on top trying to catch a grape in his mouth.

1986

PART THREE
Deafening Pictures

TV Reviews from the *Listener*, 1969–73

Panorama's trip around a hospital for the mentally sub-normal was meant to load us with guilt. We started off with naked, stricken creatures lurching across their dormitory, while Robin Day discoursed about the stench of incontinence and their tendency to eat the bedclothes. Then, after peering at a patient in convulsions, we nipped into the workroom to watch a bright nurse singing nursery rhymes to a hefty young man who glared vacantly back. Later we got around to the less spectacularly handicapped. But by that time, I imagine, most of those still watching had seen enough to recoil from the film's main contention: that the subnormal should where possible be let out into society, not institutionalized.

If the community decides it doesn't want these people around, a doctor told us sternly, then it should not be hypocritical: it should put them in the gas ovens. But suppose the community decides it wants them to stay where they are? It may be over-nice, but it is surely not hypocritical, to say that while you cannot stand living with someone who constantly excretes into his clothing, you do not feel justified in having him murdered for it. For most people it would be hypocritical to pretend anything else: to make out that we could all live with defectives if we only tried. It is this hypocrisy that produces outraged yelps whenever a charge nurse loses his temper. The gas-oven doctor did not divulge exactly how having subnormals in the community would benefit it or them. A unified society held together by bonds of compassion is a lovely idea, of course – every middle-class adolescent's dream. But if it ignores the way people actually behave, its place is in fiction, not in planning the Health Service.

The whole affair left one feeling simultaneously defiant and ashamed.

If you have £70 and some vestiges of decency to get rid of, you could spend a week at the Esalen Institute in sunny California,

where everyone paws and fondles everyone else so as to
Rediscover the Body. *Man Alive* (BBC2) went there on Wednesday. 'The trouble with adults is they think too much,' simpered
the overblown houri who officiated. Anyone who can credit that
after the merest glance at the modern world must be singularly
easy to deceive. And certainly none of her patients seemed
threatened by an overplus of intellect, though maybe that was
just the cure working. They clung together silently in gently
swaying groups – a bit of the treatment, incidentally, that
London Transport offers at a fraction of the cost. Others stood
back to back for mutual buttock-rubbing. 'That's an area you
usually don't communicate with,' struck in one rubber challeng-
ingly. Right: and for the good reason that buttock-vocabulary
soon runs out. But the fact that it was all absurd and regressive
didn't make it less moving. They blubbered and wailed and
humiliated themselves. Water poured off their noses. I was
snivelling noisily myself long before the end.

Apart from documentaries, another pastime which, to the layman, must seem to be fast outstripping common sense is
language study. Last week, *Horizon* (BBC2) made a pilgrimage to
Chomskyland, to find out how children learn to speak. Parents
misguidedly believe it is by imitation. Opposing this, Professor
Chomsky recited his well-known theory that a child's brain is
'pre-programmed' with a 'universal grammar' conveniently
adapted to any language the child may go on to speak. This
phraseology bespeaks a worthy ambition to make a child's mind
something technologically respectable like a computer. Similarly, faith in a 'universal grammar' is a scientific way of
reassuring the liberal conscience which has long felt that
national and racial boundaries are artificial. All men are computers, and all computers are equal.

A more remarkable linguist, Dr Paul Schmidt, Hitler's personal interpreter, was the subject of *Tuesday's Documentary*
(BBC1). It is almost impossible for a man who has figured in so
many newsreels that shook the world not to be disappointing
when you meet him. Besides, Dr Schmidt underwent years of
diplomatic grooming, aimed to deprive him of personality. 'I
became a piece of furniture,' as he put it, and Donald McLachlan's interview was a bit like a chat with an abnormally guarded
armchair. The Nazi war criminals, he conceded, were 'not my

cup of tea'. Mr McLachlan revealed that Ribbentrop, who had a snobbish regard for the British, tried to get his son into Eton because he thought that the youth leadership methods inculcated there would be ideal for Nazi Germany, 'which I think shows a very comic misunderstanding of Eton College, don't you?' 'Yes,' returned the armchair politely. It did, however, volunteer the opinion that Ribbentrop did not deserve to be hanged. 'He was just carrying out the instructions of Hitler.' Any armchair would have done the same.

We need more sex and violence on television, not less. Pornography, like pastoral, falsifies by half-measures. It cuts out the unpalatable bits. *Horizon*'s film on foetus surgery, *The Unborn Patient* (BBC2), spared none of the intimacies or horrors, and, consequently, it educated. Like most education, it was tough going. A perfectly respectable-looking doctor produced a needle as long as a bayonet and plunged it into a pregnant girl's stomach. Whether you just perspire quietly or totter to the drinks cupboard, it's impossible to feel detached in these circumstances, and the involvement is humanizing. Next we peered up a large vagina, while its owner yelled forlornly in the background, to watch the latest recruit to American society emerging, with electrodes already clipped to his scalp. By an extraordinary bit of luck from the film makers' viewpoint, he flopped out blue and dead, and a team of doctors pummelled him for several nerve-shattering minutes before he would undertake the office of respiration. The programme dragged its audience into the business of saving a life, and it reminded them that to be civilized you have to distrust your instincts. Instinctively one registered revulsion as the mercies and miracles were performed.

Just why we want to save babies is rather a question. When we take a look round the adult world, we seem to discover people who can be spared readily enough. The struggle for one baby's life chimed oddly with the news from Cambodia. Presumably a latent egotism makes us assume all babies will grow into people like us, and so be worth saving. Sartre recalls believing in progress, when young, on similar grounds: 'progress, that long and arduous road which led to myself'.

Besides, forcing a dead child to live reveals an unjustified prejudice in favour of life. Gale Parsons, drug addict, put the

other point of view in last week's *Man Alive* (BBC2). She valued
life so little herself that she vacated it after nineteen years. We
naturally feel threatened by people who disparage a commodity
the rest of us can't do without. Suicides are felt to be in need of
some excuse, and though Gale didn't commit suicide, she did
say she wouldn't mind dying. I fancy I wasn't the only viewer
who had to fight off waves of bourgeois impatience at her lack of
will-power and her self-pity, not to mention her ingratitude to
all the nice people who tried to help her in the fourteen
institutions she inhabited. Gale's mother took an even more
limited view. After omitting to provide her child with a father,
and leaving her to be looked after by the local authority from the
age of six months, she opined that all the girl had lacked was a
spot of discipline. 'I was disciplined at school: this is the way
children learn.' She seemed to imagine that viewers would
regard her as a particularly fine advertisement for the educational system by which she had been evolved.

Man Alive went to the funeral, of course, and gawped enthusiastically at the cellophaned flowers. 'All of us share the blame for
her death', it concluded with gloomy satisfaction. Grand confessions of this type are perfectly safe, since no one will take them
seriously and issue summonses. Still, they impede thought. If all
of us are to blame for an individual's behaviour, then that
means none of us is to blame.

You don't have to be of a pious turn yourself to see that Gale
would have been better off with something to believe in apart
from the hardness of her own lot. Unfortunately religious faith
is not available from the local authority. It was, though, recommended as a cure for 'hippies, anarchists, revolutionaries' and
other sufferers in Macdonald Hastings's investigation of the
Jesuits, *The Hated Society* (BBC1). Mr Hastings himself spoke
wistfully of the good old days of religious persecution and
martyrdom. Certainly the elderly bachelor applying to his
keeper for fifteen bob to go out to lunch with seemed a pathetic
remnant of the heroic company which, Mr Hastings assured us,
had endowed the West with such blessings as rhubarb and
umbrellas. We were treated to some glimpses of modern Jesuit
education: a master flinging exercise books round a classroom,
and massed adolescents bawling hymns. A distinguished Jesuit
historian was introduced, who asserted at one moment that the

Gunpowder Plot was probably a mere fable made up by the government to embarrass Jesuits, and the next moment showed us round the chapel where 'the Gunpowder conspirators met for their last Mass'. 'It takes just twice as long to qualify as a Jesuit as it does as a medical man,' Mr Hastings commented proudly. You can see why, if you have to learn two contradictory versions of each set of facts.

Is it wrong to laugh at death? *Talkback* (BBC1), which has rescued Sunday nights from the wordy pundits of *Ad Lib*, tackled this problem apropos of the comedy programme *That's your funeral* (BBC1), currently turning stomachs throughout the land. A representative housewife and undertaker failed to see death's funny side. 'It's just a waste of time to try to make comedy out of it.' From *The Jew of Malta* to *Loot* a lot of time has been wasted, if that's so. Michael Mills, BBC's Head of Comedy, refrained from literary parallels, however. Instead he reproved his detractors for associating funerals with death. Death, Mr Mills conceded, shouldn't be laughed at, because it's 'an act of God'. But funerals? They're man-made, and 'anything that's man-made we're entitled to mock.' By the same token, I suppose, it would be right to snigger at Michelangelo's David but wrong to makes jokes about the weather. Mr Mills's religious sensibilities came in handy once more when the housewife attacked him for reading from the burial service during a comic scene. With a forgiving smile he revealed that the service had been pre-recorded, then broadcast backwards. The disclosure of this pious ruse silenced all opposition. No one, it seemed, could muster any resentment, provided God had come out as Dog.

Arguably Mr Mills was running his theory backwards. Death, you'd have thought, not the harmless funeral, needs exorcizing with laughter.

Always anxious to make politics appear interesting, *Panorama* opened its profile of Geoffrey Rippon, our Common Market negotiator, with a version of his career set to music as a calypso. Between the greyer interviews, viewers were resuscitated by shots of the Trinidad sugar harvest. Family snaps showed Mr Rippon expanding rapidly from a weak-eyed tot in a mock-Tudor semi to Britain's youngest Lord Mayor – 'the Lion of

Surbiton'. Questioned at feeding time, the Lion downed succu-
lent forkloads, and divulged little, breaking off only to grab a
passing cigar. Later we watched him distributing pawfuls of
wines and groceries at a party for Tory workers. The passion for
provender had seemingly ousted more abstract enthusiasms.
About divorce, abortion, hanging, homosexuality, he confessed,
he had not felt strongly enough either way to vote. Peregrine
Worsthorne, trying to be kind, explained that he hadn't read
many books, and wasn't a cultivated person. 'What keeps him
awake at night?' squeaked the indignant Brian Walden. Dys-
pepsia, perhaps. Lured from his nutriment at length, the Lion
padded heavily round some Brussels streets, chins swaying, and
vented a little social philosophy. 'People are not prepared to do a
fair day's work for a fair day's pay': hence the 'tide of moral
decay' we can all feel engulfing us. His own fair day's pay, we
learned, included the proceeds of three company directorships
he was appointed to on leaving Parliament in 1964. And work? 'I
haven't had to overdo that too much.'

In search of new pastures, *Man Alive* (BBC2) penetrated Death
Row in Huntsville, Texas, to interview the condemned murderers. Some had been there for years, awaiting a Supreme
Court ruling on the death penalty. The spotless, barred cubicles,
each with its white-overalled figure, and the publicity of every
act from prayer to excretion, brought to mind a superior type of
zoo. Hygiene wedded to inhumanity. One of the keepers
described the friendships which he had formed with previous
occupants: how he used to wash, feed and shave them each day,
and finally strap them to the electric chair. 'We got real close.' He
pointed out the amenities of the place: the extractor fan above
the chair to remove the odour of friends who singed, and the
extinguisher handy lest they should ignite. Hardly less ghoulish
was the coven of influential businessmen calling itself the
Greater Dallas Crime Commission, in conclave at the Hilton
Hotel. Paunchy, smiling, they explained why they had a taste for
electrocuting people. 'I just pick my Bible up. The death
penalty's there: it was used in those days.'

No doubt the truly pious would advocate crucifixion. Death,
another Commissioner remarked, was not a cruel punishment:
'It's the end of all human life, so I think it's perfectly natural.'
Just like murder really.

The Six and Britain (BBC2), a new series on the Common Market, opened movingly with a vision of united Europe. The killing grounds have been tidied up and planted with crosses. At Verdun the tourist coaches halt near a row of sealed windows behind which the fruits of patriotism are on show, stacked in thirteen charnel houses. After this, a recitation of the pros and cons of membership was in danger of seeming tedious – a danger which Professor Walter Hallstein, First President of the European Commission, did nothing to avert. Sweeping aside the feeble burps of interruption from the other competitors, he talked with a fluency and dedication that were irresistibly soporific. When he first took the screen, some horses in a field behind him provided a measure of diversion, but later even these were removed, or overtaken by slumber.

The programme came to life momentarily with two Oxford undergraduates being questioned outside the EEC headquarters to find how their keen young intellects had sized up the situation within. Was the Common Market a bureaucracy? 'A very open bureaucracy,' one of them pronounced. 'You're allowed to look out of the windows over the whole of Brussels.' And was it powerful? 'The lift goes from 0 to 13 in about three seconds. Things like this mean power. They must do.' 'We didn't see anything really real,' countered the other, only to be taken up sharply by his companion: 'You don't think those people were real? I think they were really real.' Sadly this dialectic was cut short, but there must be a future for the pair somewhere in the world of entertainment.

The profoundly self-appreciative advance publicity supplied by the BBC's *War and Peace* team contained oddly little discussion of Tolstoy or his novel. Both the *Radio Times* piece and the televised *Preview* (BBC2) concentrated instead on why Anthony Hopkins walks to work, how you burst blood bags for realistic casualties, and other aids to understanding of that kind. It began to look as if TV's Finest Hour (or finest fifteen hours) would be as culturally respectable as *King Lear on Ice*. Happily, the *War and Peace* colour supplement found space for sections on Tolstoy and the Napoleonic age, along with a plot synopsis to straighten out viewers too caught up with bursting blood bags. But if Episode One is anything to go by, the dramatization, like the publicity, lavishes itself chiefly on incidentals. A set of soup plates (scrupulously authentic, one felt sure) were the main actors in the opening sequence, and chinaware and dress material continued to bear the brunt of the dramatic effort as the tale unfolded. Inside their period rig the characters had, as in the advance publicity, been simplified to thumbnail sketches. Count Rostov, a genial old bumbler, bumbled genially. Natasha pealed with girlish merriment. Tolstoy's penetration depends on noting exactly how people respond from moment to moment. This, TV discarded. When Natasha, for instance, bursts uproariously into the Rostov drawing-room carrying her doll, Madame Karagina, indicating the doll, asks ingratiatingly: 'Is she your little girl?' At this the child's laughter stops. 'Natasha did not like the condescending tone, and looked at the visitor gravely, without speaking.' Morag Hood's Natasha, however, bawled hilariously on. The modulation, intimating the dawn of Natasha's womanhood, was thrown away. Likewise when Tolstoy's Pierre visits his father's deathbed, he is overcome with comic embarrassment until the servants try to turn the old Count over. 'One of his arms fell back helplessly, and he in vain endeavoured to pull it after him.' Noticing Pierre's look of horror, the invalid glances at his refractory arm and manages a feeble smile, deriding his own helplessness. Only then does Pierre weep. Nothing of this happened in the TV version. The moribund Count was apparently stuffed. He neither moved nor smiled, and Pierre began snivelling quite arbitrarily. With their reactions smoothed over in this way, Tolstoy's characters became as lifelike as their soup plates.

Aside from being peopled with crockery, the first episode suffered from the serial's treatment of Tolstoy's structure. In order not to overtax viewers, the novel's action has been patiently unstitched and rearranged in little heaps around easily identifiable personages. Episode One stuck with the Rostovs, finishing up with the Rostov banquet. But by the equivalent point in the novel Tolstoy has unleashed a much livelier cavalcade, with Andrei, Princess Bolkonsky and Hélène already in circulation, Dolokhov drinking a bottle of rum on a third-floor window-sill, and Pierre waltzing with a bear cub. Bundling all this into later episodes leaves the first draughty and dull, and diminishes, besides, the figure of Pierre. Robbed of any chance to display his Herculean muscle-power, Anthony Hopkins ran the risk of seeming merely Bunterish, the Owl of the Moscow Remove, all twitter and giggle. His legendary dissipation amounted to a quiet game of cards with Anatole Kuragin. Still, Mr Hopkins is the only participant so far with the remotest chance of giving depth to his role.

Dr Bronowski's series *The Ascent of Man* (BBC2) has been a brilliant enterprise by any standards. Taken together with the published scripts (invaluable, since pictures on the box so often deafen the viewer), the thirteen films provide an educative sequence of the kind TV seems ideally fitted for, but almost never manages. Peregrine, polymath, Dr Bronowski has the added advantage of looking like everyone's loved grandpa. He hunches in cuddly chuckles, or rows himself round the set with expressive hand-waggles. Popping up on Easter Island one minute, dripping in an Icelandic chasm the next, he transmits visually the speed and breadth of his mind. And from his account of the history of science a secular, mechanical theory of culture can be pieced together which is bleakly challenging.

It begins in Bronowski's view of the relative status of art, science and religion. A fact noted in his book on Blake was that Blake, though he wrote of dark satanic mills, had never seen one. He imagined them filled with looms and driven by water, when they were actually steam spinning-mills. Having been no further north than London, the only mill he knew was the Albion Flour Mill. The liveliness of this criticism sprang from its matching art against science, and in *The Ascent of Man* humanity's spiritual history is repeatedly diagnosed as science in disguise. A myth like that of the phoenix, for instance, is traced to the discovery that metal can be reshaped in fire. The prayers and rituals ancient metallurgy surrounded itself with were, it's suggested, not magical but practical, fixing the sequence of technical operations like a set of chemical formulae. The wheel became a heavenly symbol in art and myth, an image of the sky itself for Babylonians and Greeks, because its discovery had solved a technical problem. In each case, technology was the prime factor, and imagination supplied a muddled gloss on it, like Blake's mills.

This approach lost some of its plausibility when Dr Bronowski turned his attentions to medieval cathedrals. He regarded them purely as manufactures, built by an intellectual aristocracy of technicians – Freemasons – who 'stood apart from the dreary formalism of pulpit learning', and closely resembled modern physicists. His suppression of the religious motive behind the structure was conspicuous, and when religion appeared in his narrative it was usually shown to be destructive. It persecuted Galileo and killed science in the Mediterranean world; in Islam it forbade the study of anatomy. That Christianity was a civilizing force, Dr Bronowski does not apparently concede, and he dismissed contemporary outbreaks of religion in a testy aside about Zen and ESP. Bronowskian man advances by accumulating gadgets. Science replaces religion in his scale of values, and to an extent it replaces art: 'Physics in the twentieth century is an immortal work. The human imagination working communally has produced no monument to equal it; not the Pyramids, not the *Iliad*, not the Ballads.' Humblingly for the innumerate, Dr Bronowski can respond to a page of equations as if it was orchestral music, and he has persuaded himself that art, in its very origins, was an adjunct of technology. The Altamira cave paintings, he believes, were a training scheme for hunters. The hunter was brought into the dark, and a light flashed on the pictures, so that 'he saw the bison and the boar as he would have to face them'. On this view, it's worth noting, a stuffed bison and boar would have been even better 'art' than the pictures.

The responsibility for providing moral guidance, traditionally connected with art and religion, can be perfectly well undertaken by science in Dr Bronowski's opinion. The role of physics in the twentieth century, he specifies, has been to prove that an exact picture of the material world can't be constructed. At any wavelength we can intercept a ray only by an object about as large as the wavelength itself. Hence all information is imperfect, dogma is obsolete, and the only moral attitude sanctioned by science is uncertainty. True, science has no way of persuading dogmatic persons of this. While Heisenberg was developing the Principle of Uncertainty, Hitler was working in a quite contrary direction. The morals of science could not prevent Auschwitz; but, Dr Bronowski might reply, neither could Christianity.

More surprising, in a scientifically uncertain world, is Dr Bronowski's certainty. He seems sure that Western man's development has been an 'ascent', though the title of his first programme, *Lower than the Angels*, itself suggested that the metaphor belongs to an outmoded world picture. In his encounter with the nomadic Bakhtiari tribe in Persia, he plainly felt that he was superior to the tribesmen, though this conclusion was reached by the simple process of selecting as the criteria of superiority commodities which he happened to possess – metal saucepans, quantum physics – and which the Bakhtiari did not. His eagerness to establish his higher manhood betrayed him into assertions which he could not possibly substantiate. The Bakhtiari life lacked variety, he claimed: 'Every night is the end of a day like the last'. Since, from his own account, the tribe crosses six ranges of mountains each year, marching through snow and spring flood-water, this seemed an unlikely proposition. And, anyway, he should not have allowed himself to pronounce about what life is like for a Bakhtiari tribesman, since one lesson he extracts from modern physics is that there is no 'God's-eye view' of events, each observation being relative to the observer. Elsewhere, he praised Wallace for sympathizing with the culture of Amazon tribes at a time when the Victorians deemed them 'savages'. But his own disrespect for the Bakhtiari seems Victorian, as do his optimistic cast of mind and his belief in progress.

PART FOUR
Books and Bookmen

Pope's fallibility

Alexander Pope's wet nurse Mary Beach, an otherwise wholly unnotable person, deserves a niche in literary history because it was probably from her milk that Pope contracted tuberculosis of the bone. The effects were spectacular. A dwarf and hunchback, he had to be laced every morning into stiff canvas bodices to keep him upright. These were replaced, as his spine gradually collapsed, by a sort of iron cage which locked round him like the chains of a hanged felon, or so it seemed to a friend who saw the shrivelled corpse lifted out after death.

To escape from the grotesque tragedy which was his body, Pope perfected a series of immaculate masks and voices. There was the manly patriot, the graceful arbiter of taste, the sly wag. In satire he aimed to sound serenely superior, immune to his foes' cruel taunts. In portraits, of which he commissioned more than sixty (a record at the time for an uncrowned head), he turned his fine, hard features to the viewer, and kept his deformities hidden. His mania for elegance in diction and versification, which changed the face of English poetry, provided another refuge from his ungainly self. So, in its way, did the famous grotto – actually a damp passage under the Richmond-Twickenham road – where he would linger in the shades.

But what Pope was really like behind these disguises, what he believed in, and how he behaved at critical junctures are, we gather from Maynard Mack's large, woolly *Life**, problematic. About his childhood, for example, nothing is known except that he was once frightened by a cow. By imagining other things that might have occurred, Mack manages to pad out the early years to a decent bulk, but a sense of vacancy lingers.

Then there was Pope's Catholicism – or was there? As the son of Catholic parents he incurred penal taxation and other legal harassments. He could have avoided these by renouncing Rome, but always refused to. Yet his religion, in so far as he had

Alexander Pope: A Life by Maynard Mack (Yale).

one, seems to have been a tepid theism, far from the faith of a Catholic, and he professed to oppose Papal power.

Perhaps he stayed Catholic so as not to hurt his parents. Personal affection always meant more to him than principle, which is one of his most admirable traits. But around his loves, hates and principles other unanswered questions cluster. What were his relations with Martha Blount, believed by some to be his wife or mistress? On the matter of principle, is it true that Pope, the fearless satirist, agreed to give up his attacks on ministerial corruption because Sir Robert Walpole threatened him with prosecution? The answer to this last query seems almost certainly yes, much as Pope's admirers might wish otherwise, but the mode of arm-twisting Walpole used remains unknown.

Mack is not to blame, of course, for his subject's tendency to slip out of sight. The clouds of fantasy and gossip Pope raised around himself are responsible for this – and anyway Mack throws in biographies of almost all Pope's friends for good measure. What may more justly rile readers is Mack's bid, backed by much homespun moralizing, to establish Pope as a Culture Hero – a guardian of True Standards who, would we but heed him, might yet save our degenerate age from its infatuation with pop stars, TV evangelists and Arts Council grants. This approach seems ill-advised. Pope's cultural standards are no secret, and they scarcely qualify him as a model.

He was dishonest and irresponsible. When publishing his translation of the *Odyssey* he concealed, from mercenary motives, the fact that half the work had been done by collaborators. He made Theobald the leading dunce of 'The Dunciad' because Theobald had rightly exposed the errors in Pope's amateurish edition of Shakespeare. The task of rescuing what Shakespeare wrote from the chaos of early printed editions required expert knowledge of Elizabethan English and a scientific grasp of textual criticism. Pope lacked these; Theobald had them – and was mocked accordingly. So too with Pope's vaunted classicism, which was compounded of superstitious reverence for the past, plus a disposition to ridicule genuine research. Pope's day saw the start of techniques – in philology and archaeology – which were to open up the ancient world. He completely missed the significance of these, and installed Richard Bentley, one of the great classicists of all time, among 'The Dunciad''s prize pedants.

Like his friend Swift's, Pope's hostility to advances in knowledge was remarkably consistent. Even his quip about Lady Mary Wortley Montagu (that one must be either 'Poxed by her love, or libelled by her hate') seems less funny when we realize it includes a sneer at her campaign to introduce inoculation against smallpox, which she had observed on her Eastern travels.

Needless to say, none of these lapses escapes Maynard Mack, who must know more about Pope than anyone else alive, and more than Pope knew about any subject whatsoever. It is to Mack's credit (though not an aspect that has apparently occurred to him) that his mighty tome with its panoply of footnotes would have seemed, to the author of 'The Dunciad', a glorious opportunity for mirth. It represents just the kind of laborious scholarship Pope loved to poke fun at.

Mack would have us believe Pope a serious thinker, and he quotes approvingly a comparison of him with T. S. Eliot. But the peculiar challenge of Pope for our age is that his greatness (and there is no point in denying he was a great poet) was perfectly consistent with his having no worthwhile or original thoughts at all. He was brilliantly superficial. This presented no problem to his own century, which did not demand profundity in its poets but could enjoy them, like painted porcelain or music, on purely aesthetic grounds. 'Never was penury of knowledge and vulgarity of sentiment so happily disguised', wrote Dr Johnson of Pope's 'Essay on Man' – and meant it as praise.

That kind of admiration is less easy for us. Mack taxes us for neglecting the 'Essay'. It shows, he says, that poetry is 'not our thing'. But that is mere carping. It argues no disrespect for poetry that we should hesitate to recognize as poetic the 'Essay''s decorated platitudes. Its immense contemporary success – dozens of editions, translations in twenty languages – is symptomatic of what now makes the eighteenth century seem more out of date than any other. How can we take seriously a philosophic poem that urges, as its world view, that 'Whatever is, is right'? How could Pope, given that he spent half a lifetime writing satire?

And satire itself seems duller nowadays than it did even twenty years ago. It depends so clearly on misrepresentation – on preset attitudes, like the clown's fixed grin. Mack himself is not blameless here. He might have done more justice to Pope's victims, especially Lord Hervey, whom Pope disgustingly travestied as Sporus. 'An effete courtier and literary dabbler', notes Mack. But Hervey's Memoirs contain, though no reader of Pope or Mack would guess it, some of the most witty and entertaining writing in the language – rather more witty and entertaining, one would have to admit if pressed, than anything in Mack's *Life* of Pope.

1985

Scott: a giant eclipsed

Most great writers are two people, if not more: their art grows out of the splits in their personalities. The two halves of Sir Walter Scott* came from separate geographical regions. On one side he was a rationalist and lawyer, breathing the classic air of Georgian Edinburgh. The other part of him belonged to the wild Border Country, steeped in feud and folklore, to which he had been sent at the age of three to regain his health after contracting polio. Throughout his life these contrasting cultures waged war inside him. Repressed, and terrified of the passions, like all good Augustans, he was, at the same time, madly exorbitant, swaggering around in bogus regimentals, pouring his fortunes into the absurd mock-feudal estate at Abbotsford, and imagining in his later ravings that he was King Lear.

He was over forty before he began to write novels, but once he started he thundered through them at incredible speeds, notching up sales figures like a giant's fever chart. Sheer heroism kept him at it. Racked by stomach pangs and gallstones, he lay groaning on a sofa while he dictated. When, by dint of reckless mismanagement, his printing and publishing firms failed to the tune of £130,000, he vowed he would pay his creditors to the last farthing by the labour of his pen. And he did.

Andrew Wilson has the advantage of being a novelist himself, and he traces the man in the works with a novelist's insight, following the seismic fault in Scott's character as it zigzags through his writings. It's an idea that could well be explored further than Mr Wilson, in this slim and stylish book, has time for. Every novel Scott wrote resolves itself, at some level, into a fight between the free human spirit and the forces that conspire to stunt it. On the one hand are rebels, smugglers, gypsies, Saxons, Highlanders, lunatics and zealots: on the other, the civilized barbarities of law and commerce. Faced with this opposition Scott did not (except when his imagination had begun to ossify) resort to anything as simple as a consistent

*The Laird of Abbotsford: A view of Sir Walter Scott by A. N. Wilson (OUP).

viewpoint. Somewhere beneath his waistcoat an extremely sensitive moral pendulum was fitted, and it prevented him from seeing only one side of the question. He realized that savages were cruel, ignorant and squalid, as well as noble, and that civilization widened life's possibilities as well as cramping them.

These truths, hateful to cultured progressives in all ages, are repeatedly brought to our notice by Scott just as the torrent of his narrative threatens to drown them. Mr Wilson picks as an example the moment in *Rob Roy* when the hostage Morris is flung screaming from the cliff, with a boulder round his neck, by Helen Campbell and her outlaws. Till then, outlawry had seemed rather fine. Suddenly we see it for what it is: terrorism. Scott, as Mr Wilson observes, shrewdly anticipated the problems we associate with modern Africa and Ireland.

Which brings us to the great mystery about Scott – his total eclipse at the present day. The Waverley novels were hugely influential, trailing in their wake dozens of operas, hundreds of paintings, miles of Gothic villas. A cultural Krakatoa, they permanently changed European sensibility. Yet now they prop up broken furniture in every bookseller's back room. Why? Largely, I think, because people regard them as monuments, so assume they must be rather solemn. Nothing could be more unfair to Scott. He writes with such dash that you have to keep reminding yourself he's a serious author at all. Ideally he should be read at top speed, with lots of skipping – a practice he recommended. That way, even his more lurid historical fictions become compulsive – like watching *son et lumière* from a Big Dipper. A master of stage lighting, he throws glare and gloom round the merest incidentals of his action – the salmon-fishers in *Guy Mannering*, for instance, spear their prey at night by the blaze of tar barrels, looking like fiends from Milton's Hell.

His grander figures are insurgents from a primitive world (to which, not seldom, one wishes they would speedily return): Redgauntlet, for example, with his sinister expandable eyebrows, or Lady Glenallan, who hands her waiting woman a golden bodkin with orders to stab the newborn Glenallan heir. Mr Wilson finds Lady Glenallan 'incredible', but she terrifies me. As Chesterton said, it's no good complaining that Scott's effects are unlikely, when they hit you between the eyes like a stone.

It would be good to think that Mr Wilson's book might

prompt a resurgence of interest in Scott, but I doubt if it will. Indeed, for all his wit and poise I'm afraid he may put some people off. For one thing, he underrates Scott's faults. He applauds his 'Shakespearean' qualities without seeming to realize what a dreadful mistake it was for Scott to imitate Shakespeare, or how excruciating the 'Shakespearean' comic characters Scott cobbles together are. Scott's love of pastiche distinguishes his genius radically from Shakespeare's: it is precisely his wish to be like Shakespeare that makes him unlike.

More upsetting is a prim and pompous strain in Mr Wilson, which shows itself in his criticism of other authors. He alludes sniffily to D. H. Lawrence's 'orgiastic fantasies' (can he have *read* any Lawrence?), and reproves Stevenson for introducing a puerile impossibility into *Treasure Island* by making Jim Hawkins swim across the bay, dragging the *Hispaniola* behind him. Actually, no such episode occurs in *Treasure Island*; Mr Wilson has dreamed it up. It's a tribute to his book's liveliness that it survives such lapses, leaving an impression of keenly communicated enjoyment. In that respect it's quite like Scott.

1980

The truculent genius of Thomas Carlyle

Carlyle, Professor Kaplan tells us,* was a man of compassion and humanity who deserves our respect. That makes a change from the standard view, which is that Carlyle was so poisonous it's a wonder his mind didn't infect his bloodstream. However, after digesting Kaplan's weighty book you feel pretty clear that the standard view was right. Carlyle was a racist, with a rare talent for misreading historical trends and selecting for applause precisely those that were to bear the most hideous fruit in our century.

He idolized Teutonic 'valour', wishing like Hitler to see a mighty Germany subjugate the rest of Europe. He detested Jews, and favoured depriving them of civil rights. A friend once glimpsed him outside the Rothschild mansion, engaged in a fiendish mime of extracting teeth – the torture formerly used to make Jews reveal their hidden treasure. It's typical of Kaplan's pussyfooting that he risks only a vague allusion to this disquieting incident.

With similar compassion and humanity Carlyle opposed the abolition of negro slavery, and when Governor Eyre of Jamaica killed several hundred blacks after an uprising, he remarked that it might have been better had Eyre shot 'the whole Nigger population' and flung them in the sea. A wish to see people subjugated also lay behind Carlyle's enthusiasm for 'heroes' or divinely gifted leaders who, he believed, embodied the 'vital energy of the universe' and could rightly claim unquestioned authority over the rest of mankind.

Naturally the main question raised by Carlyle is why he had such disgusting ideas. Kaplan, while blandly refusing to register disgust, offers some plausible explanations. Illness was partly to blame. Carlyle's bowels were a perpetual battleground, swept by mighty onslaughts of flatulence, colic and constipation. From youth he crammed himself with medicines, which must have fearfully intensified the tumult within. His wife Jane also

*Thomas Carlyle: A Biography by Fred Kaplan (CUP).

enjoyed almost permanent ill-health, so that for long stretches Kaplan's book resembles a contribution to medical rather than literary history.

Then there was sex, or rather there wasn't, for Carlyle apparently suffered from incurable impotence. So sternly had he repressed his physical instincts, under the influence of his holy old mum, that he had, it seems, no inkling of what was expected of him on the wedding night, and wrote afterwards for enlightenment to his brother who had studied medical textbooks. Despite this scientific aid, the forty-year-long marriage probably, Kaplan thinks, remained unconsummated. Carlyle's tirades against 'phallus worship' and the cesspool of modern sexuality acquire a comic pathos in the light of his personal handicap, but it can have been no joke for him or Jane. His hatred of the body and the material world, which is the key to his thinking, cannot be separated from rage at the humiliating performance of his own guts and genitals.

The Carlyle marriage sounds like hell on earth. There was affection on both sides, but nerves and tempers clashed and Carlyle's pig-headedness would have driven many women mad. Jane contemplated separation. Especially galling was Carlyle's middle-aged infatuation with Lady Harriet Ashburton, to whom he wrote strange masochistic love letters, wisely ignored by their recipient.

Carlyle's mother and his marginally less awesome father had much to answer for besides his marital failure. They brought him up to believe his family was in receipt of special grace from God, and the pride of religious election fuelled his immense conceit. He confided to his mother that he had a mission, and compared himself to Christ. The narrowness and bigotry of his Annandale peasant background permanently impaired his capacity for thought. He always associated science and progress with the Devil, harbouring particularly dark suspicions of the railway services, which he considered monuments of 'brutal heathenism'.

His truculent insistence on his own genius dimmed his respect for everyone else. His memoirs of acquaintances are a storm-path of vituperation. Coleridge was an 'inspired ass', sunk in 'putrescent indolence'. Nothing seems to have intrigued him so much about the great Romantic as the continual sucking motion Coleridge had to resort to to stop his saliva spilling over. Lamb was a 'despicable abortion', Scott 'almost worthless',

Wordsworth 'small', Shelley 'a ghastly object'. Tennyson's poetry was unbearable: Carlyle left the house to avoid having to hear him read *Maud*. *David Copperfield* was 'the wateriest of twaddle', *Bleak House*, 'a new dud of a book'. No one, even with Carlyle's rather crude sensibility, could have been so unerringly wrong about literature if jealous self-regard had not rotted his judgement.

His peculiar psychological sickness required not only that he should believe himself 'totally above the reptile world of authors', but also that he should despise human life and its pleasures. To have valued anything beyond his own mind would have threatened his monolithic self-esteem. He saw himself doomed to live on a 'dirty little uncomfortable planet', the other inhabitants of which he condemned out of hand. Ten days in Germany were enough to convince him that all Germans were vapid and dull; the French were 'fops and pastry-cooks'; America, which he never visited, was a nation of 18 million bores.

It would be hard to select a set of prejudices more calculated to make their owner wretched, and Carlyle seems to have moved around in a permanent puddle of gloom, which slopped over on to close associates. His portraits and photos, assembled by Kaplan, form a gallery of tragic masks, culminating in Julia Margaret Cameron's famous shot of the bearded sage as a soggy-eyed hedgehog. The obvious failure of Carlyle's doctrines to bring joy to their chief proponent might, you would think, have deterred imitators. But in fact he strongly influenced Victorian thought, for reasons which it is now almost impossible to puzzle out.

Presumably his teaching happened to combine vagueness and uplift in just the right proportions for the age. His prophetic fury seemed reassuringly biblical in a time of waning faith, but it did not entail any inconvenient curb upon one's daily actions. Man was meant to discover the divinity within him, emerge into 'the eternal blue of ether' and inaugurate at some unspecified period a new heaven and new earth. As a programme this seemed harmless and bracing, and you could happily assent to it without attempting to remedy the present injustices of society.

Indeed, Carlyle discouraged practical measures. Reforms such as the extension of the franchise to working men earned his vehement opposition on the grounds that politics were just materialism in disguise. So Carlylism provided a way of assuaging one's social guilt while continuing to exploit the masses just as before. Its emphasis on individual will and energy chimed exactly with the spirit of Victorian industrial capitalism: in this respect it was an outgrowth of the system it proported to condemn.

Kaplan offers no clear summary, let alone a reasoned critique, of Carlyle's thought. He keeps urging us to admire the 'fire' of his rhetoric, but the reader is never persuaded that Carlyle could distinguish between fire and hot air. Still, Kaplan has assembled and stuck together a mountain of information about Carlyle's private life, and if he cannot make his scarred misanthrope seem humane, he does make him look terribly human.

1983

A writer on the front line

William Howard Russell was thirteen stone of unresolved contradictions: a war correspondent who hated war; a sexual prude who fathered three illegitimate children; an ace journalist so disorganized that he could never learn to master a railway timetable. Yet if you took this amiable muddler and put him on a battlefield he would emit streams of faultless prose as unerringly as a water-cannon, and with an authority that made it clear, as Bismarck sourly conceded during the Franco-Prussian war, that Russell knew more about what was going on than the commanders-in-chief. Alan Hankinson does not try to sort Russell out.* He presents him in all his raw inconsistency; and he comes out of it potent, enigmatic and alive.

He started work as a reporter at twenty-one, and an early assignment was the Irish famine of 1846. An impoverished Irish lad himself, he might have been excused partisan fervour, but his descriptions show his flair for unswerving and appalling fact. One 'strange and fearful' consequence of hunger, he reported, was seen in the famished children, whose faces and bodies became covered with long, fine hair. This, with their dwindled limbs and enormously swollen bellies, rendered them 'bestial to behold'. War, after that, must have seemed light relief, and the Crimea gave Russell his chance. *The Times* sent him out, assuring him it would be over in a few weeks. He stayed two years, and came back famous.

At the time war was still a spectator sport, and Russell had a knack of choosing the best seat. He viewed Balaclava from a high ridge, with his telescope, watch and notebook beside him, and the masses of soldiery spread out like toys in the valley below. Between the cannon bursts, the champing of bits and clink of sabres floated up clearly through the bright air. The result was one of the great battle accounts of all time. Russell watched the Russian cavalry falter and break before the Suther-

Man of Wars: William Howard Russell of 'The Times' by Alan Hankinson (Heinemann Educational).

land Highlanders – 'that thin red streak topped with a line of steel' – and his phrase, modified to the 'thin red line', became a watchword of jingoism. He also saw the Light Brigade immortalize and destroy itself within twenty-five minutes, charging the wrong guns. The fault, Russell disclosed, lay in Raglan's orders, which had failed to make it clear that the Brigade should attack the battery to its right, not the one at the valley's end, which was covered by fire from three sides. To Raglan and his staff up on the heights, this was too obvious to need stating, but it was obscure to the cavalry officers on the ground.

'What can any novelist write so interesting?' sighed Russell's friend Thackeray on reading his Crimea despatches in *The Times*. Tolstoy, serving with the Russian army, evidently pondered the same problem. The panorama of Borodino, and other battle scenes in *War and Peace*, show fiction adapting itself to the new realistic expectations created by journalism. Twice more after Balaclava Russell secured a bird's-eye view of history as it took one of its uglier turns. At Sadowa he climbed a handy medieval tower to watch the Prussians wipe out 24,000 Austrians against a backdrop of flaming villages and cornfields. At Sedan he sat with Bismarck on a hill overlooking the Meuse and saw the beautiful blocks of French cavalry, drawn up by the river, being pounded to blood and dirt.

But it was as critic of official policy that he earned most fame and hatred. His revelations from the Crimea about the lack of supplies and medical care aroused alarm at home. Whole regiments, he divulged, were being 'murdered slowly and in accordance with military discipline'. Queen Victoria raged against his 'infamous attacks', and Prince Albert pronounced him a 'miserable scribbler'. For all that, public feeling ignited, the Aberdeen coalition fell, and Russell became the only journalist to have brought down an English government. It gave him no pleasure. 'Cursed is he that delighteth in war,' he wrote morosely to his wife.

Imperialism and its theories of racial superiority disgusted him just as much. He observed the system at first hand when *The Times* sent him to witness the suppression of the Indian Mutiny. Evidence of British barbarity met him everywhere. Stiffened corpses hung from trees on the line of march, and an English officer was seen to shoot through the head a Kashmiri boy who had thrown himself at his feet for protection. Another officer boasted to Russell that when fifty-seven sepoys surrendered to him he had disarmed them, lined them up against a wall, and got his Sikhs to slice them to pieces. The British-Indian papers vilified Russell for publicizing these punitive measures, but his voice carried political weight and helped stop further reprisals.

Strangely, Russell's conscience did not prevent him from sharing the loot. When Lucknow fell he was up with the vanguard, stuffing his pockets full of jade and diamond in one of the palaces. His only regret was that he couldn't get more. A trooper offered him a fabulous assortment of gems for 100 rupees, but Russell, as usual, lacked ready cash. Also anomalous, given his condemnation of war, was his respect for the military virtues. This emerged most scathingly when he encountered cowardice. Covering the American Civil War for *The Times*, he was present at Bull Run, where a Northern army turned tail rather than face Stonewall Jackson's militia, and continued to flee till nightfall, tumbling over one another in terror, though no one was pursuing them. Russell wrote up the 'scandalous' retreat with withering accuracy, after which his stay in America became hazardous. His life was threatened, and the Northern papers declared he had caused their army to panic by galloping from the field himself.

Being married to Russell, as to most of the great Victorians, must have been awful. While he was off enjoying himself he would write to his wife telling her how he longed to see her 'dear old red nose' again. The need for sexual purity, and the dullness of her letters were also frequently touched on. Repeated childbirth, depression, and kidney failure finally did for her: when her screams became intolerable she was packed off to a nursing home to die. Russell had rather a jolly time afterwards, pursuing several amours, while deploring in letters to the press immodesties like the can-can.

He liked billiards, overeating, and aristocratic company. A crony of the Prince of Wales ('Tum Tum' in Russell's diaries), he accompanied him on a pleasure trip up the Nile with a flotilla of blue and gold steamers, and 3,000 bottles of champagne as part of the provender. The Prince also took him along as official historian on a state visit to India, and Russell designed a splendid uniform for himself to match his dignity. It was cut on the slim side, and while mounting an elephant he split the trousers down the back releasing an impressive festoon of shirt tail. Luckily the Indian princes took this to be part of the regalia.

At sixty-three he married an Italian countess half his age, and against all the odds it was blissfully successful, lasting for twenty-three years. She played him dreamy melodies on the piano, and kept a firm grip on his social engagements. They found a mutual interest in hypochondria, and toured the European spas sampling the mud baths. 'I suppose there is no absolute truth in any history,' Russell once said. But he did his best to put that right. Not a reflective man, he never tried to square his excitement over warfare with his disapproval of it. But he was fearless, merciful, and matchless in his profession. His life must have been even more enjoyable to live than it is to read – which is saying quite a lot.

1982

How they destroyed Thackeray

The Victorians destroyed Thackeray.* It was a needful act of self-defence, for he saw through everything they believed in. As a young writer he showed them, with deplorable wit and clarity, that their patriotism was arrogance, their religion humbug, and their class distinction tyranny. This was the Thackeray Marx praised for delivering 'more political and social truths than all the professional politicians, publicists and moralists put together'. Obviously it could not be allowed to go on. His masterpiece, *Vanity Fair*, was roundly condemned by the Victorian middle class for its 'cynicism', so after that, as he was anxious to make a fortune, he decided to become the sort of soggy, benevolent ironist his public wanted. The transformation was so successful that he never wrote anything remotely resembling a great novel again.

He was richly rewarded for his treachery, reeling from dinner party to dinner party, and lionized by the great hostesses. It killed him eventually – struck down, at fifty-three, by apoplexy, after a Christmas Eve binge. But by then he had guzzled blissfully for fifteen years, swallowing enough wine, he calculated, to float a 74-gun ship. He adored all the appurtenances of greed – the grand rooms ablaze with lights, the pretty women, the 'gay and airy gossip'. William Allingham, the Irish poet, recalls dining with him in Paris and noting his rapture at each culinary detail, beginning with the flourish with which the waiter set down their dishes of Ostend oysters.

He aspired to stuff others as well as himself. The childhood memories included here show that no juvenile was safe if Thackeray spotted it within sniffing distance of a sweetshop or pastrycook's. Regardless of age and sex it would be dragged inside and crammed with tooth-rotting dainties. Many a pale-faced tot must, one fears, have puked over its bed linen as a direct outcome of the great man's bounty. This passion for giving instant pleasure can pretty clearly be seen as an expres-

Thackeray: Interviews and Recollections ed. Philip Collins (Macmillan).

sion of Thackeray's guilt and insecurity. So can his own gluttony. He gorged to console himself for all he had lost – his
betrayed ideals, his youth, his poor mad wife locked up with her
keeper in Camberwell.

Isabella's insanity put a distressing strain on him. It left him
wifeless but unable, as she was still alive, to marry again. 'It's *a*
woman I want, rather than any particular one' he complained in
a letter to his mother. Professor Collins's memoirists are for the
most part decent citizens, keen to hush up anything unseemly,
so they divulge little about this predicament or its effects. At
Thackeray's funeral, we learn, a crowd of garishly dressed
women in scarlet and blue feathers gathered so thickly around
the grave that 'the true mourners and friends' could not get near.
Unfortunately none of these Jezebels has bequeathed us an
Interview or Recollection, and of the hundred or so accredited
friends in Professor Collins's pages only one gets round to
mentioning that the urethral stricture that caused Thackeray
such agony, and sent him so frequently to his doctor, resulted
from a venereal infection.

Corporate censorship of this sort has the effect of making
Thackeray's forays into Bohemia, or the glimpses we're allowed
of them, seem embarrassingly tame. He enjoyed, we're told,
glee-singing in Evans's Cider Cellars which, to judge from the
accounts here (and in *The Newcomes*) must have been one of
London's least thrilling dissipations. More adult pastimes, such
as his long and unavailing campaign to lure his friend's wife
Jane Brookfield into bed, go virtually unmentioned. After *Vanity
Fair* the Thackeray who didn't get into the novels was immeasu-
rably more interesting than the one who did, but he's to be
found in the private correspondence rather than in these loyal
and guarded reminiscences.

Not, of course, that Philip Collins should have chosen differ-
ently. He gives us, besides the big names, chance acquaintances
dug out of the remotest crannies of Victoriana. The range is
formidable, and makes the general air of cover-up the more
impressive. 'Old Thack's' apologists evidently felt they faced a
ticklish task. Noticeably, they seldom quote him. There's praise
for his 'sparkling fancy', and suchlike vacuities, but verbatim
accounts of his conversations are avoided, even (or perhaps
especially) when he shocked his hearers. Charlotte Brontë
reports that he defended himself like 'a great Turk and heathen'
when she took him to task; Carlyle declares he had 'no

convictions'; John Chapman recalls him as a secret free-thinker who concealed his religious doubts lest they should harm his popularity; Edward Fitzgerald – a close friend – describes him, in private, as 'naturally prejudiced in favour of the dirty and the immoral'. It's hardly what you'd expect of the author of *Henry Esmond*, but infuriatingly not one of these witnesses records what Thackeray actually said to prompt their judgements. Typically the collection ends with a letter from John Blackwood rejecting some samples of Thackeray's talk sent in by a contributor. Blackwood declines to publish them because, he explains, though Thackeray used to say such things in a 'half-mocking way', they'd be an improper tribute to his memory.

What sort of things? Probably it was his nihilism that most pained the Victorians. He had a contempt for human life that would have done credit to one of the more ascetic Church Fathers, and would not be out of place in Beckett. 'There's nothing new and there's nothing true, and it don't much sinnify', he would drawl. It's one of the most vivid scraps of old Thack to survive: you can almost smell the cigar smoke. Literature was a favourite target for his sneers. To an American friend he defined the difference between Shakespeare and an ordinary mind as the difference in the lengths of two maggots. Milton was a 'damned bore'. He liked, he used to say, 'second-rate books, second-rate women, but first-rate wines'.

Partly this was the raffish pose of the old Carthusian who believed himself too good for the trade of letters. Thackeray remained a swell, though a swell in difficulties, as an unswell friend observed. But it wasn't just that. In reality he cared dreadfully about his literary reputation. Dickens's matchless popularity tormented him. He couldn't win, so he pretended not to bother – and perhaps sometimes managed not to. Undeniably this nonchalance had its appealing side. Whereas Dickens possessed neatly-bound volumes of his own works ranged in order on his shelves, Thackeray could never lay his hand on a copy of his. 'Fellows borrow or steal them,' he would shrug. 'I try to keep them, and can't.'

It's good to think that he tasted success in the end. His American lectures were a hit, and as editor of the *Cornhill*, four years before his death, he achieved spectacular sales. Friends remember him dancing in the street with excitement, and riding round in a cab with his legs stuck out of the window. In Paris he had to be restrained from rushing into jewellers' shops and buying 'a pocketful of diamonds'. He always liked playing the fool, and distrusted solemnity. Impromptu bawdy was a speciality. "'Tis true 'tis titty, titty 'tis 'tis true', he remarked of a prominent example of female portraiture. Philip Collins finds this vein in Thackeray schoolboyish and no doubt it is, but at least it's less dull than *The Virginians*. One rather wishes his friends had recollected it more.

1983

Loti: a many-splendoured thing

Pierre Loti's life reads like fiction, and much of it may be. Lesley Blanch* has had access to his secret journals – or what remains of them after systematic purges by his embarrassed relatives. But Loti himself described the journals, at an early stage, as dreams and longings rather than authentic records, so their exact status remains a puzzle. In this fix Mrs Blanch takes the valiant step of accepting everything Loti writes, including the torrid imbroglios in the novels, as essentially true. That may not be rigorous scholarship, but it certainly peps up the story.

Born Jean Viaud into a provincial Huguenot family consisting mainly of elderly ladies, Loti felt that nature had let him down. 'I was not my type,' he mourned. He wanted to be a husky sailor lad. Instead he was a short French naval officer whose built-up shoes and rouge only made his lack of huskiness more striking. As a young man he tried to remedy this by signing on for a gruelling body-building course, from which he emerged a miniature Hercules with a nervous breakdown. While recovering he worked briefly as a circus acrobat, 'a Hamlet-figure in black velvet', as Mrs Blanch imagines him. Actually his trapeze gear comprised bathing trunks, lace cuffs, and a green wig with pom-poms – an ensemble which might have created rather a stir on the battlements at Elsinore. Loti's spiritual home was not the tragic stage but the theatre wardrobe.

Ashore in foreign ports he enjoyed skulking through the kasbahs in an Arab burnous, or lurking inconspicuously around the mosques in his Turkish outfit, covered in daggers and gold embroidery. Nearer home he would mutate into a Breton fisherman and carouse with fellow salts. The naval authorities seem to have handled their thespian colleague with saintly forbearance, though his affection for young ratings earned mild censure.

Loti, an ex-crony explained to Mrs Blanch, loved both men and women passionately, and if there had been a third sex would have loved that too. He adorned his cabin in boudoir-style with red silk hangings, gilt mirrors, and a grand piano, which rendered access difficult, and he introduced personnel

Pierre Loti: Portrait of an Escapist by Lesley Blanch (Collins).

unusual on French warships. An Arab taxi driver from Suez came aboard at night to fan him while he toiled at his manuscripts. Despite these quirks, Loti was a distinguished officer and a stickler for the service. A latish photo shows him virtually coated with medals, and clutching a chair, seemingly to avoid tilting sideways under the weight of metal.

The navy provided Loti's gateway to romance. Steaming round the French colonial empire vastly extended his female acquaintance. In Tahiti the dizzy perfumes and plenitude of 'come-by-chance brown bodies' (in Mrs Blanch's phrase) quite overcame him. He apparently contracted marriage 'in the Tahitian fashion' with a voluptuous fifteen-year-old, Rarahu, who, like most of Loti's loves, was gently off-loaded when the fleet sailed. In Senegal he found a supply of deliciously willing little negresses, and also tangled with an inflammable Creole lady – or so Mrs Blanch surmises, for Loti later destroyed the pages of his journal relating to this conflagration.

But his great love, and the heroine of his most famous novel, was Aziyadé, the Circassian beauty whom he snatched from the harem of her Turkish overlord and enjoyed – if Loti's account can be trusted – in a sort of floating bed, stuffed with oriental soft-furnishings, while Samuel, his trusty boatman, gravely rowed the preoccupied couple round the bay of Salonika. Samuel's reward on these trips was to make love to Loti after Aziyadé had finished with him. This amour inaugurated Loti's lifelong devotion to all things Turkish. He later defended Turkey over little lapses like the Bulgarian atrocities, earning public honour from the sultan who was charmed by his obliging infidel friend.

Islam appealed to Loti's conservatism. He liked its backwardness and its tyranny, 'far from that wind of equality, stinking with coal dust, that blows from the West'. He also approved its insistence on male supremacy. He married only so that his wife might enrich the world with some juvenile replicas of himself. Apart from that, she bored him. To make doubly sure of issue, he persuaded a doctor friend to select a healthy peasant girl, installed her in a house inconsiderately near to the one where his wife resided, and begot three sons on her. These lordly ways did nothing to diminish his spell over women. They wrote incessantly, offering to elope with him, to bear his children, or to become his slaves.

Things, not people, were what he treasured, though. The old ladies back home grew frantic over the cartloads of exotica that

arrived – gigantic tapestries, fearsome weapons, the catafalque
of an emir specially delivered by smugglers from Damascus.
'Tante Claire and I beg you to tell us what to do with the giraffe
skins,' wrote his mother plaintively. Gradually Loti converted
the Viaud house at Rochefort into a colossal souvenir. There was
a Turkish room, crammed with divans and narghiles; a
Pagoda room, all scarlet lacquer and porcelain; a Japanese
salon; a Renaissance hall and, crowning fantasy, Loti's own
personal mosque with Aziyadé's tombstone (she had pined to
death when he left her) as its showpiece.

Sumptuous parties graced these settings. At the opening of
his medieval room guests had to come bearing their own silver
goblets and knives, as at the court of Louis XI, and feasted on
stuffed peacock and lampreys. For Loti, nothing was real unless
it wore fancy dress. He had his cats photographed in frilly robes
and bonnets, printed visiting cards for them, and arranged for
one to be christened. When his first son died, aged four days, he
gave the little corpse the full carnival treatment, laying him out
like a prince of the Orient on cloth of gold. Just before the coffin
was screwed down he took a plaster cast of one minuscule foot
for his memento collection.

Loti much regretted his lack of religious faith – he went to
India to consult fakirs, and once entered a Trappist monastery
(which he soon left, finding the food inadequate). But his
voluptuous, dream-like (and untranslatable) prose creates an
illusion of spirituality which flattered the comfortably-off reading public of his day. Proust used to quote whole pages of
Aziyadé at dinner.

The novels have dated, but he is still one of the world's
greatest travel writers, stylish and surprising in his observation.
Sailing the Indian Ocean at night, he notices, beneath the warm
waters, a continual luminous spray – the wake of sharks and
other big, fast predators. Crossing the Arabian desert, he spies
what seem to be myriads of small blue flowers, which prove to
be crushed fragments, shed through the centuries, of the turquoise glass-bead amulets that camels wear to avert the evil eye.
Like Conrad, he both hated colonialism and relives for us the
glamour of the great colonial adventure. This is his first biography in English, and he has been lucky to find a chronicler as
romantic, as addictively readable, and almost as smitten with
the East as himself.

                                                              1983

Stevenson: the optimistic traveller

In the last completed sentences of *Weir of Hermiston*, the novel Stevenson was still writing on the day he died, we learn that 'the curtains of boyhood' have begun to lift from the hero's eyes. They never lifted from Stevenson's, and that is the key to his appeal. He loved violence and romance, generous friendships, flashing steel, and blood gushing out 'hot as tea' (as it gushes from the dastardly Case in *The Beach of Falesa*). These wild dreams were a natural outlet for an invalid child, reared in sickrooms, who had to be shielded from other boys and their rough games. He grew up all coughs and bones – so like a scarecrow, it was said, that you expected him to creak in the wind – and spent his short life trekking the globe to find a climate in which his lungs would work properly.

Such trials would have cowed a lesser spirit, but they merely whetted Stevenson's zest for living. His great aim was to get off the feather bed of civilization and feel the world's granite underfoot. Sleeping out beneath the stars, washing in cold water, seeing the dawn come up – things no normal person enjoys after the age of fifteen, and precious few before that – filled him with rapture.

They are the raw material of two captivating early books, *An Inland Voyage*, where he explores the Belgian waterways with a friend and a couple of sailing canoes, and *Travels with a Donkey*, which takes him and his unwilling baggage-carrier through some of the less hospitable bits of France. Both books radiate a pagan joy in the outdoors, and pity for fellow men who lie choked between walls and curtains. Both, too, like Orwell's forays among the tramps half a century later, were experiments in seeing society from below. Turned away from smart inns because of his vagabond appearance, Stevenson began to sympathize with the vicious feelings of the deprived.

He loathed the bear-hug of custom, which squeezes the souls out of men. Typically, he started married life in a ruined shack, stuck on a mountain in California. (He described it in *The Silverado Squatters* – another book so full of open air that you breathe more deeply while you read.) His wife, a cigarette-rolling American divorcée ten years his senior, with a background of mining camps and frontier adventures, sent shivers through the staid Edinburgh Stevensons at first. But she offered just the mixture of mothering and wildness he craved for. With her, and a hired yacht, he was able to give his nomad urges full scope. They roamed, tattered and barefoot, through the South Sea islands, finding 'depth upon depth of unimaginable colour, and a huge silence'. On Samoa they bought 300 acres of jungle, with ravines and waterfalls and a tumbledown hideaway at the centre of it, where they finally put down roots. Just a year after their arrrival another refugee from civilization, Paul Gauguin, landed on Tahiti.

Because he lived close to death, no scruple of life was too mean to set Stevenson's spirit soaring. Marooned Ben Gunn in *Treasure Island*, who dreams nightly of cheese – 'toasted mostly' – has something of his creator's ardour for common pleasures. The same enthusiasm entered his relations with people. 'No class of man is altogether bad,' declares David Balfour in *Kidnapped* – a lenient opinion considering the brigands he is surrounded by, but certainly Stevenson's own. He believed you had to take the good and evil together in everyone. To isolate one from the other could only spell disaster, as *Dr Jekyll and Mr Hyde* (a story that came to Stevenson in a nightmare) shows. Besides, not to see the other fellow's viewpoint was a sign you were only half alive yourself. Slow to think ill of any creature, Stevenson had been some time in California before he learnt that the timorous beasties that buzzed in the undergrowth when he took a stroll were actually rattlesnakes.

He loved children, and took their games seriously. *Treasure Island* began life as a pirate map, produced with the aid of his stepson's paintbox. He forbore becoming a father himself, it seems, only because he suspected his child would be infirm and could not bear the thought of it suffering. With this tenderness and courage went cheerfulness. It enraged him to hear people bleating about their sorrows. Every dank, dispirited word was, he said, a crime of *lèse-humanité*. The business of art was to send us on our way rejoicing. His talent for looking on the bright side is illustrated by his fictional borrowings from life. His friend W. E. Henley, who lost one foot and underwent excruciating surgery to save the other, found himself immortalized as Long John Silver.

The optimism of Stevenson's art is one of the traits which Jenni Calder deplores.* He spoiled himself, she maintains, by his anxiety to be 'pleasing'. To be sure, some anxiety on this score would not have come amiss in her own book, for it is drably written and repeats itself wearingly (the word 'bourgeois', in a pejorative sense, being an especial favourite). Stevenson, a rigorously elegant stylist, would have been most upset. Mrs Calder responds warmly to the personal qualities of her subject, but disparages his work. He remained, we are told, 'on the wrong tack' as a writer almost all his life, though had he only pulled himself together he might have become 'akin to Joseph Conrad'. That seems a rum do – for who wants two Conrads? Imagine Conrad trying to write *Treasure Island*. Still, for lovers of Stevenson this book has the very considerable merit that after gnawing at it for a while you will almost certainly find yourself skulking off to re-read some Stevenson instead. That's always a shot in the arm.

1980

RLS: A Life Study by Jenni Calder (Hamish Hamilton).

The man who stood for beer and liberty

Chesterton had a body like a slag heap, but a mind like the dawn sky. He saw the world new, as if he'd just landed from another planet. Mankind's very existence struck him as wildly improbable. How could anyone take seriously, he demanded, an intelligent being which sustained itself by stuffing alien substances through a hole in its head? His amazement at normality unlocked for him the poetry of Edwardian London, which becomes in his books a magical stage-set, alive with barrel-organ music and fiery orchards of gas-lamps. But Chesterton's innocent eye rested with most incredulity on the poor. Like the fair-minded cannibals who visit Europe in Montaigne's essay, he couldn't understand why the poor didn't simply fall upon the rich and cut their throats. Wealth filled him with almost physical loathing: he dreamed of bloody revolutions which would smash the 'fat white houses' in Park Lane.

This hatred came partly from his Christianity, partly from his conviction that the rich were, in any nation, the scum of the earth. But it was fuelled too, by his phobia about international finance. When he first saw the neon signs in New York, trumpeting the monopolies of the rich, he remarked what a glorious sight they'd be if only you couldn't read. He believed there was a worldwide conspiracy of millionaires intent on reducing man to docile uniformity and stamping out patriotic urges. The poor, not the rich, were necessarily the real patriots, he argued: the rich could always scuttle off to the Caribbean in their yachts if times got bad. Great Jewish families like the Rothschilds, with ties that spanned national frontiers, appalled him. They were treason personified: all Jews, he suggested, should be made to wear Eastern dress, so that they couldn't pass as loyal natives.

Margaret Canovan, in her acute anatomy of Chesterton's politics,* apologizes for these extremes, while sensibly insisting

G. K. Chesterton: Radical Populist by Margaret Canovan (Harcourt Brace Jovanovich).

that our knowledge of later horrors makes us incapable of judging his anti-Semitism fairly. His support for Mussolini can likewise, if we switch off hindsight, look quite healthy. It stemmed solely from sympathy with the poor. Mussolini, Chesterton reported, had proved more independent of the rich and done more to coerce employers than any English government. He admired Fascism's contempt for parliamentary rule: Parliament, he'd always thought, was a charade run by a governing clique who were in league, as like as not, with the dark plutocrats of his nightmares. When his brother Cecil unearthed some crooked share dealings involving government ministers, it confirmed his worst fears.

In fact he probably saw through his own obsessions half the time. In his novel *The Man Who Was Thursday*, the creepy conspirators are all, it turns out, honest policemen in disguise. What remained stubbornly sane about him was the treatment of the poor, though his sanity took the form of battling against all current proposals for their relief. Socialism was no good, he decided, because it aimed to take capital out of the hands of the few and put it into the hands of fewer – the politicians. The abolition of private property was a mad idea: the poor existed precisely because someone had abolished theirs. Everyone needed something to express himself through, if it was only a roll of wallpaper or a cabbage patch: property was the art of a democracy. As for the reforms being introducd by the Liberal party, they were just high-minded elitism. They compelled the poor to be thrifty, hygienic and sober, exactly as potential employers would wish. Chesterton stuck out for beer and liberty. The philanthropist, he warned, is not a brother but a supercilious aunt.

He was right, too. The best part of Mrs Canovan's book is her catalogue of the consistently repressive attitudes displayed by the philanthropic reformers. The unemployed, it was proposed, should be segregated from their families to stop them breeding and confined to remote labour colonies where idlers would be firmly disciplined. Such schemes were favoured by Socialists like Beatrice Webb as well as by Liberals. The same tyrannical paternalism inspired the movement for the prohibition of the sale of alcohol, and measures like Lloyd George's National Insurance Act, which involved compulsory deductions from wages but denied unemployment relief to anyone who'd been discharged for 'insolence' or left his job 'without just cause'. Old age pensions, introduced in 1908, were to be withheld from those who had been in prison or 'persistently failed to work'. Under the Mental Deficiency Act, a prime Chestertonian bugbear, 'defective' children of the poor could be forcibly removed and subjected to remedies like craniectomy – an operation which killed a quarter of them and left the rest no brainier than before.

The assumption behind all these charitable enterprises was that the poor needed reformative treatment. Chesterton thought they needed a house and a bit of garden like everyone else. This humdrum, sensible opinion reflects his lifelong respect for the common man, as against intellectuals and other cranks. He helped to found the Distributist League, which campaigned to create a prosperous English peasantry by settling the destitute on smallholdings. A beautiful idea, and a sure flop politically.

Sadly Chesterton watched his League dwindling into a talking-shop for simple-lifers and vegetarians. But then, he'd never reckoned himself a practical politician. Asked what he'd do if he were made Prime Minister, he said he'd resign at once. He remains a vital force because he held aloft great glaring half-truths about poverty and wealth without which justice dies, and which shuffling practicality prefers to ignore.

1978

A Victorian clerk's tale

'The one thing certain is that mankind remains a race of low intelligence and evil instincts.' Not quite the view you'd expect from the author of *Three Men in a Boat*, but it was Jerome K. Jerome's considered opinion. Like many humorists, he suffered from melancholy, and laughed only to stop himself weeping. He had a grim childhood. His father lost the family fortune and moved to the East End, where the fierce faces in the streets and flaring naphtha lamps struck terror into little Jerome's soul.*

Christianity also petrified him. His mother, a devout woman who used to petition the Almighty in winter to bring down the price of coal, vividly impressed upon her son the disadvantages of eternal damnation. Face down on the pillow at night he would gibber 'I do believe' over and over again, ending by screaming it aloud in case God had not heard his smothered whisperings. 'It caused me', he states simply, 'to hate God.'

His parents died in quick succession, leaving the fifteen-year-old neurotic to cope alone. He got a job with the LNWR at Euston, creeping back to his empty digs each evening where, he recalls, desolation would strike him like a physical pain. When he could stand it no longer, he joined a travelling stage company. He later said he had acted every part in *Hamlet* except Ophelia. But rascally stage managers kept absconding with the funds, and the players often had to beg their way by the roadside. At nineteen Jerome found himself back in London, penniless, famished, and sleeping in dosshouses.

That might have been the end of him, but sheer chance got him started as a jobbing journalist at three-halfpence a line. To bring his earnings somewhere near subsistence level he doubled as a solicitor's clerk. The writing itch had taken hold, though, and he would polish his phrases as he trudged the

Jerome K. Jerome: A Critical Biography by Joseph Connolly (Orbis).

pavements at night, stopping beneath the street-lamps to write them down. As this suggests, the easy, flippant style he perfected cost him relentless toil. From the start, the critics hated it and him. Even when he had won worldwide fame as a humorist, they could not forgive his 'vulgarity'. The *Morning Post* cited him as an example of the sad results to be expected from over-educating the lower orders.

It was a shrewd point – for Jerome was consciously wooing a new readership: the perky clerks and shop assistants, the Mr Pollys and Lupin Pooters, whose stripy blazers and half-starved features still gaze triumphantly from a thousand sepia photos. The genteel highbrows of the next generation – Forster, Virginia Woolf, Eliot – were to sneer at this whole breed. In their eyes, the house-agent's clerk who misbehaves so regrettably with the typist in *The Waste Land* is a typical specimen. But clerks were Jerome's class, and he liked them – especially the jaunty, stoical way they took life's knocks.

His humour shows them struggling ineffectively in a hostile universe where slot machines, bicycles and tins of pineapple chunks conspire to humiliate mankind. The superiority of inanimate objects always impressed Jerome. On a skiing holiday he watched his skis slithering down the mountainside, and thought how much better they got on without him. Animals also fare well in his fiction. He sympathized with them for having to share the globe with the human race, and liked stories in which they got their own back. One of his favourites was about a dog which arrived each morning at the baker's with a penny in its mouth to buy a penny bun. One day the baker, thinking the poor beast wouldn't know the difference, tried to palm him off with a halfpenny bun instead. The dog walked straight out and fetched a policeman. It's no coincidence that Montmorency the dog is the only wholly fictional character in *Three Men in a Boat*. The trip was strictly dogless, but writing it up Jerome couldn't resist giving the dumb creatures a spokesman.

Dollops of sentimentality regularly alternate with the humour in Jerome's work, but he learnt to laugh at his mawkishness. Indigestion, he explained, had an infallible effect upon his heart. When he wanted to write anything truly pathetic he would eat a large plate of hot buttered muffins about an hour beforehand. Then, by the time he sat down to work, a feeling of unutterable grief would have overcome him. Besides self-mockery, changes of scene helped to ease his depression. He was a compulsive traveller, and the sprees with George and Harris grew more adventurous as funds increased. They tramped through the Ardennes and up the Danube, and their cycling tour in the Black Forest became *Three Men on the Bummel*. Jerome's blend of innocence and irascibility accompanied him on his journeys, as did his contempt for self-esteem.

Americans, especially, struck him as obsessed with their own bigness. He declared he had once met an American in an Alpine resort who observed appreciatively that Switzerland would be quite an extensive country if it were rolled out flat. When he visited the States, he enjoyed being unimpressed by the grandeur. 'The Rockies are imposing but lack human interest', he reported. 'Niagara disappointed me. I had some trouble finding it. The tram driver promised to let me know when we came to the proper turning, but forgot.' What sickened him was the unabashed racism. In the South he met men who would describe, amid laughter, how they had roasted 'buck niggers' alive over a slow fire.

He went to Russia twice, and in *Russians as I Know Them* forecast the Revolution twelve years before it happened. The educated classes and thinkers who were working to bring it about were, he found, perfectly aware that they would be crushed by it. But they had come to hate injustice better than they loved themselves. He admired them, but his own leftist sympathies were more guarded. He prized personal effort, and feared Socialism would eliminate it. *The New Utopia* is set in a drab socialist England of the twenty-ninth century where all individual initiative is forbidden, and it has been made illegal to wash yourself. Private washing, it was found, led to two classes, the clean and the dirty, and this bred recrimination and social antagonism. So now everyone is washed twice a day by a government official.

Jerome's life saw spectacular changes. In his boyhood, stage-coaches still ran, and London was semi-rural. They hunted deer around Highgate, and a path led through cornfields to Swiss Cottage. He lived to take part in the First World War: at fifty-seven the British army wouldn't have him, so he signed on in the French, and drove an ambulance on the Western front. His autobiography *My Life and Times* teems with tales of the crowd of writers he knew – Wells, Shaw, Kipling, Barrie, Conan Doyle, Rider Haggard. It is a bran-tub of a book, and Mr Connolly wisely lifts a lot from it. Truth to tell, he hasn't much to add himself. He sheds as little light as Jerome on the dim figure of Jerome's wife and leaves out some of the best stuff. But until a wise publisher reprints *My Life and Times* this is an agreeable substitute.

1982

The Heavenly Hound

In creating Sherlock Holmes,* Conan Doyle created a substitute God. Holmes's deerstalker and pipe correspond to the identification marks carried by lesser gods (thunderbolts, winged heels etc), but his sexlessness and high cultural tone assimilate him particularly to the Judaeo-Christian God, as does his appreciation of music (though Holmes's fancy is for the violin rather than the harp). Like God, he usually consorts with an inferior, more human male companion, renowned for his healing powers (Watson/Christ). Like God, he has a fixed habitation (221b Baker Street/the New Jerusalem) the furniture of which is a subject for loving contemplation by devotees. It may be protested that people don't actually pray to Holmes, but in fact letters requesting his assistance still arrive at the Baker Street address. The Holmes saga, in common with other holy books, has an episodic structure, being a string of triumphs and miracles rather than an organized whole, and it includes a passion-death-resurrection sequence. In 1891 Holmes plunged to his destruction over the Reichenbach Falls, locked in mortal combat with the arch-fiend Moriarty, only to be restored to life by popular request within a decade.

Another of Holmes's Godlike attributes is omniscience, though Conan Doyle tried to deny him this at first. The proto-Holmes of *A Study in Scarlet* is a half-comic figure, steeped in chemical lore, but ignorant of art and literature, and so little acquainted with astronomy that he does not know the Earth goes round the Sun. A mere three years later, in *The Sign of Four*, Holmes has learned to quote Goethe and chat brilliantly about Miracle Plays and Medieval pottery, and in the last full-length novel, *The Valley of Fear*, he informs Watson that all knowledge is the detective's province.

Before the invention of fictional sleuths like Holmes, readers had to make do with tales of detection in which God played the star part. Popular literature had swarmed with these ever since

The Sherlock Holmes Collected Edition by Arthur Conan Doyle (John Murray and Cape).

the Middle Ages. One of my own favourites comes in Bunyan's *Life and Death of Mr Badman* and concerns Dorothy Mately, an employee in a Derbyshire lead-mine, who is engulfed by a divinely-inspired landslide shortly after denying that she has stolen twopence from a workmate. They dig her body out and find the twopence in her pocket. Unlike Bunyan's God, Holmes doesn't soil his hands with execution, but his taste for justice is quite as ruthless.

The key difference between Holmes and the previous Great Detective is that Holmes uses science and God didn't. Holmes's status as scientist receives emphasis from the start. Watson first encounters him in a tangle of test-tubes and retorts, crying 'I've found it!' like a modern Archimedes. What he's found is a reagent precipitated only by haemoglobin, which provides an infallible test for bloodstains. Len Deighton, in his helpful introduction to *The Valley of Fear*, points out that Holmes was often working on the frontiers of forensic chemistry. A test for distinguishing animal and human bloodstains was actually evolved during the next four years. With similar foresight, Holmes deduced in *The Norwood Builder* how an astute criminal could fake fingerprint evidence to frame his victim – at a time when only three convictions had been made on fingerprint evidence anywhere in the world, none of them in Britain. And in *A Case of Identity* he hit on the fact that a typewriter leaves individual marks on every document it types, long before any real investigation of the subject was published. Small wonder that the crime laboratories at Lyons were named after Holmes's creator, and that the Egyptian Police trained on his methods.

Holmes belongs to an age in which the protection of life and property has passed from God to science. But one of the things he increasingly had to afford protection against was science itself, or those abtruser aspects of it which have always, and rightly, seemed threatening to the layman. The 'king devil' Moriarty, besides being the controlling brain behind the underworld, is the author of *The Dynamics of the Asteroid*: a book, Holmes reports, 'which ascends to such rarefied heights of pure mathematics that it is said there was no man in the scientific press capable of criticizing it.' We may note, though Mr Deighton doesn't, that some ten years before Conan Doyle wrote those words there had appeared Poincare's two papers 'On the Dynamics of the Electron', and Einstein's 'On the Electrodynamics of Moving Bodies', which introduced the world to relativity theory. Holmes's homely dabblings in bloodstains and cigar-ash pertain to a friendlier branch of science, and in identifying the twentieth-century physicist with Satan he was, as in other matters, a conservative.

But it was not only science that made the new God Holmes necessary. The growth of London was another determining factor. For megalopolitan life brings with it anonymity and bewilderment and it needs a detective, with his comforting attention to personal minutiae, to trace, as Holmes himself once put it, 'the strange coincidences, the plannings, the cross-purposes' that bind men together in the city's twilight labyrinth. It's significant that the earliest fictional detective should have made his appearance in a novel that dwells, time and again, on the perplexities of London fog, *Bleak House*. Fog swirls repeatedly around Holmes and Watson as they pursue their prey through dank courts and alleys. The world they inhabit is crepuscular, bemired, sprouting horrible rows of brick villas with diseased plants and raw clay paths in front of them, and as like as not a corpse in the back parlour. 'The monster tentacles which the giant city was throwing out into the country,' Watson calls them. Watson heeds the desolation even more than Holmes (who has his cocaine to help him escape): he is haunted by the mindless crowds, 'the endless procession of faces' flitting across the bars of light from shop windows. Besides, London acts as a magnet for criminals of every clime. In three of the four Holmes novels, and in numerous shorter pieces, it transpires that the villains have come from abroad to wage their vile vendettas. The city harbours an unnatural medley of races and creeds, and the standard of immigrant drops markedly during Holmes's career. The early work contains nothing direr than the little black Andaman Islander in *The Sign of Four*, with his exotic blow-pipe and darts. But by 1915 Holmes was up against murderous trade-unionists from the States, convinced that their atrocities were part of a class war, and armed with sawn-off shot guns. Other things, besides physics, had taken a sinister turn.

These four volumes of *The Sherlock Holmes Collected Edition* (there'll be nine in all) are pleasant to own, handsomely bound and printed, as befits quasi-biblical texts, with endpapers reproducing some original illustrations, and brief but reverent introductions by selected celebrities. The reverence falters only in John Fowles's Afterword to *The Hound of the Baskervilles*: a strange, carping piece in which he complains that the novel, and the Holmes stories generally, lack 'concentrated wisdom' and 'deeper content'. To remedy this, he suggests 'more could have been made of the hound symbolism'. Conan Doyle ought to have rendered Holmes himself more houndlike by concentrating on his 'snapping boredom', and so forth. Personally, I can't believe the novel would have benefited from having Holmes sniffing around in it like a dog. The creaky 'symbolism' Mr Fowles wants to import belongs to an old religious world of mystic links and archetypes. It would be quite alien to the new God Holmes, for whom truth is solid and single, like a laboratory bench. Mr Fowles also faults Conan Doyle's knowledge of Dartmoor, a region about which, he intimates, he knows a thing or two. He doubts whether you could drown in the Grimpen Mire, having been in and out of bogs himself unscathed, and he feels that Conan Doyle should have known that bitterns boom only in spring. Actually, a glance at the text shows that he knew this perfectly well. It's the villainous Stapleton who suggests (in October) that the hound's fearful cry might just be a bittern booming, and it's plain that he has selected a ludicrously inadequate explanation because he wants his victim to believe there really is a phantom hound so that he'll be helpless with terror when he eventually claps eyes on Stapleton's own phosphorescent pup. Mr Fowles will have to think harder if he's to outsmart Holmes.

1974

The rhymes of the ancient mariner

'I must go down to the seas again,' chanted Masefield with briny zest in 'Sea-Fever'. It seems, however, that he was never keen to go down to them at all, and hated them when he got there. His nautical career has always remained vague, despite his expansive autobiographical output.

Gossip circulated by Laurence Binyon, credited him with running away to sea as a boy and enjoying 'wondrous adventures'. Constance Babington Smith, who, to judge from her style, has as much poetry in her nature as a knitting machine, is nevertheless admirable at clearing up mysteries. In *John Masefield: A Life** she has worked through all Masefield's surviving correspondence and diaries, and firmly scotches Binyonish bunkum.

Masefield was a dreamy, tender lad, especially after the death of his beloved mother when he was six. Ragged by schoolmates for his poetic bent, he attempted suicide by consuming laurel leaves. His Aunt Kate, a 'repulsive hag' in Masefield's view, and a muscular Christian, decided that sea life would toughen him, and sent him to train on an old wooden hulk, the *Conway*, moored on the Mersey. His first voyage was aboard a four-master called the *Gilcruix*, bound for Chile.

The moment she set sail he was desperately seasick. Bouts of nausea kept recurring, and he also got sunstroke. Rounding Cape Horn the vessel ran into a month of continuous storm, with forty-foot-high, ice-packed seas. At her first port of call, Iquique, Masefield was discharged from the crew suffering from a nervous breakdown.

And that was the end of his life under sail: it had lasted three months. After a spell in hospital at Valparaiso, he travelled home by steamship, classified as a Distressed British Seaman. Aunt Kate, deeply contemptuous, bundled him off to New York to join another ship, but before it sailed he deserted. He became successively a vagrant, barman and carpet factory operative, and

*John Masefield: A Life by Constance Babington Smith (OUP).

arrived back in England aged nineteen with tuberculosis, malaria, £6, and a revolver to blow his brains out with if he didn't get a job.

If Masefield hadn't failed as a sailor, he would never have become the rapturous, bewitched sea poet commemorated in Ronald Hope's elegant volume *John Masefield: The Sea Poems*.* In reality the mindless brutality of sea life had revolted him. But he blamed his own weakness and, as an atonement, idolized the sea's beauty all his days. Failure fed romance, as it always does. Putting himself across in the poems as a lyrical old salt, he could fill a role for which life had proved him too delicate. 'Dauber', his best poem, portrays an innocent, victimized young sailor, who is plainly Masefield himself but who escapes the indignity of a nervous breakdown by falling to a fine death from the yard-arm.

What one misses, generally, in the sea poems is any hint of the stinking awfulness of ships and their occupants, though this must have struck Masefield forcibly during his brief and bilious sojourn among them. There's pitifully little rage. He seems to have been fathomlessly patient and good, and weighed down by his own incompetence. Marrying a woman twelve years his senior, he explained that 'for such a bun-headed person as myself' a mature partner was 'a jolly good thing'.

In the years of obscurity and starched collars when young Masefield, revolver safely stowed away, was working as a bank clerk, the friendship of W. B. Yeats gave a glowing centre to his life. Recounting the evenings at Yeats's flat in Woburn Buildings, where poets, painters and occultists gathered in the lamplight and sipped wine from dark brown and green glasses, Miss Babington Smith's narrative rounds into a richness which her cramped method doesn't normally allow. But the real treasure of her book comes later with her selection from the letters Masefield wrote home during the First World War. Though too old for military service, he insisted on going out to France as a Red Cross orderly, working a few miles behind the lines. In his descriptions of the defiled landscape, of the wounded, like heaps of bloody rags, carted into the casualty stations, of the long slow filthy hospital trains, full of mad-eyed whimpering men, we encounter a Masefield scarcely dreamed of

John Masefield: The Sea Poems ed. Ronald Hope (Marine Society/ Heinemann).

before. The letters throb with love for the 'poor blinded bleeding stinking heroes' he tends, and their realism makes much of his poetry look like damp tissue paper.

As part of his war service he undertook a lecture tour of the USA to stir up support for the English cause. Once more his letters home are charged with power: this time, the power of hate for the local people, particularly in the German-dominated areas of the Middle West. Chicago disgusted him; Pittsburgh, he said, was 'where the Devil was born'. His portraits of American types are bracingly hostile: the males 'oily with Mammon'; their mates, culture-hungry harpies glittering with false teeth and spectacles. It's as if Masefield has at last been able to unleash his inner bitterness which his wistful flutings about tall ships always kept muffled.

That's not to disparage the sea poems as a whole, of course. Often they splash and surge splendidly. It's especially good to see 'The River' among the pieces Mr Hope reprints – a tense, almost Conradian narrative about some men trapped in the deckhouse of a wrecked ship which is gradually being sucked into an underwater quicksand. Confident that help will soon arrive, the sailors jeer at one of their number who patiently scrapes the solder from a metal hatch-cover – a possible escape-route. In fact they all drown except the lonely toiler, who dives through his hatch to safety just as the vessel sinks. It is 'Dauber' in reverse. The derided outsider survives, as Masefield has survived when his stalwart seamates have all long been forgotten.

1978

The Czech who kept bouncing

The son of an alcoholic Czech schoolmaster, Jaroslav Hašek* was
born physically complete but without a sense of responsibility.
Clown, cabaret artist, drunkard, bigamist and literary genius, he
detested authority, especially that of the ramshackle Austro-
Hungarian Empire in which he grew up. As a lad he registered
his protest by heaving paving stones through windows and
urinating against public buildings. When not helping the police
with their enquiries he tramped penniless through Central
Europe, chumming up with Hungarian gypsies and Slovakian
peasants, who served as raw material for his first short stories.

Back in Prague he naturally gravitated towards the Anarchists, but proved too unprincipled even for them. He disappeared one day on the Anarchist office bicycle, and bartered it
for booze. Unhampered by any genuine radical convictions, he
happily wrote for the more remunerative bourgeois papers,
adapting his views accordingly. When the Social Democrats
rejected an article guying the National Socialist leaders, he
inserted the names of the Social Democratic leaders instead and
sold it to the National Socialists.

As rebels will, he married a prim conventional girl, Jarmila
Mayer, who fancied she'd reform him. He settled down briefly
as editor of the family magazine *Animal World*, but the temptation to play the fool soon prevailed. His account of the discovery
of a fossilized antediluvian flea caused a sensation among
zoologists and was translated and republished abroad, and
when he advertised for sale a pair of thoroughbred werewolves
the office was flooded with applications. His most elaborate
hoax involved the establishment of a new political party. In
mockery of the orthodox Left's gradualism, it styled itself the
Party of Moderate Progress Within the Bounds of the Law, and
one reform it advocated was that politicians should no longer
use animal names when vilifying one another since this was an

The Bad Bohemian: A Life of Jaroslav Hašek by Sir Cecil Parrott (Bodley
Head).

insult to animals. Everyone voting for the party was promised the free gift of a small pocket aquarium.

Even with these diversions he found the treadmill of married life intolerable, and tried to commit suicide by jumping off Charles Bridge in Prague, only to be saved by a passing theatrical hairdresser and lodged in the local lunatic asylum. After that his marriage broke up and he went back to bohemianism and the bottle. His cabaret turns in Prague nightspots were unreliable: he would turn up sozzled and disgust the audience by undoing his filthy footwraps or giving a lurid lecture on cholera and its effects. Jarmila bore him a son, Richard, whom he hardly ever saw, and who didn't know for many years that Hašek was his father. A pathetic late snapshot shows the pudgy, sheepish Hašek trying to strike a paternal pose beside the youngster he abandoned at birth. Understandably Jarmila vowed that when it came to planning Richard's education she'd be sure not to encourage in him any love of art.

At the outbreak of the First World War Hašek volunteered for service with the Austrian Army – his personal file classified him succinctly as a 'swindler and deceiver' – and he got himself captured by the Russians as quickly as possible. Transformed overnight into a militarist and patriot, he declared his ardent support for the Tsarist regime and gratified his captors by drumming up recruits for the Czech Legion, which fought on the Russian side.

The Bolshevik revolution produced another personality-change. Appointed editor of *Red Europe*, Hašek demanded merciless suppression of anti-Soviet elements, and chose himself a sturdy new wife from among the proletariat, omitting to mention his previous marriage. As a Commissar with the Red Army, he turned his propaganda against the Czech Legion, which was now the enemy since it had declined to lay down its arms at the comradely invitation of Stalin and Trotsky.

Hašek's arrival in post-war Prague was timed to coincide with a leftist coup, but if fizzled out. He was hounded as a traitor, and lived in terror of public disgrace and imprisonment. He also found it difficult explaining to his wives how there came to be two of them. Sullen, vicious and resentful, he typically subsided into drink and self-pity, blubbering that his life had been a 'damned zigzag' and that no one understood him. 'But you're cheating me' were his last words – spoken to the doctor who refused him cognac.

As a human being Hašek was undeniably a washout – but that's merely to say that he wouldn't take seriously the impressive array of institutions which the human race has invented to conceal from itself its own futility. Like the orderly-room cat in *The Good Soldier Svejk* which defecates on the Imperial Battle Map and then claws it to shreds, he rips great holes in the papery fabric of civilization with gales of ironic laughter. Through the rents he shows us common humanity's sly, daft, unconquerable face – represented here by a photo of Straslipka, the radiantly stupid-looking Czech army batman who was Svejk's real-life prototype.

This illustration is only one of countless tie-ups between Hašek's masterpiece and his life which Sir Cecil's volume reveals. No one outside Czechoslovakia has attempted a full-scale biography before. Besides demanding rare linguistic skills, the task calls for a mastery of highly complicated original sources overlaid with decades of conflicting legend – for under the Germans Hašek's books were outlawed and burned, whereas by the Communists he has been virtually canonized. Sir Cecil coolly untangles him from the coils of rumour, and manages, while performing this delicate scholarly operation, to transmit the raucous glitter of the beer-gardens and night-dives and *cafés-chantants* which were Hašek's element. The result is a triumph, and – like all first-rate scholarship – enormously enjoyable.

1978

The diseases of Thomas Mann

'We do not even know why the stomach does not digest itself' notes Thomas Mann, boning up on the mysteries of physiology for the medical sections of *The Magic Mountain*. Mann's own stomach did not digest itself, readers of these diaries* will quickly gather, because it was too busy coping with the ample alternative provender he presented it with. Double-smoked pork, roast goose, Sachertorte – the punitively rich diet is itemized with loving care, as are the cakes, pastries and chocolate bars Mann polishes off to keep himself going between scheduled blowouts. Agonies of constipation and heartburn invariably follow, which he combats with chest powder and other nostrums.

The long-term damage proves more harrowing: 'I am suffering both physically and psychically', he reports, 'from the fact that all No. 4 underwear is now too small for me.' But bright spots occur too. 'The adhesive powder for the denture works well,' he ruminates appreciatively in 1937.

Eating is not, of course, the only bourgeois comfort he treasures. His Munich mansion exudes cultured ease and cigar smoke. The great author strolls on its sunlit terraces, while little white-frocked Mann maidens frolic through the rose gardens. At night there are theatres, operas, recitals. Possessions matter deeply. Each birthday and Christmas, the diaries catalogue the seasonal haul of luxury articles – the glittering cigarette lighters, tea-making kits, leather goods.

When he visits the States it is the opulence of the arrangements – his suite on the liner piled with flowers, cherries, presents, books – that enchants him. Buying a new wrist-watch can make him, even at forty-four, 'as excited as a child'. The poetic intensity that commodities acquire in Mann's fiction (the dazzling shop windows in *Felix Krull*, say, or the candlelit Christmas tree in *Buddenbrooks*, which has been called 'a Manet

Thomas Mann Diaries 1918–1939 ed. Hermann Kesten (André Deutsch).

in words') flows directly out of the rapt materialism of the diaries.

Sometimes you can actually see it happening. In 1920 he develops an 'almost sinful passion' for his friend Richter's new gramophone, and this transmutes into the 'little black sarcophagus' breathing its 'ghostly music' that so captivates Hans Castorp in *The Magic Mountain*. In quest of more advanced gadgetry Mann tours the X-ray unit at the local hospital – an experience that inspires the devastating episode where Castorp, watching his cousin Joachim have a chest X-ray, notices a black bag, rather like a jellyfish palpitating on the screen, and recognizes it, appalled, as Joachim's 'honour-loving heart'.

That image typifies the sardonic undercutting of spiritual values that has always upset sentimental critics of Mann. His famed coldness and irony do not obtrude overmuch in the diaries, though he is capable of complaining, on his way through the streets, of the 'odious smell of people', and his calculations in 1918 over whether his wife should have an abortion or a sixth child do seem somewhat detached for an expectant pa. (In the end she had the child, Bibi, who became a concert violinist.) He records his rare marital consummations and the early onset of impotence (at forty-five) with the same objectivity as he chronicles haircuts and the inefficiency of the central heating.

His homoerotic desires fracture his calm marginally more: a Hermes-like dandy, glimpsed at the club, raises hopes for a while, and a brawny gardener in the park gives him 'quite a turn'. His son Klaus's radiant adolescent body sets off the worst tremors, especially on summer holidays when the boy will persist in lounging around half-naked. But throughout these trials Mann continues honest and rational: 'I find it quite natural that I should fall in love with my son.'

He kept diaries from his schooldays in Lubeck till shortly before his death, but systematically destroyed most of them, thinking them too intimate. The surviving batches, anthologized here, cover 1918–21 and 1933–9, periods of political upheaval which severely test his powers of adjustment. 1918 sees a Communist uprising in Munich, looting, red flags and the murder of aristocrats. Grenades and gunfire disturb the nights, and the mob comes unpleasantly near the Mann residence.

Mann confronts the crisis with eager muddle. It comforts him to think that, if they are having a revolution, Germany must be

in the forefront of something, and he's also glad that a leftist
coup will annoy the detestable victors at Versailles. He feels like
rushing into the streets shouting, 'Hurrah for Communism!',
but desists in case the activists should not realize as clearly as he
does that writers like himself must be exempt from political
pressure. Once troops have crushed the uprising, Mann's democratic ardour vanishes like snow. The 'scoundrelly heroes of the
masses' should be shot like vermin, he feels: military dictatorship is preferable to 'the rule of the *crapule*'.

In 1933, when the second lot of diaries start, Hitler has just
been given dictatorial powers following the Reichstag fire.
Mann and his wife, holidaying in Switzerland, are warned that
he would be in danger if he went back to Germany, because of
what the Nazis call his 'pacifist excesses'. After a summer of
wandering, the Manns settle in Zurich.

At this stage of his exile he still hopes to return, daily
scanning the German papers for signs of the regime's collapse.
He feels patrician scorn for the Nazis. They represent 'the petty
shop-keeping class', their faces 'much uglier and racially
inferior' to those of ordinary Germans. On the other hand,
there's just a chance they may be on to something 'deeply
significant and revolutionary'. It's no calamity, Mann tells
himself, that they have put a stop to the domination of the legal
system by Jews.

What keeps him vacillating is fear that his Munich house will
be confiscated if he comes out openly against Hitler. Separation
from his adored belongings torments him, and he sheds tears at
the 'ghastly *déclassé* existence' he endures in Switzerland. Not
until 1936, with hopes of avoiding confiscation virtually gone,
does he publish an article in the *Neue Zuricher Zeitung* denounc-
ing Nazi Germany.

Readers in no immediate danger of losing their homes and
property may feel virtuously superior to Mann for temporizing
so long. But in fact his attachment to possessions nourished
everything that was wisest in his art and thought, arming him
against the vanities of metaphysics and fanaticism. From his
sane materialistic stance he saw the Nazi movement as a prime
example of the German spirit's zest for wallowing in 'the
manure of myth', its lust for everything 'misty and vaporous'.

The diaries, with their snowdrifts of mundane detail, celebrate the supreme banality of human existence which, however
it may irk us, is the only alternative to death. They are, as Rilke

said of *Buddenbrooks*, 'an act of reverence towards life', scrupulously trivial and often beautiful, especially in the accounts of
scenery and weather. Mann wanders through gold-drenched
autumn afternoons, watching the thistle flowers fade into fuzzy
down, or, bathing in the North Sea, exults in the great soft wind,
the waves 'like beasts of prey', the carpets of foam. Passages like
these transport you to another place, another time, and make
you thankful that Mann was so afflicted by the need to turn life
into words – the one disease every great novelist must suffer
from.

1983

Edwin Muir: one foot in Eden

We think of Edwin Muir as a modern poet, but he grew up in a mythical land – like a child in a tapestry surrounded by centaurs and unicorns.* He was born on a farm in the Orkneys nearly a hundred years ago. The islanders made no great distinction between the ordinary and the fabulous. Fishermen talked with mermaids; fairies were seen dancing on the sands on moonlit nights; and the devil sometimes appeared at threshing time – a coal-black figure with a fine upcurling tail.

To young Muir, the very animals had a visionary air. Insects were fragments of night darting about in the sun, and the farm horses with their bearded feet and smoking nostrils towered like heraldic beasts. Being a delicate child, he was shielded from most of the sex and slaughter of farmyard life, but he once stumbled upon a pig screaming like a circular saw from a slit in its throat, and this sank into his subconscious with all the rest.

Throughout his life these animals invaded his dreams, assuming weird science-fiction disguises which, he came to believe, represented ancestral memories of a time when animals and men were more closely related. His autobiography devotes much more space to dreams than to such relatively superficial events as the two World Wars. This absorption in the inner life, which you'd normally expect only in a monastery or an asylum, came naturally to Muir, perhaps because his early years lay so far beyond the touch of the ordinary world. The islands slept in a timeless haze. By winter lamplight his mother would sing ballads that had been passed down orally for centuries, using, Muir recalls, a much richer voice than the careful one she put on for singing from print. They lived on herrings, potatoes and porridge, eaten from communal bowls, without knives or forks, and they also had plovers' eggs, crabs and lobsters in abundance, never realizing they were luxuries.

When Muir was fourteen, this idyll ended: the family gave up its farm and moved to Glasgow. Even to the locals it cannot, in

*An Autobiography by Edwin Muir (Hogarth Press).

the early 1900s, have seemed a jocund spot, and it overwhelmed
Muir like a putrid avalanche. On his island, he had never seen a
road, let alone a slum. Within two years his mother, father and
two brothers had all died, as if the uprooting had damaged them
beyond repair. Numbed, he stumbled from one office-boy job to
another, ending up in a bone factory at Fairport. Decaying
bones from all over Scotland arrived at the railway sidings,
festooned with slowly-writhing yellow maggots which seagulls,
screaming up from the estuary, swallowed by the hundred-
weight. Bones, and uneaten maggots, were then shovelled into
furnaces to make charcoal for refining sugar. A rancid stink
hung over the town like a blanket.

Giant maggots soon joined the cast of Muir's dreams, performing with such *brio* that they brought him close to mental
breakdown. In his waking hours he struggled to educate himself. He scrutinized literary periodicals in a Gorbals reading
room foggy with steaming down-and-outs; he joined debating societies; he became a Socialist, and wept over statistics
in his morning tramcar. One day, when his malign Fates had
nodded off for a moment, he came upon A.R. Orage's paper *The
New Age*, wrote to Orage, and got a kind reply sketching plans
for future reading. It was a lifeline, and Muir grabbed it. In the
next few years he began contributing to *The New Age* himself,
married a college lecturer Willa Anderson, moved to London
and, to counteract the maggots, got himself psychoanalysed.

At the start of the twenties Muir and Willa threw up their jobs
and left England. They drifted round Europe – Prague, Dresden,
Salzburg – in a golden reverie, learning German and earning
their keep by translating for publishers. (Their translations of
Kafka were to introduce him to English audiences.) Muir, at
thirty-five, began writing poems, and Virginia Woolf took his
first collection for the Hogarth Press. In their cocoon of work and
happiness, faint rumbles reached them from the outside world.
Inflation had soared, and they began inviting German acquaintances round in relays to give them a square meal. Hysterical
stories about Jewish profiteers circulated – but no one guessed
that Germany was getting ready for its own demonic version of
the Fairport bone factory. In the event, several of the Muirs'
friends from this period died in the gas chambers.

Few writers give such an impression of wisdom and gentleness as Muir. He had, as he said in a poem, 'one foot in Eden'.
The trouble with the poetry, though, is that his other foot seems

to be stuck in a pond of archetype and parable, only murkily connected with actual living. This reissue of the 1954 autobiography will give new readers a chance to discover the portion of his work that bears the stamp of experience most sharply. He notices the unremarkable things which fix scenes in the mind's eye – swifts cutting scimitar shapes in the sky of Rome, or oxen shambling deep in marble dust at Carrara.

He distrusts ideas, because they help men to formulate detached and deadly images of one another. Modern inhumanity breeds in the pure atmosphere of ideas, as he realized while watching the Communist takeover in Prague in 1948. The impersonality with which the Communists treated their victims was not animated by anything as human as hatred; it was clean and logical. Against this cold rigour he pits his own belief that people are immortal souls, and that if they were not, human life would be 'a nightmare populated by animals wearing top-hats and kid gloves, painting their lips and touching up their cheeks, and talking in heated rooms'. That does not, of course, amount to an argument – but it is an unsettling vision, and like so much else in Muir it goes back to the dream-haunted Orkney farm.

1980

Perish every laggard

E. M. Forster was thirty, and had published three novels, before he altogether understood how copulation took place. Till then he was under the impression that the man placed his stomach against the woman's and warmed her. This innocence derived largely from his upbringing. His father died when he was one, and he spent his childhood, indulged and imperious, in (as he later put it) 'a haze of elderly ladies'. It was a refined haze. A pair of his female relatives once complained that they were kept awake at night by the 'coarse voices' of crickets. Foremost among the ladies was his father's aunt, Marianne Thornton (aptly nicknamed 'Monie'). Bossy but astute, this last survivor of the Clapham Sect discerned the infant Forster's idolatrous attachment to objects – his 'memory for old toys and love for sticks and stones' – and her legacy of £8,000 eventually enabled him to become a writer. He repaid her kindness by satirizing the clannishness of the Thorntons in *Where Angels Fear to Tread*.

Forster's mother, who came from a rather jolly Bohemian family of painters and sailors, played a major role in suppressing what virility he might have had. Under her influence he learned to refer to his penis (if at all) as his 'dirty'. He wore shoulder-length curls and lace-collared suits, and was lagged with mufflers at the least threat of inclement weather. Passersby mistook him for a girl. But though his long love-affair with his mother proved irksome as he matured, it made his childhood, as P. N. Furbank relates,* radiantly happy. After the shortest absence he would smother her with kisses as if they had been parted for years. His childish wit and capriciousness burgeoned in the tender warmth she created round him. Besides, from her and her lady friends he acquired a close understanding of snobbery and innuendo, which was of infinitely more service to a future novelist than an acquaintance with the reproductive organs. On visits to friends, and later travelling

---

E. M. Forster: A Life, Vol. 1 by P. N. Furbank (Secker and Warburg).

together in Italy, he and his mother applied themselves with
zest to the dissection of their fellow mortals, and young Forster's
ear for trivia became valuably acute. 'Conductors say '"two
pence"' not '"tuppence"' his diary sagely records.

Another great advantage of his pampered childhood was that
it rendered him exquisitely vulnerable when he came to mix
with boys of his own age. They quickly identified him as their
natural prey. A cousin known as Blowdy Wags, his earliest
persecutor, blew a whistle in his ear, at which he screamed and
cried for hours. 'This horrid boy', Forster later testified, 'was the
first to demonstrate to me that I was a coward.' At prep school he
found himself an unskinned prawn among fully-armed crusta-
ceans, and was thus admirably placed to gather unlimited
information about cruelty and loneliness. The experience also
gave him a perspective on the English class system. By the time
he had been withdrawn, in floods of tears, from his second prep
school – an establishment for 'the sons of gentlemen' – he had
persuaded himself that 'If only they were not the sons of
gentlemen they would not be so unkind'. Almost certainly he
was wrong. Workers' children would probably have torn him to
pieces. But the special kind of brutality he needed to know
about for his writing was the kind that good breeding breeds,
and prep school taught him this.

So, with conspicuous efficiency, did Tonbridge (later
'Sawston School' in *The Longest Journey*). It had been taken over,
shortly before Forster's arrival, by a new headmaster, the Rev.
'Joey' Wood, DD – a beetle-browed eminence, attentive to team
spirit and the more socially desirable parents. He was fond of
modelling his sermons round the words of the school anthem
('Perish every laggard . . .'), laying stress on the lines which
exhort Tonbridgeans to seize 'harp or sword or pen' for life's
battle. According to Forster, the Rev. Wood always recommended the sword as the noblest choice, because it might lead
to the death of a fellow creature. Under his aegis bullying was
virtually part of the academic curriculum, senior pupils being
allowed to kick new boys as one of their privileges. Forster, in
later life, refused to talk about the miseries of the place beyond
admitting that he had been pelted with chestnuts. Other Old
Boys proved more forthcoming. 'Forster? The writer? Yes, I
remember him. A little cissy. We took it out of him, I can tell
you,' a schoolfriend reminisced when questioned by Mr Furbank in the 1950s. As he moved up the school Forster got better

at merging into the background and avoiding trouble. He became buttoned-up, droopy and mute.

At Cambridge he blossomed, but it was a withered sort of blossoming. He parted company with his religious faith (it had never been much to write home about) under the influence of friends like Nathaniel Wedd, who characterized Christianity as 'the bloody swinish bunkum that the prize idiots of the two Universities use to cloak their erotic tendencies'. The other 'grand discovery' of his young manhood was his homosexuality. There had been hints of it before – idyllic tumblings and ticklings in the straw with the gardener's boys at Rooksnest (the old gabled house near Stevenage which Forster adored as a child, and transformed into Howard's End). But at Cambridge he met Hugh Meredith, who was to become his first lover. Their love never progressed beyond kisses and embraces. To Forster it spelt emancipation, though: until he met Meredith he had not dared to acknowledge this part of his nature at all.

Acknowledging it did not bring him much happiness, it seems. He stayed shy and frustrated, would glance wistfully after workmen and burly bargees, loiter in public lavatories, and comfort himself with long erotic day-dreams. Fear of blackmail haunted him – with reason, for the forces of purity were strong and underhand. One day at the Savile Club he happened to say something about a 'charming boy', and noticed a member staring at him: later, when he went to have his hair cut, the barber hinted that he would like a loan of £10. Then there was the incident of Ernest Merz. Forster and Merz, a King's contemporary, walked home together one night in 1909. What passed between them isn't known, but next morning Merz was found hanging in his rooms. He must, Forster explained to a friend, have been 'insulted disgustingly' by someone.

Telling his love was inevitably an ordeal, for contempt and abuse might lie behind every friendly face. He went through agonies after he had blurted out his passion to Syed Ross Masood, a dashing young Indian whom he coached in Latin and lusted after for years. Luckily Masood gave him the gentlest of brush-offs, and they stayed friends. His allure drew Forster to India in 1912, and with an account of the blazing, bewildering spaces he found there (along with Godbole and Chandrapore and the courtroom *punkah*-boy and the Marabar Caves – 'not all that remarkable', he said), Mr Furbank's narrative ends. Masood put the idea of a book about India into his head, crediting him with an uncanny grasp of the oriental soul. Besides, Forster perceived in Masood's anecdotes a new angle for attack on the British character. Masood used to tell how he had been relaxing in a railway compartment when a British officer bounded in shouting, 'Come on! get out of this.' 'D'you want your head knocked off?' enquired Masood: whereupon the officer exclaimed, 'I say, I'm awfully sorry! I didn't know you were that sort of person.'

Whether, apart from bringing Masood into his life, Forster's homosexuality advantaged him as a writer, it's hard to decide. Arguably it helped him to the isolation a satirist needs. On the other hand, it made him fed up with the kind of book he had been producing. Analysing the causes of his sterility in 1911, he put high on the list: 'Weariness of the only subject that I both can and may treat – the love of men for women and vice versa.' Further, homosexuality took him in an unfortunate way because it made him sentimental. When he approaches it as an author, the stringency drips out of him, and a fearsome cheeriness supervenes – witness the jinks the lovers get up to in *Maurice*: 'Maurice smote him on the ribs, and for ten minutes they played up amongst the trees, too silly for speech.' Quite so. Perhaps it would have been better for the novels if he had never found out about sex at all.

Of Mr Furbank's biography one can say with confidence that it won't be surpassed. Forster himself invited him to write it. It draws on all the available diaries and correspondence, as well as on innumerable conversations. Graceful, intimate, evocative, it is that rare thing, a study of a major writer by a major critic who was also a close friend. We shall not be brought so near to the young Forster again.

1977

Eric, or Gigantic by Gigantic

The trouble with sex, so far as Eric Gill was concerned, was that he could not stop thinking about it. Its incidentals, big and little, aroused his ungovernable curiosity. Female pubic hair, for example, when he first discovered its existence from a photograph, filled 'all the nooks and crannies of thought' for months on end, and the loving care he expends on this feature in his models indicates its lasting fascination. Most men, he estimated, spend their days in virtually perpetual tumescence. But occasionally he suspected that he might be singular in this respect, and as a lad it worried him. 'What does God think? Oh dear!' he moaned, recording yet another masturbatory lapse in his diary.

He began his professional career carving letters on tombstones – not, you might think, an especially inflaming task, but the pressure of his erotic yearnings drove him, at the age of thirty, to seek respite in the Catholic Church. He and his wife became novices in the Third Order of St Dominic, and with other questers after piety and discomfort set up a working community at Ditchling in Sussex – later they found a bleaker site in the Black Mountains. Day began with Prime at 6 a.m., and ended with Compline in the Chapel.

In the intervals of prayer, Gill busied himself with his engraving blocks, sculpture and drawing, while the females, whom he believed unfitted as a sex for higher creativity, baked bread, churned butter, and tended the pigs and poultry. The Order frowned on frivolities of dress, which suited Gill, for he had strict sartorial ideas. He despised trousers, favouring instead smocks, run up for him by a dressmaker, and loose scarlet silk underpants, which he would discard in summer to keep himself from overheating.

Gill's susceptibility, and his attempts to quell it, caused some confusion in his standards. Like D.H. Lawrence, whom he admired, he had a prudish streak. He fulminated against tight skirts, bare arms, scent, and the display of feminine garments in shop windows ('should be punishable by law as an unwarrant-

able indecency'). On the other hand he preached the purity of
the human body, enjoyed nude tennis or photography sessions
with friends and their families, and accumulated a handsome
collection of erotica. He was a keen observer of courting couples
in Hyde Park, and rigged up a mirror in his studio to get a better
view of his own illicit love-making. Genitals always engrossed
him. He made many drawings of his own and other people's, in
various stages of arousal, sometimes decorating the self-
portraits with orchid-like colours and whimsical titles ('Eric
Erect', 'The Front Yard').

Puritanism and prurience conflicted, too, in his more public
artworks. He had a mania for clean, hard outlines. In his nudes
he smooths away personal details, such as the face, and aspires
to symbolic form. Sculpture, he taught, should induce worship
of an idea, freezing the human shape into a religious emblem.
He did not start life-study until he was forty, and he found the
'dimples and what-nots' of flesh-and-blood models fearfully
distracting. His rigours of technique and theory represent a
desperate lunge in the direction of self-control.

But his natural appetites got the better of him whenever he
approached the erotic zones. He arranged his models in such
strenuously revealing poses that even hardened viewers blen-
ched. John Rothenstein recalls Gill showing some particularly
acrobatic studies to a group of friends, and inviting their
admiration 'with all the candour of a child'. In the shocked
silence Rothenstein found himself enquiring weakly as to the
girl's identity. 'Oh,' replied Gill, 'she was the Deputy Librarian
at High Wycombe.' When Gill was finishing off his sculpture of
Prospero and Ariel for the front of Broadcasting House, he asked
the BBC Governors up on to the scaffolding for a preview. The
amplitude of Ariel's private parts raised instant consternation
and disbelief, and the Governors withdrew to deliberate. After
calling on the experience of one of their number, who was an
ex-public-school headmaster, they decided that Gill had exaggerated, and ordered him to cut the lad down to size.

For Gill such exhibitions were ultimately religious. He seems
to have joined the Catholic Church under the impression that it
had abolished the opposition between flesh and spirit and was
out to promote a mystical form of sexual intercourse. In his
sacred art he pursued this idea zestfully. His crucified Christs
are often naked, and unmistakably masculine in their endow-
ments. One wood-engraving shows a girl embracing the hang-

ing figure. The reaction of Gill's fellow Catholics to these novel icons surprised and pained him – not least when his curvaceous illustrations for the Song of Songs were suppressed by the Prior Provincial of the Dominican Order. But with typical ingenuousness he agreed that some of the figure-drawing could have been improved ('it's a pity about her belly . . .').

The most exasperating part of Gill was his theories. He had one for every aspect of art and life, and they were inexhaustibly muddled and arbitrary. He considered both modern industrial society and the Renaissance serious mistakes, and desired a return to the twelfth century – a period about which he was at best hazily informed. His ideal of the medieval craftsman, derived from Ruskin and William Morris, led him to despise the 'fine arts', and long for a time when the same sturdy artisan would paint, sculpt, lay bricks and cobble boots. Art, he never tired of arguing, should be useful, not just decorative.

Luckily, his own art freely ignores this dictate, and his insistence that the artist must live in the thick of humanity comes ludicrously from one who could survive, in practice, only in a sheltered community of freaks and cranks. He knew so little about the masses that he imagined they were going to rise up in protest against machine-made goods, and demand the right to support themselves by handicraft.

His own quarrel with industrialization was choosy. He loved railway engines, and joyfully took on the job of painting the Flying Scotsman's nameplate, with a ride in the driver's cab as reward. Some of his most elegant work was the design of typefaces for machine printing. The bare outlines of skyscrapers, pylons and hangers excited his ascetic instincts, and in the end he accepted the title of Designer to Industry.

But if he was inconsistent he also radiated sincerity. He truly hated the dead soul of European capitalist society, and two trips to the Holy Land late in life intensified his yearning for some alternative. David Jones remembers seeing him, unaware of being observed, kissing the diseased stump of a beggar woman's hand. The other-worldliness of Indian art inspired him: he might really have been happiest as a nameless craftsman carving countless supple charmers on one of the great Hindu temples. Perhaps in another incarnation that is what he did.

What he did in this one, Malcolm Yorke's book splendidly

illustrates.* The rich realms of Gill, in sculpture, wood-engraving, drawing and lettering, are spread out and expertly glossed. Naturally the sculpture suffers most in reproduction, and some of it, as Mr Yorke notes, is now shamefully inaccessible. He tracked down 'Mankind', once Gill's most acclaimed work, under wrappers in the Tate Gallery's store on an industrial estate in North Acton. Since then it has been rescued by the Whitechapel Gallery, and visitors to 'British Sculpture in the 20th Century' have had the chance to wonder at it. A huge naked female torso, carved from two and a half tons of Hopton-wood stone, apple-smooth and delicate as a leaf, it dazzlingly vindicates the marriage of sensual music with unageing intellect that Gill battled to bring about.

1981

*Eric Gill: Man of Flesh and Spirit by Malcolm Yorke (Constable).

Passionate contradictions

D. H. Lawrence was born one hundred years ago next Wednesday. Eastwood is celebrating its son with a three-week festival and a grand procession mounted by the Welfare State theatre group. Hardly the nuance Lawrence would have chosen – but then, he is an uncomfortable focus for popular merrymaking of any complexion. His reputation as an apostle of permissiveness, gained in the wake of the *Lady Chatterley* trial, would have shocked him. He believed that boys and girls should be kept apart, that marriage was sacred, and that to teach people the biological facts of sex was criminal. Couples should couple in 'dark secrecy' and ignorance.

His political ideas also present problems for the designers of carnival floats. His religion of the blood led, Bertrand Russell claimed, straight to Auschwitz. As Lawrence saw it, the only hope for civilization lay in magically potent leaders, like himself, whom mankind must blindly obey. Most people were slaves by nature, anyway. The great mass of humanity should never, he stipulated, learn to read or write: all schools should be closed at once. The higher (white) races must subjugate or destroy the lower, which will otherwise swarm like vermin and suffocate them. These ideological leanings meant that when the New Left canonized Lawrence in the fifties, it required a rather selective reading of the sacred texts.

Luckily no one disagreed with Lawrence more hotly than Lawrence. It clearly occurred to him at times that a person who believed what he did ought to be in a criminal lunatic asylum (one Lawrence spokesman suggests this possibility to another in *Aaron's Rod*). Anthony Burgess* bravely seizes on self-contradiction not as a massive blemish but as the key to Lawrence's greatness. It saved him from the dead consistency of machines, which he dreaded, and brought the quick flame of life to his writing. His clumsy style, with its prolixity and repetition,

Flame into Being: The Life and Work of D. H. Lawrence by Anthony Burgess (Heinemann).

worked the same marvel, breaking through the techniques of literature to the naked, feeling, inconstant self.

Burgess traces Lawrence's vivid inner splits to the days in Eastwood. He combines his father's working-class aggression with his mother's gentility. Ringside attendance at their combats apparently taught him, early on, to see reality as a pattern of warring viewpoints. The enriching effect of domestic bedlam continued in his own marriage, where Frieda was always ready to pelt him with crockery if he got above himself. Even at his most dogmatic, Lawrence retains the taunting emphasis of someone who knows he may have to dodge a saucepan any moment, and in novels and stories where a Lawrence figure and a Frieda figure jointly appear every statement exists in a combat zone of possible contradictions.

Burgess is himself the kind of big, untidy writer critics niggle at, and this may have helped him to savour Lawrence as a working model of human inconsistency. Not that his reading reduces the books to feeble, see-both-sides fairness. Lawrence's furious fixations survive, and Burgess admits to finding them crazy at times. That, too, is a kind of compliment to Lawrence, because his stature depends on his being the first great European writer to launch a frontal attack on reason. He aims to show how much more of reality can be accounted for if humans are regarded as irrational complexes of blood and nerve.

At heart, Burgess would like us to believe, the inaugurator of this revolution remained a decent, gentle, animal-loving Englishman. Eastwood would probably like to believe that too, and Lawrence's actions, as opposed to his theories, mostly support it. Despite his ravings about salutary spillings of blood, he was disgusted when he went to a bullfight, and wrote it off as a low dago business. His idealization of peasant values received a rude shock when he went to Italy, and found that peasants excrete in the open air. 'Dirty disgusting swine' was Lawrence's comment, and the foe of industrial civilization went on to complain that there were no real shops in the Italian countryside.

Burgess's account leaves out the short stories – a mistake, since they are matchlessly ardent and acute. That aside, this is the most understanding introduction to Lawrence so far. As a biographer Burgess's appeal lies not in any new facts (though he did once meet some elderly and evidently tactful Eastwooders who recalled Lawrence's father as 'a real old English gentleman'), but in the closeness he feels to Lawrence as a professional writer. Like Lawrence he started as a provincial underdog – brought up in a pub – and was called 'mardarse' at school. Like Lawrence he married a foreign aristocrat, and lives in voluntary exile abroad. Just as Lawrence suffers from being identified with a single book, *Lady Chatterley's Lover*, so Burgess would like to repudiate *A Clockwork Orange* – a joke, he says, knocked off for money in three weeks, and made into a sex-and-violence movie, which has typecast him in the public mind.

Whereas Burgess widens his focus to take in the crowd of people inside Lawrence, Sheila MacLeod* strives to reduce everything Lawrence said to the simplest terms, so that she can condemn it. She represents the feminist angle, and complains, quite rightly, that Lawrence made some disgraceful allegations about women – as he did, of course, about almost everything else. Actually she seems to have missed some of the worst. Lawrence claimed for example (with, one imagines, a wary eye on Frieda) that 'women, when they speak or write, utter not one single word that men have not taught them'. Heaven knows what shock and horror would have ensued had Ms MacLeod hit upon that. On the other hand, when she finds women in Lawrence's fiction who display strength, intelligence and generosity, she seems to think they do so unbeknown to Lawrence and have somehow escaped from his jealous masculine control.

She tramples all over Lawrence's intensities in her sensible, flat-soled shoes, distributing praise and blame among the characters with unerring bathos. The passionate kiss Mrs Morel gives Paul in *Sons and Lovers* arouses her gravest suspicions: 'as the mother of two grown-up sons myself I find her conduct inexcusable.'

What are the perfect conditions for enjoying Lawrence? Burgess rightly urges that he should be read entire, in chronological order, and at one go. Sheila MacLeod digested all the shorter fiction as a teenager on her parents' lawn, and it gave her anorexia nervosa. My own solution is a Mediterranean beach. I remember taking in all Lawrence (or everything buyable in Penguin) one long hot summer in Kos. At the time the island had beaches so deserted (maybe it still has) that they tempted the shyest to shed all, and bake. You could lie for hours and see nothing more animated than a prickly pear. True, any writer

Lawrence's Men and Women by Sheila MacLeod (Heinemann).

seems pretty good in this situation (except Jane Austen, who instantly impels you to replace your swimwear). But for Lawrence it is ideal. Drugged by heat, the mind sinks back into the body, and your only problem is keeping the Coppertone from gumming up the pages. And as you follow Lawrence, sun-dazzled, through book after book, you realize that he does not need any commemorative celebrations, however well meant, because he is, simply, still alive.

1985

Seer Sucker

What mainly strikes you, reading Volume 2 of Sybille Bedford's biography of Huxley,* is that all the fizz and glitter were in Volume 1. Gone are the gambols at Garsington, the banter in Bloomsbury. Gone the scintillating cynical novels that set the flappers flapping and electrified the bright young things. The agonies are mostly over too – his mother's early death, his brother's suicide, his own blindness (struck down at sixteen by *keratitis punctata*), the Braille and the bravery, and the hopeless *grande passion* for Nancy Cunard. Even Europe has slipped into the past, and with it have vanished the scarlet Bugatti and the villa at Sanary, the vines and tuberoses and the picnics on summer nights by the phosphorescent sea, the Albany apartment (such a saving to live there, Maria Huxley used to say – so convenient for Fortnum and Mason's), and the cottage by the Seine where James Joyce would come and explain his mad notions of etymology, reflected upside-down in the mirror-top dining table. These revels ended in 1937 when the Huxleys scuttled for safety to California, terrified, it seems, by their friend Gerald Heard's craven tales about what would follow the outbreak of war. Heard went with them.

True, they could have contributed little to England's defence had they stayed. Huxley himself was half-blind, and his son Matthew, when eventually conscripted into the US forces as a non-combatant (his conscientious objections having been disallowed), found even the routine immunization jabs too much for him and had to be invalided out. Still, their flight to the States can't be invested with much dignity, and its aftermath was totally depressing. They rented a kitsch house in Pacific Palisades, Los Angeles, with luminous dogs as lamps and clocks that ticked fans up and down over naked girls, and Huxley was soon swallowed up in worthless, lucrative projects – adaptations for Metro-Goldwyn-Mayer (*Pride and Prejudice*; the Madame

Aldous Huxley: A Biography, Vol. 2: 1939–1963 by Sybille Bedford (Chatto and Windus/Collins).

Curie story, starring Greta Garbo), a happily abortive musical version of *Brave New World*, then, later, think-pieces for *Esquire* ('Thanks to the nude ladies,' he shamefacedly joked, 'they can pay very well'), and endless, dismal bids to write a Broadway hit. Had the Huxleys stayed in England, Sybille Bedford loyally boasts, 'food rationing, clothes rationing, shortage of drink, drabness and the rest wouldn't have mattered a scrap to them.' That's poppycock, of course: such things would matter to anyone who wasn't permanently in a coma, and since Sybille Bedford soon joined the Huxleys in California I can't see that she's in a position to judge. But supposing the Huxleys wouldn't have fled of their own accord, why was Gerald Heard so influential? Shouldn't Huxley's famed scientific brain have suspected some alarmism when Heard predicted that, for instance, the Luftwaffe would annihilate the British Home Fleet in a single hour? A study of Heard's motives, career and personality should be pivotal in any biography of Huxley. Mrs Bedford, instead, leaves a hole. We hear, in passing, of the monastery Heard founded at Trabuco after he arrived in the USA, of trouble over his having favourites among the monks, and of the community being disbanded by direct decree from God. For the rest, there's a loudly tactful silence.

The omission is particularly riling since on every other conceivable topic, right down to Maria Huxley's shopping lists, Mrs Bedford is a perpetual fountain of tittle-tattle. What we can be sure of is that Huxley's decline into woolly-headed mysticism and blue jeans was something Heard industriously abetted. Even back in the thirties he had been responsible for encouraging Huxley to seek increasingly cranky cures for his own and the world's ills, from F.M. Alexander's kinaesthetic therapy and J.E.R. McDonagh's colonic lavages, to homeopathy and hypnotism and Sedobrol (a sedative French Oxo cube), and Dick Sheppard's Peace Pledge Union. Once Huxley had got to the States, his fads and quackeries multiplied dizzily: animal magnetism, dianetics, flying saucers, acupuncture, entelechy, sessions at the Vedanta Temple of Swami Prabhavananda, and, of course, mescalin. On this last touchy topic Mrs Bedford is commendably cagey, raising and quickly shelving the issue of whether Huxley could and should have known more about the potential dangers, physical, genetic and social, of mescalin and LSD before so volubly advocating their use. Again it's his scientific nous that comes into question. One very much wants

to know (and Mrs Bedford evidently can't tell us) how well
educated he was scientifically – apart, that is, from having an
eye for fascinating facts in the *Encyclopaedia Britannica*, which
he had reputedly read right through. The evidence is confusing,
and the lay reader keeps wondering why Huxley's ideas haven't
been taken up, if they're so brilliant. He's credited here with
discovering, among other things, a cure for cancer (semi-
hibernation, produced by a mixture of Chlorpromazine, Phena-
cetin, Aspirin and Demarol, combined with hypnosis), and the
answer to the world's power problems (wind – utilized via a
wind turbine that can produce, so he says, 1500 kilowatts). Are
conventional scientists keeping Man oil-burning and cancer-
ridden just out of cussedness, or what?

It seems to me that what intrigued Huxley about science,
apart from its potential, was its inhumanity. It allowed him to
regard people as chemical experiments, sets of data. That's what
keeps supplying the novelty in his novels. Take Irene in *Those
Barren Leaves*: 'Her frock was sleeveless. The warmth of her bare
arms drifted off along the wind; the temperature of the
surrounding atmosphere rose by a hundred-billionth of a
degree.' Woman as thermal generator. Scogan's bright remarks
in *Crome Yellow* come from the same stable: 'Screams of pain
and fear go pulsing through the air at the rate of eleven hundred
feet per second. After travelling for three seconds they are
perfectly inaudible. These are distressing facts; but do we
enjoy life any the less because of them?' Just the reverse. It's
frightfully exciting to see life in that way (or to read about it in
the *Encyclopaedia Britannica*) because it makes you feel so
modern and rational. Even more bracing is the prospect of
tampering with the human character by chemical means. Huxley's moral attitude to this changed, apparently. In *Brave New
World* the Central London Hatchery and Conditioning Centre is
presented as an awful warning; and when Dr Obispo in *After
Many a Summer* boasts that a course of thiamin chloride would
have cured the Romantic poets of their poetry-writing, we're
supposed to think him insensitive. But a few years in the United
States rotted Huxley's sense of human decency enough for him
to put across (in *Island*) the psychological grading of all children
under five, and subsequent daily dosing with drugs to eliminate
unacceptable character-traits, as positively Utopian arrangements. However, whether he approved or disapproved of such
things doesn't eventually matter: what remained constant was

his need to imagine them. The belief that human beings could be artificially controlled never failed to entrance him. It was a facet of his Olympianism, fitting in with his wearily aloof attitude to practical politics.

Another Olympian feature was the fun he got from imagining human beings hurt or debased. 'Do you notice', Orwell remarked, after reading *Ape and Essence*, 'that the more holy he gets, the more his books stink with sex. He cannot get off the subject of flagellating women.' Unless Mrs Bedford is keeping something back, Huxley didn't flagellate them in real life. As might be expected from his sadistic fantasies, he was a gentle, weakly person, constantly riddled with minor ailments, from toothache to lumbago. But scenes like the whipping of Lenina, 'that plump incarnation of turpitude', in *Brave New World*, receive Huxley's fond attention because they provided him with a way of feeling superior to the seductive, passionate, irrational element in humanity, while at the same time indulging it. You find a similar vindictive luxury in his comments about the eventual fate of mankind. Mrs Bedford remembers him coming back 'full of glee' from a scientific conference, announcing that a virus 'conveyed by air travel' would wipe out the human race even quicker than the bomb and the population explosion.

It's a glee that shakes one's faith in the picture of saintly seer and social saviour that admirers of the later Huxley keep trying to build up. Besides, you only have to look at the way he lived to see that his yearnings for small, self-supporting communes and the beauties of a pre-industrial state are so much eyewash. For a foe of industrialism he was remarkably fond of fast cars – a series of powerful Oldsmobiles replaced the pre-war Bugatti; and there's something absurd about fulminating against mankind's 'craving for pleasure' when you're staying at Claridges. When not off colour, his capacity for pleasure seems to have been pretty large ('My God, the Huxleys ate well!' their daughter-in-law recalls, picturing 'their huge freezer stuffed with breads and meats'), and he knew so little about looking after himself that he thought the way to wash a drip-dry suit was to take a shower in it and then stand about in the open air. By long practice he had become adept at being a burden to his wife and anyone else prepared to wait on him. Poor Maria even had to fix him up with mistresses ('You can't leave it to Aldous,' she would say, 'he'd make a muddle'), and almost the last thing she did before she died was to remind Betty Wendel to keep a fresh ribbon on her typewriter so that Aldous wouldn't have trouble reading. Aldous, of course, speedily fitted himself out with a new wife, Maria's spirit having intimated to him, through a medium, that she was in favour of it.

He regarded himself as a member of the 'small theocentric minority' who were 'simply not concerned with the things that preoccupy the great mass of human beings', and who could not be expected to fight or do any of the other unpleasant jobs necessary for the survival of a civilization. At the same time, his theocentricity did not involve a God who issued any inconvenient commands or prohibitions. He simply existed 'at the heart of things', and when you got through to Him, by way of mescalin, you learnt that 'in spite of Death, in spite of Horror, the universe is in some way All Right'. Pangloss, though, managed to believe that, even without the use of drugs. What Huxley never offers is a reason for believing that the beatific vision he got with drugs was any closer to 'the heart of things' than what he felt when he had toothache or lumbago. Why should the psychological outcome of one kind of chemical upset be more valid than that of another? It's a question the earlier Huxley wouldn't have allowed himself to evade.

                                                                    1974

How the style refines

Evelyn Waugh's *Diaries** are, predictably, snobbish, malicious, offensive and highly enjoyable. He met, and disliked, a great many people, and his pages crawl with squashed celebrities, from Noel Coward to Edmund Wilson. Beverley Nichols ('a mercenary, hypochondriacal flibbertigibbet') is a typical casualty. So is Edith Sitwell, whom Waugh found 'wholly ignorant'. She informed him that port was made from methylated spirit: 'she knew this for a fact because her charwoman told her.' Of Waugh's numerous loathsome acquaintances, Randolph Churchill emerges as arguably the least engaging. His rudeness to servants was habitual, and on one occasion during the war in Italy he expressly stopped his vehicle in order to urinate in front of some local women – 'Because', he explained, 'I am a Member of Parliament.' Drunk or sober, his conversation was intolerable. To keep him quiet, Waugh once bet him £10 he could not read the Bible right through, whereupon Churchill set to work, persistently exclaiming 'God, isn't God a shit.' 'Randolph's coughing and farting', Waugh feelingly notes, 'make him a poor companion in wet weather.' Randolph eventually entered hospital to have a lung removed, and it was announced that the trouble was not malignant. Waugh observed that it was characteristic of modern science to find the only unmalignant part of Randolph and remove it.

Pen-portraits of this quality are a beguiling feature of the *Diaries*. More importantly, these 800 pages portray the evolution of a major novelist. True, there are gaps – quite apart from those left by editing out libellous matter. Waugh destroyed his undergraduate diaries, apparently because of their homosexual content. His humiliating first marriage, which ended after twelve months when his wife went off with a BBC news-editor, and the *Gilbert Pinfold* 'lunacy' of 1954, are also blanks. What remains is still totally absorbing. No parallel case comes to mind of so

The Diaries of Evelyn Waugh ed. Michael Davie (Weidenfeld and Nicolson).

distinguished a writer leaving us, in its day-to-day form, the raw material of his novels. We follow Waugh from prep school, through Lancing, and his capers with the Bright Young People, to the self-proving treks in central Africa and the South American jungle during the thirties, and then, with the outbreak of war, to Libya, the Battle of Crete, and Yugoslavia, where he was attached as liaison officer to Tito's partisans – a role for which his social prejudices and manner made him perhaps the least suitable choice in the British army.

Waugh's character, it seems, became warped quite early. His schoolboy reflections on the 'blatantly semitic' spectators at the Lancing–Brighton cricket match, the 'blatantly risen-from-the-ranks' officer who inspected the OTC, and the 'vile Southend trippers' who had the ill luck to share his railway compartment, all indicate traits that were to prove permanent – as do his feats of piggishness in the tuck-shop. His religious sensibilities appear in childhood, too: 'Went to church. We struck a horrible low one. I was the only person who crossed myself and bowed to the altar.' This, at the age of eleven, foreshadows the conversion to Catholicism and the class attitudes that went with it. What did change – indeed, died – was the child's capacity for enthusiasm.

With young manhood came a sense of life's futility, which Waugh sought to exorcise, or reinforce, by grim bouts of drunkenness and dissipation (and by a half-hearted suicide attempt, in the course of which he swam out to sea, but turned back because of jellyfish). He and his friends spent much of the twenties ingesting choice foodstuffs and fine wines, which were rapidly and regularly converted into streams of vomit. 'Never have I seen so many men being sick together . . . They threw about chairs and soda water syphons and lavatory seats' – this entry accurately conveys the tone of the period.

To voice his new bitterness, Waugh perfected a laconic rhetoric of denigration which becomes one of the chief pleasures of his style. At first it rises little above abuse: 'to Lord's, where the cricket was slow, and the crowd almost entirely made up of shits'. Even here, though, the judiciousness of 'almost entirely', coupled with 'shits', has a lively effect. And as the technique developed it enabled Waugh to convey his peculiar vision of people and places with speed and power – the Welsh school where he taught in the twenties, for instance, largely composed of pitch-pine, linoleum, and 'an army of housemaids who scurry about the passages laden with urine'; or Athens, seen on a trip in 1927 – 'all the drinks taste either of camphor or medicine and everything smells of drains'.

Like any style, it prevents much of the truth from being told. We hear nothing in the *Diaries* of Waugh's relationship with his God which, to judge from the punctiliousness of his religious observances, must have mattered to him deeply. The style also inhibits the expression of emotion. After the birth of his daughter in 1941, Waugh noted: 'The baby died shortly after my arrival. I saw her when she was dead – a blue, slatey colour. Poor little girl, she was not wanted.' What he felt, behind the meagre phrases, we have no way of judging. Likewise with the acid outbursts directed at his surviving children: we cannot tell whether his professions of disgust at their company are a requirement of the style, or whether he was indeed emotionally maimed.

Increasingly, the style's dominant function is to expose the absurdity of existence. People disintegrate into strings of incongruous attributes. 'She had a thick beard, a bald dog, a drunken husband, and a paederastic son' – that, for instance, is Waugh's way of commemorating a lady who entertained him in Scotland (and whose name Mr Davie has kindly erased). If freaks were not forthcoming, they had to be invented. In the footnotes to this edition, an aggrieved band of Waugh's acquaintances firmly disown the gallstones, weak bladders and other imperfections he wished on them. He became adept at wresting bizarre collocations from the most innocent landscape: 'went to see the phallic giant at Cerne Abbas. Two little girls with long bare legs sat on his testicles.' His forays into half-civilized continents gave additional scope to his faculty. In Africa, Waugh, like Conrad, found that humankind's attempts to impose significance upon chaos wore satisfyingly thin. Conrad's young Russian, in *Heart of Darkness*, cherishing his manual of seamanship in the depths of the jungle, is kin to the religious maniac Waugh met in the wilds of British Guiana, or the English lady he discovered in Abyssinia, wearing a large brooch presented to her father when Lord Mayor of London on the opening of Epping Forest.

Warfare, like foreign parts, offered a glimpse into chaos. The 1939–45 diaries give extensive coverage to the Dakar expedition, various commando operations, and the retreat from Crete. Throughout, the record of military disorganization and incompetence is almost unbroken, and it is plain that Waugh took savage pleasure in chronicling it. His picture of the last days in Crete is unforgettable, with hordes of demoralized British troops streaming down the coast roads, and the C-in-C, General Freyberg, seated apathetically at the mouth of a cave, distributing half-cupfuls of sherry and signed photographs. Significantly when, a year or two later, news of the war began to improve, Waugh lost all interest in it.

Besides stirring the absurdist's imagination, battle gave Waugh an opportunity to prove his courage – a quality by which, again like Conrad, he set great store. He had long had worries on the subject. 'I am a contemptible, clever little coward,' he noted, desperately, at Lancing. For a man so censorious, and so enamoured of the aristocratic virtues, it was imperative that he should not lose caste in his own eyes by running away. Hence, perhaps, the strong contrast, in his account of the action in Crete, between his own coolness and the quivering panic of almost everyone else. Not that Waugh's courage is in doubt. A man of forty who volunteers for parachute training, and makes two jumps, is patently braver than most. But Waugh's parading of his fearlessness in the Cretan affair seems overdone. Maybe he felt awkward about the fact that his unit eventually fought its way through the 'rabble' (i.e., allied troops) on the beaches, in order to board the available craft and escape. Or maybe resentment over his enforced resignation from the Commandos, which followed, led him to stress his soldierly mettle in this episode.

That he had to resign, despite his soapy letters to highly placed friends, plainly riled him. He seems to have been surprised to find that he was considered inefficient and insubordinate as an officer, and that no one wanted to serve with him. Rather in the same way, he repeatedly complains on his birthdays that the expected multitude of gifts from loving friends has not arrived. It is one of his few winning traits, and perhaps a condition of his greatness as a writer, that he does not appear to have realized what an intolerable person he was.

1976

The mouse who made the mousetrap

Murderers, Agatha Christie suggests,* should be made to choose between downing a cup of hemlock and offering themselves for vivisection to aid medical research. On care of the aged, she favours the Eskimo method: a bumper meal is cooked for dear old mum, who then trots off over the ice and doesn't come back.

These bracing views typify Mrs Christie's social outlook, and come as a surprise, given the soft upbringing her memoirs depict. Parents and nannies cosseted her, and the big family house in Torquay was a child's paradise. Her father, having inherited a fortune, never had to master much in life beyond whist and putting on his dinner clothes, and though he left his dependants 'very badly off' when he died, it was the kind of poverty which allowed them to spend winter in Egypt and send Agatha to a Parisian finishing school.

She might easily have turned out a wastrel like her brother Monty. Instead she had bags of grit, and made herself into a singer and concert pianist of almost professional excellence by the time she was twenty. Then, deciding she'd never be quite first rate, she briskly gave it up and turned to authorship. In that role she's had some 2,000 million readers so far, and been translated into more languages than Shakespeare. She puts her literary creativity on a level with embroidering cushion covers, and insists that writers should regard themselves as tradesmen.

Her hard-headedness shows in her eyes. Even in early photos they look out, old and cold, from the child's petal-like face. They appraised the world detachedly. Lovers who proposed to her always put her in mind, she says, of sick sheep. The First World War further toughened her. As a nurse with the VADs she found herself lugging amputated legs to the incinerator and slaving in the dispensary, where she gained invaluable knowledge of poisons and the psychopaths they attract. One boss used to carry a lump of curare in his pocket, to make him feel powerful.

*An Autobiography by Agatha Christie (Collins).

Her tales of these black days are sometimes appallingly funny. The Lady Mayoress of Torquay, it appears, fell symbolically on her knees before the first batch of heroes to arrive at the hospital from the trenches, and humbly unlaced the boots of the nearest soldier. As he was an epileptic suffering from no wound of any kind, he was decidedly put out to find his footwear being removed in mid-afternoon.

The collapse of her first marriage after the war, and the nervous crisis it brought on, get little coverage here. That's probably no loss, for she is always firmly superficial about personal relations – which is one reason why her detective stories provide such a relaxing read. Houses, furniture and utensils move her far more deeply, and she resurrects her youth through intense memories of them – the mauve nursery wall-paper, the solid mahogany lavatory seats, the knee-length black alpaca bathing dresses. She makes the tragedy of age hinge on possessions too. In one haunting sequence she remembers turning out cupboardfuls of moth-eaten velvets and mouldy jam in her grandmother's house, after the old woman had gone blind.

Travel occupies a lot of the book: a world tour, taking in Honolulu and the Antipodes, with her first husband; archaeological digs at Ur, Ninevah and Nimrud with her second. Far horizons grow solid as they clatter through her typewriter, because she never romanticizes what she finds. The Orient Express, she reports, was infested with bed-bugs, which fed hungrily on their fellow passengers; the exquisite Hawaiian girls stank of coconut oil. Her account of the Palace Hotel at Damascus, with its vast marble halls and weak electric light epitomizes the disappointments foreign parts generally manage to have in store. Of course, since she loves objects, her flat-heeled approach has its magic too. Gently cleaning, with orange-stick and face-cream, an ivory head just dug from Nimrud's sludge after 2,500 years, she sounds like someone raising the dead.

But inside the shell of practicality a more tremulous Agatha lurked. She could hardly bring herself to enter a shop, and had to grit her teeth when arriving at parties. In dreams, a sinister gunman dogged her, and she would wake shrieking. Once when she was on holiday as a child a kindly French guide pinned a live butterfly to her hat as a treat. It flapped there for hours, and she wept, spellbound with horror, not daring to object.

Her inarticulateness, she thinks, made her a writer; and the choice of the detective story as a form must have been determined, too, by her over-acute sensibility. Being limited and mathematical, it kept her imagination in check, while allowing her to get her own back on the slaughterers of innocence. She seldom permits herself to think deeply, and the reflections in this volume – about joy, femininity, and the thrill of dining with the Queen – are like being hit over the head with a net curtain. Luckily they're rare, and won't worry those 2,000 million readers anyway.

1977

Inferior soap

Much of the thrill of Auden's poetry in the thirties derived, one imagines, from its tough, knowing voice. Whoever this young Mr Auden might be, he certainly wasn't mistily mystic like Yeats or dried out like Eliot. He knew about communication systems and industry and power stations and troop movements and espionage and the big European cities. He sounded battle-hardened and ascetic – addicted to moorland and crouching behind sheep-pens. And of course he must be deeply involved in politics. That's how it might have struck an innocent peruser in the pre-Second-World-War years.

This chunky, amicable volume,* on the other hand, brings together a host of pals to remind us what Uncle Wiz's back-ground and life-style were really like. Daddy was a doctor, and quite nicely off. There were maids, who slept in the attic, smelling, one of Wystan's brothers recalls, of 'inferior soap'. Wystan, as a snap cherished by his prep-school mistress shows, was a portly unathletic child in an Eton collar. During the hols he enjoyed going on hikes and bike rides over the moors with his mother and brothers, and made a speciality of poking around old mine workings and abandoned machinery. The grim, ravaged landscapes of the poems derive from these gentle excursions. Wystan's knowledge of military affairs was limited to the Gresham School's Annual OTC Camp, and jaunts like the Gresham School Sociological Society's visit to a boot factory at Norwich provided him with his understanding of the workers.

For much of the time in the thirties he was a prep-school master, an occupation which he greatly relished. Far from being hardened, he was almost entirely unable to look after himself. On the Iceland trip – in the company of schoolboys as usual – he squelched around in several layers of clothing plus his pyjamas, equipped with a blue-and-yellow pneumatic a tent which blew down on him when he tried to erect it. The schoolboyishness, or

*W. H. Auden: A Tribute ed. Stephen Spender (Weidenfeld and Nicolson).

schoolgirlishness, stayed on in later life. Auden's sense of what was done or not done always smacked, Louis Kronenberger attests, of the nursery or the schoolroom; and Orlan Fox remembers the 'private schoolgirl jokes' like 'Au reservoir' which he and WHA used to share.

Not that this necessarily adds up to an adverse criticism of Auden's poetry. In a sense it does just the opposite. To make out of such soft, private materials poems that voiced the fears of a doomed, hag-ridden continent was a triumph of art over life – like making a rifle that really fires out of plasticine.

It's possible, of course, to take a more moral view, and protest that poets shouldn't write about things of which they're ignorant. Orwell, following this tack, jibbed at Auden's mention of 'necessary murder' in his poem 'Spain'. No one who had actually seen murder, he argued, would refer to it so glibly. Orwell's whole quarrel with parlour Bolsheviks of the Auden and Spender cut was that they had never experienced anything beyond public school and university and a few trips abroad. Hunger, hardship, exile, war, prison, persecution, manual labour, were just words to them. They were the kind of people who fomented political feelings, but always contrived to be somewhere else when the trigger was pulled.

That Auden did so contrive can't be gainsaid. The plasticine rifle was never taken into battle. But why should it have been? There's no law that decrees that poets ought to have physical courage, and it seems wiser to accept that Auden hadn't than to maintain, as his brother does here, that he left England shortly before the outbreak of hostilities because he couldn't stand 'the narrow intellectualism of the English establishment'. It would have been more dignified, too, if Auden himself had not tried to justify his flight by turning Christian and fulminating about 'the masochistic murderee and the sadistic murderer' that lurk within every soldier. The really gruesome and craven episode in Auden's career seems to me not his quitting England in 1939, but his joining the US Army, with the rank of Major, when the war was drawing safely to a close, and swanning round the German cities in a jeep, inspecting the bomb damage. Somehow it had become possible, apparently, to be a soldier, without turning into a 'masochistic murderee', etc.

At all events, Orwell's criticism strikes at Auden's character rather than at his poetry, and Orwell conceded as much by calling 'Spain', despite his objections, 'one of the few decent things that have been written about the Spanish war'. To succeed, when the experiences the poems laid claim to had not been gone through, meant getting the voice exactly right – clinical, confident – and that required a dedication to technique that reflects one whole side of Auden's personality. Friends bear witness to his passion for anagrams and crosswords and the *OED*. But the obsession with exact fit stretched beyond words. It extended, for instance, to the clock. He was fanatically punctual. Guests who arrived even half a minute late for dinner underwent reproof, and at nine precisely he would waddle off to bed, clutching a bottle of wine, no matter what company remained. He connected punctuality with his mother: 'Mother would never have allowed that' was a common remark with him even late in life. And it seems to have got mixed up with his sexual drives: one of his recurrent dreams involved trying to catch a train for which he was late, and ended with him ejaculating as he realized he had missed it.

His concern about sewage disposal was another aspect of his long love-affair with perfect technique. On Ischia he had a flush system installed, at great expense, the tank of which had to be recharged from goat skins carried on donkeys. He was severe if he suspected a guest of wasting toilet paper, and would scrutinize the diameter of the roll with a jealous eye. The interest went back to undergraduate days. John Betjeman remembers that at Oxford Auden was always asking him for the return of a book with coloured illustrations of soil pipes and domestic privies, which Betjeman had borrowed and lost. When, much later, he was invited to Japan, Auden gave, as a reason for refusing, his belief that the lavatory seats there would be too small for his bottom. As in matters of metre and form, exact fit was important.

Only when he was deliberately letting his hair down would Auden allow himself to make light of excretory decencies. The results were not always appreciated. It is rumoured that, in the Common Room at Christ Church, he used to disconcert bishops and other distinguished guests by enquiring whether they peed in the hand basin. Many years before, during the Spanish Civil War, he was arrested by two militia men in the gardens of Monjuich for urinating behind a bush. This incident, which is related by Cyril Connolly, revealed, or so Connolly believes, 'the misunderstanding between the revolutionary poet who felt disinhibited by the workers' victory and the new bureaucracy to whom the people's gardens deserved more respect than ever before.' That Auden should have imagined that urinating in public was the mark of a 'revolutionary', and indicated one's solidarity with 'the workers', sheds some light on the pitch of maturity which his political and social thinking had attained, and illustrates the symbolic significance with which, in moments of stress, he could endue his evacuatory system.

But the Monjuich episode was an aberration. Generally, as we've seen, he was keen on toilet fittings and toilets fitting. The concern with fit fits, too, with his passion for tea-cosies and egg-cosies, recalled here by Dr Oliver Sacks. Once when Auden saw Sacks riding a BMW with a jacketed tank he remarked 'I have never seen a bike with a bike-cosy before', and added philosophically, 'it's absolutely right, it belongs where it is'. He liked to sleep under an Auden-cosy, composed of the bedroom curtains, carpet, and even the pictures from the wall, piled on the bed.

Of course, these worries about punctuality and privies aren't, in Auden's case, marks of a tidy mind, but rather the contrary – signs of a deep disquiet over his relations with other people and with his own physical functions. As an adolescent he went in for outrageousness. 'Mrs Carritt, my tea is like tepid piss,' he told a don's wife with whom he was staying. On another occasion, in a public bar full of agricultural workers, he ordered 'best bubbly all round to celebrate the anniversary of my birth'. Such sallies were treated by his chums as rather a hoot. But what they actually reveal is the need to strike an attitude, to find a definite self for his various insecurities to inhabit. This was what he looked for in the world of ideas, as well. He would snatch up theories like a jackdaw – Freud, Marx, Homer Lane, Groddeck – swallow them whole, and regurgitate them in a magisterial voice so that his friends tended to become converted too.

It could have horrible results. Cyril Connolly remembers discussing with young Auden his own difficult relationship with his father. Auden, going through a Groddeck phase, was dogmatic: 'Those people just batten on one, real emotional harpies, they've got to be taught a lesson. Stand up to him, make him see you don't need him any more.' Shortly afterwards, Connolly relates, his father lunched with him in Soho:

a treat he always enjoyed, and on the way back I stopped the taxi outside my door in Chelsea (he lived in South Kensington). He clearly expected to be invited in for a talk and a brandy but I bade him an abrupt farewell and gave the driver his address. Clutching his two thick cherrywood sticks with the rubber ferrules, his legs crossed, his feet in pumps, for owing to arthritis he could not stoop to do up the laces, he fingered his grey moustache while a tear trickled down his cheek. I don't know which of us felt more unhappy.

Nor do I, of course, but I hope it was Cyril.

This capacity to take you in with firmly enunciated half-truths is one of the strengths, if wayward strengths, of the poetry. As long ago as 1937 Christopher Isherwood remarked (in a piece about which he now seems to feel a bit ashamed) that the first thing you needed to understand, reading Auden's poetry, was that he was a 'schoolboy scientist': his science, that is, doesn't go at all deep, but he has acquired a vocabulary and a technique of approach which is 'really all he needs for his writing'. It allows the brilliant subterfuge to be carried through, though a corollary of this situation is that the poems aren't worth much attention as structures of ideas or expositions of theories. Indeed Isherwood recounts that when Auden showed him poems, he would pick out the lines that he liked, and then whole new peoms would be constructed which were simply anthologies of Isherwood's favorite lines, entirely regardless of grammar or sense: and that, he concludes, 'is the simple explanation of much of Auden's celebrated obscurity'.

But if a vocabulary and a technique were all he needed for writing, they weren't all he needed for living. The Audenesque aphorisms, that could be shatteringly successful in poems, were a handicap in conversation, particularly if those present had heard them before, as in later years they often had. A man who asserts that 'Only the Hitlers of the world work at night', or that 'No gentleman can fail to admire Bellini', really needs to be told that he's talking hogwash. But as Auden grew more distinguished there were naturally fewer and fewer people prepared to point this out to him, and he was allowed to pontificate in lonely splendour.

The loneliness was endemic. He had early been made to recognize his homosexuality as something shameful and dissevering. Robert Medley recalls how at school Auden, who was not normally keen on swimming, showed an unexpected eagerness to do double dives with him, a trick which entailed sitting on his shoulders and hugging him with his legs. 'It was as near as we, or most of us, ever got to an embrace at Gresham's', Medley observes. It bore fruit in some erotic verses which unfortunately came to the notice of Auden's father, and he proceeded to lecture Medley and his son on the undesirability of close friendship between males. It can't have helped much.

Despite, or because of, this sense of separateness, Auden hugely wanted to be loved. Few things, of course, make it harder to love someone than that. Of the infinite varieties of unrequited love, he had a deep and sad understanding. Hannah Arendt writes finely about this aspect of him, and about the infuriating substitution of admiration for love that he increasingly encountered as his reputation became more intimidating. This volume does not contain a personal memoir by Chester Kallman, with whom Auden formed his most stable and devoted relationship, so we cannot tell why that union terminated. What's clear is that he was fearfully lonely at the end. David Luke depicts him, after his return to Christ Church, pathetically sitting down to his glass of port after dinner each night, 'while the rest of us swallowed coffee, glanced at a newspaper and hurried off'. In the town he would sit alone at a cafe table, curiously gazed at by the young. The shade of Cyril Connolly's father could, I suppose, feel that the whirligig of time had brought in its revenges.

1975

Socialist and Sahib

Eric Blair's will requested that no one should write his biography. How they squared their consciences with this, Professor Stansky and Mr Abrahams don't reveal. Their example, though, has prompted Sonia Orwell to square hers. She has recently announced that she and Professor Bernard Crick are preparing a life of Orwell to correct the 'mistakes and misconceptions' of this one. The dust-jacket of *The Unknown Orwell** briefly makes out that it isn't 'a violation of the will' because it covers only the years (birth to 1933) before Blair called himself George Orwell. As a defence, that seems to lack relevance as well as candour. But it's late to strike righteous attitudes when one has willingly devoured the biography. Besides, Orwell takes his own revenge: he depicted his life so potently that mere scholar-critics look arthritic in his wake. Even the 'unknown' years were later worked into masterpieces like 'Such, such were the joys' and 'Shooting an Elephant'. Confronted with these, the Stansky-Abrahams method is to ferret out Orwell's kin, school chums, Indian Police mess mates and so on, and check his recollections against theirs. Their verdict, repeatedly, is that he 'exaggerated'.

Hardly surprising, really, given a set of dullish interviewees who would by nature regard anything vivid as an exaggeration. Sometimes, indeed, they were worse than dullish. Mrs Vaughan Wilkes, ex-doyenne of St Cyprian's Preparatory School (now happily burned down), had the authors to sherry and enlarged upon the comforts of the place, including her own cure for home-sickness. This was to kneel before the sufferer and grapple him to her bosom (an unusually mobile article, apparently, which earned her the nickname of 'Flip'). The child was expected to gasp 'O Mum!', or weep gratefully. Little Orwell, she recalls, simply tried to get away, and the price of resisting Flip's overtures was to be labelled 'not affectionate'. It was the affectionate Flip who later had Orwell beaten for bed-wetting.

The Unknown Orwell by Peter Stansky and William Abrahams (Constable).

At St Cyprian's, we may note, he first encountered the paraphernalia of coercion which turns up in *1984*. As described in 'Such, such were the joys' it involved spies, informers, a privileged oligarchy and systematic torture, all masquerading as love and paternalism, coupled with the calculated suppression of sex. Readers who hail *1984* as a warning against state control would do well to reflect that it has its roots in private education. St Cyprian's was riddled with snobbery and money-worship, and Orwell soon understood his inferior status. 'I had no money, I was weak, I was ugly, I was unpopular. The conviction that it was *not possible* for me to be a success went deep enough to influence my actions till far into adult life.' Professor Stansky and Mr Abrahams pooh-pooh this morbid hindsight. Did not Orwell's letters at the time convey how jolly ripping things were? Did he not win a scholarship to Eton? But, we may ask, what sort of critic takes exam results and letters to parents as a surer index of a child's inner self than the events which the grown man still can't forget a quarter of a century later?

The book riles when it claims to know better than Orwell what Orwell felt. But its informants were not all Flips, and it undeniably collects evidence to suggest that Orwell toughened up his experiences when turning them into prose. The gang of farm lads and errand boys, it points out, whom George Bowling goes fishing with in *Coming Up for Air*, were really genteel young Henleyites. George's big delinquent brother Joe shrinks, on inspection, to respectable Humphrey Dakin, who married Orwell's sister in 1920. Mr Dakin remembers Orwell as 'a rather nasty little fat boy with a constant grievance'. Seemingly he wasn't asked, in his interview, whether he and Orwell used to stamp on young thrushes – a favourite sport of George and Joe. Another tough Orwellian fancy, perhaps. Then again, a friend of Orwell's from Burma was interrogated, and called to mind their naive attempt to become tiger-hunters. Armed with a Luger and a 12-bore, they bullied an elderly villager into taking them out in his ox cart. After some hours of waiting, no tiger had presented itself, and Orwell's companion adds: 'I imagine the wily old Burman had no intention of going anywhere near where such an animal may have been lurking'. This, as Professor Stansky and Mr Abrahams comment, hardly prepares us for 'the successful tiger shoot that figures so decisively in *Burmese Days*' (leopard shoot, actually, but the slip doesn't affect their point). In *Burmese Days*, too, the nigger-hating cockney, Ellis, blinds a native schoolboy who has been teasing him by striking him across the eyes with a stick. What looks like the germ of this (though the authors don't venture the connection) has been related by Dr Maung Htin Aung, Vice-Chancellor of the University of Rangoon. One afternoon in 1924 he saw Orwell accidentally knocked downstairs at Rangoon railway station by a schoolboy who had been fooling around with his friends. Orwell 'was furious, and raised the heavy cane that he was carrying, to hit the boy on the head, but he checked himself, and struck him on the back instead'. Some undergraduates on the platform protested, and Orwell discussed the incident with them at length. Truth, once again, was tamer than fiction.

Dishonesty, of course, doesn't enter into it. Orwell was writing a novel: his gift was making fiction seem fact. *Down and Out in Paris and London* – not quite a novel – poses questions of truthfulness more awkwardly. The authors are keen to urge that Orwell's forays among the destitute weren't brought on by economic necessity, as he pretended. He could easily have got a job, and anyway was kept intermittently in funds by his mother and Aunt Nellie. Back from Paris, he didn't plunge into squalor, as in the book, but settled comfortably at his parents' Southwold home, watched over by golf-playing, poodle-breeding Mrs Blair – evidently a fond mother. He kept his down-and-out costume in a suitcase at Ruth Pitter's flat and donned it largely, the authors feel, to gather material for his writing. Maybe: but Orwell freely admitted that *Down and Out* wasn't all authentic ('nearly all', he said). And to start questioning his motives is merely to back one's own canniness against his assertion that dossing down with tramps was a way of mastering his snobbery, as well as expiating the five years he had spent knocking natives about in Burma.

Hanging them, too, one might have added – but in the authors' opinion the famous piece called 'A Hanging' is an invention, not an eye-witness account. Mabel Fierz, they report, remembers Orwell telling her he had never attended such an execution, and ex-police colleagues agree it would have fallen outside his normal duties. Orwell might, they concede, have gone along out of curiosity. But readers anxious to take 'A Hanging' as reportage, instead of imaginative literature, will have to assume that Orwell lied to Mrs Fierz. That seems unlikely, though one would admittedly like to disbelieve some of his other disclosures to her. Can he really, for instance, have been beaten on his first day at Eton for batting badly at cricket? Cricket-loving Etonians will know, I suppose.

Eton was the one phase of his life Orwell didn't write up. The authors repair this gap, zealously expounding the ancient rigmaroles of the place. Orwell's surviving classmates, like his Indian Police colleagues later, concur in pronouncing him a 'misfit'. He cultivated cynicism – 'the first person', one shocked contemporary attests, 'I ever heard running down his own father and mother'. Another acquaintance, a clergyman, deemed him 'a real stinker'. These are reassuring testimonials, in the circumstances. We should hardly expect Orwell to have entered with much spirit into the flagellatory pleasures of Eton, or, from what we hear of them, into the off-duty amusements of the Indian Police. His first Commanding Officer, a subordinate lovingly recalls, 'was a non-drinker and smoker, but on two glasses of lemonade on a Mess night, a holy terror if it came to a rough and tumble'.

What moderns are rather more likely to regret is how much Orwell *could* fit in to this sort of ambience. At Eton he earned himself a name as a 'sadistic' footballer, and was 'absolutely delighted' when awarded his colours for the Wall Game. Soldiers and uniforms thrilled him – even the uniform of the Indian Imperial Police. 'Those straps under the boot give you a feeling like nothing else in life,' he told Anthony Powell. This brand of masculinity, apt to reduce liberal intellectuals to titters, is closely connected with the assurance of Orwell's prose, and with his political independence. Swopping between socialist and sahib sometimes, it's true, landed him in inconsistency. In 1938, for instance, he maintained that the masses should refuse to fight the capitalist-imperialist war, and urged Herbert Read to start organizing illegal anti-war activities. Once hostilities commenced, however, he applauded 'patriotism and the military virtues', and denounced 'the boiled rabbits of the Left'. But more often this mixed allegiance makes his thought challenging and unpredictable. He fancied 'sleek young rabbits in 1,000-guinea motor-cars' even less than lefty rabbits. Orwell was a misfit by vocation.

1972

Oxford's beer and baccy brigade

The Inklings were a group of dons and hangers-on who met in C. S. Lewis's rooms at Magdalen, and in various Oxford pubs, during and after the Second World War. Regulars included J. R. R. Tolkien, Charles Williams, Nevill Coghill, and Lewis's brother Warnie who appears in snapshots of the clique as an amiable, baggy-trousered walrus. Mr Carpenter takes an affectionate but keen look at their doings, and at their pugnacious, inhibited leader, Lewis.* He's alive to the intellectual wealth on show, but intrigued by the blind spots.

In literature the Inklings favoured myth and fairy tale, and their contempt for the modern movement was, generally speaking, equalled by their ignorance of it. Tolkien's reading had not advanced chronologically much beyond Shakespeare, whom he thought overrated. Lewis disparaged most moderns indiscriminately, but nursed an especially intense hatred for T. S. Eliot, whose 'bilge' he denounced at Inkling covens. Mr Carpenter traces this prejudice to Lewis's early tutoring days, when Eliot had been the darling of Oxford's pansy aesthetes. Always nervous of homosexuals, partly because of his own warm feelings for men friends, Lewis took to garbing himself in dung-coloured macs and shabby headgear to advertise his irreproachable normality. Pooh-poohing Eliot was, from this viewpoint, just an extra coating of mackintosh.

These rather personal considerations had a drastic effect on the Oxford English school. By energetic lobbying Lewis managed to purge the syllabus of every modernist taint. Under his aegis, literature in Oxford stopped at 1830. Tolkien backed him up stoutly. Another of their triumphs was the election of the Rev. Adam Fox, a charming, ineffective Inkling, to Oxford's Professorship of Poetry, in preference to the great Elizabethan scholar E. K. Chambers. Juntos and jobbery had fascinated Lewis from his schooldays on, and Mr Carpenter sees Fox's

*The Inklings by Humphrey Carpenter (Allen and Unwin).

election as gamesomeness rather than deliberate irresponsibility.

The Inklings set great store by manly conduct, which they associated with pipe tobacco, mugs of ale, and tramps through the countryside. They enjoyed bawdy jests, composed by Tolkien in Icelandic and several other languages, and they excluded women from their circle as intellectual inferiors. Women, Lewis felt, would disturb their male intimacies. He liked to think of himself and his friends as warriors. 'Long before history began we men have got together and done things,' he wrote, 'we Braves, we hunters, all bound together by shared dangers and hardships – away from the women and children.' It seems an unlikely way to visualize a discussion-group of ageing academics, and in his actual relations with women Lewis was the reverse of intrepid. For most of his adult life he worked as unpaid housemaid and errand boy for a tyrannical lady called Mrs Moore, some twenty-five years his senior. They first set up house together in 1918, and Lewis's voluntary servitude lasted till 1950, when Mrs Moore fortunately went mad and was removed to a nursing home. Theirs wasn't, it seems, a sexual union in the normal sense, but Mrs Moore evidently satisfied Lewis's desire for maternal domination, and this accords, perhaps, with other boyish traits in his character such as his shyness of emotion and his enthusiasm for gangs like the Inklings.

All Inklings were keen Christians, relishing nothing so much as a good set-to on some doctrinal point. 'The fun is often so fast and furious,' reported Lewis, of their pub sessions, 'that the company probably thinks we're talking bawdy when in fact we're very likely talking theology.' Within this aura of chortling holiness, though, their brands of Christianity differed markedly. Tolkien was a devout Roman Catholic; Lewis, an Ulster Protestant, inclined to refer to Papists as 'bog-rats'. In religion, as in other respects, Charles Williams was the exotic of the bunch, with his black magic and his troop of female disciples, whom he would threaten with whipping and other rigours to kindle their spirituality

Personal magnetism is a hard thing to recapture in a biographical sketch, and though Williams, to judge from the ardour of his votaries, must have been virtually radioactive with it, he emerges from Mr Carpenter's admiring pages as a prize prig and freak. He had, however, a much subtler mind than most

Inklings, and this, together with Lewis's worship of him, bred jealousies. Tolkien spoke of him in later life with frosty disdain, evidently resenting his immensely superior understanding of literature, and his consequent refusal to take Tolkien's own fanciful outpourings seriously.

The chief trouble with Mr Carpenter's intimate, parochial study is that what really matters about its chief figure, Lewis, gets lost among the biographical facts. If you concentrate on Lewis's life it's too easy to find yourself contemplating him as some sort of mental case. How else can you regard a university tutor who, when a pupil refused to admire Arnold's *Sohrab and Rustum*, seized two swords from the wall, thrust one into the defaulter's hands, and engaged him in armed combat until he had actually drawn blood? Lewis did his serious living in his books. He was a prodigiously zestful scholar-critic who romped through great tracts of world literature like a combine harvester. Life was scarcely more than a bothersome incidental which gave him time to write volumes like *The Allegory of Love* and the *History of English Literature in the Sixteenth Century*.

Still, Mr Carpenter scintillates beside Lewis's previous hagiographers, Roger Lancelyn Green and Walter Hooper. He has beavered away gamely among Inkling documents and survivors, and come up with a constantly enjoyable volume. He says, incidentally, of Lewis's late and tragically brief marriage to Joy Davidman that there's no evidence as to whether it was consummated. It would be prurient to question the point, were it not that Lewis himself seems to have been eager to place it beyond doubt. 'No cranny of heart or body remained unsatisfied', he wrote of his marriage in *A Grief Observed*.

1978

Sir Galahad of soppiness

The English have always suspected that people engaged in the arts are, in the main, rather soppy. Numerous verifiable cases of soppiness, especially from the twenties and thirties, have confirmed this belief, and among them Denton Welch must rank as a star performer. In a typical journal entry,* dated 1943, he meets some soldiers on manoeuvres near Tunbridge Wells, and twitters with delight at the 'prettiness' of the leaves and twigs stuck over them for camouflage: 'the effect was wild and pastoral and fancy dress'. The point to grasp, though, is that here, as often, Welch is being a ninny by design. He means to convey his contempt for militarism and his stubborn faith in beauty. He knew readers would deride his 'missish slop', but he refused to be brutalized. He was defiantly, courageously soppy – the Sir Galahad of soppiness – and that is what makes him different.

That, and his ruined life. What most people remember about Welch is that a motorist knocked him off his bike when he was twenty, fracturing his spine. But that tragedy, which happened in 1935, was his second, the first being his mother's death when he was eleven. His early childhood had been a series of delicious adventures with her – to China, Korea, Canada, staying in expensive hotels – and her loss blighted his growth, so that he always remained, in some respects, a child. His accident left him a semi-invalid, but there were pain-free spells when he could walk, cycle again, write his novels, and take up his career as a painter which had begun before he was crippled.

The journals, extending from 1942 to 1948, when he died, cover these years of partial recovery. Though this is billed as the first unexpurgated edition, it is hard to see what even the most sheltered reader might wish to expurgate. Welch lives quietly in Kent, regularly walking or cycling through the countryside,

*The Journals of Denton Welch ed. Michael de la Noy (Allison and Busby).

either alone or with his great friend Eric, a land-boy. His routine
varies little. At lunchtime he stops in some damp patch of
woodland, spreads his mac, pumps up his patent air cushion,
and tucks into tenderized prunes, nut loaf, and other vegetarian
goodies.

Then he sets off again, and as like as not comes upon an
unclothed male, either taking a dip in the river or just lying
about in the fields. Nothing much ensues. Welch gazes appreciatively at his new acquaintance's 'pearly' or 'junket-white' or
'nacre' skin, engages him in conversation, and occasionally asks
him home for a chaste vegetarian tea. Whether these idyllic
encounters actually occurred seems questionable. The editor
presents the journals firmly as autobiography, otherwise one
would scarcely have expected wartime Kent to be so productive
of friendly naturists.

Welch's highly coloured sensibility makes it difficult to guess
what he will be disturbed by next. At a church hall meeting the
sight of the parishioners' hats and the smell of their clothes
overwhelm him, and he flees panic-stricken from the building.
Dining with Herbert Read at the Reform Club, he is upset by the
waitresses, who strike him as 'excessively female, almost
exuding a smell'. Unsparingly subjective, he lets his moods
flood over everything he looks at. After a grim visit to some
relatives he flounces off past a flock of sheep 'bleating and
chewing degradedly' – an awful libel, one feels, on the innocent
ruminants – and he is equally appalled by some 'degraded'
brooms, 'abandoned and horrible', which he finds when poking
around for memorial tablets in an empty church.

This touchiness, and his sexual ambivalence, both recall the
young D. H. Lawrence, but there is one massive difference.
Oddly for someone so wedded to the open air, Welch has almost
no interest in trees, flowers or anything natural. Nature was, it
seems, too robust and vulgar. 'How I loathe nature-lovers', he
snaps. He feels a kinship, rather, with broken, discarded things
– odd pieces of fine china, for which he scours junk shops; an
eighteenth-century doll's house which he spends weeks repair-
ing. He seeks out derelict mansions at the ends of overgrown
lanes, and mopes happily amid the peeling wallpaper.

Often they have been abandoned by the military, and the
soldiers' graffiti add a male tang which he plainly savours. Eric
and he are also aficionados of churchyards, nothing exciting
them more than a crumbling vault inside which can be glimpsed

stacked coffins. Once they actually find a skeleton, the skull lying on its side, 'demonishly lustful', and the ribs curling up 'like birds' fingers'.

The mingling of love and death in Welch's psyche pretty clearly relates to his mother's loss. His writing is most deep and alive when he goes back to his romance with her – Shanghai, and wind-up gramophones in Edwardian Gothic planters' houses; rambles in the peanut fields, and cream cakes for tea. The feel of her gloved hand as he clasped it – suede leather warmed from within; and the musty, elaborate upholstery of ancient taxis, with sliding glass screens, in which he and she sat cosseted – these memories are a magic burrow down which he can escape from the raw landscapes of Kent, the drone of bombers heading for the invasion beaches, and of doodlebugs bound for London.

Living on the fringes of normality he relishes other eccentrics, and collects a rich crop. The doctor's wife cycles around the village in a mauve riding habit, and pours milk down the drains to succour German prisoners confined below. A friend's friend likes licking girls all over, in Hyde Park. Welch becomes involved with a self-styled RAF fighter ace and direct descendant of Montaigne, who turns out to be a local farmer's son and is carried off gibbering by the police.

His brushes with the sane are less interesting, but there is a memorable lunch with Edith Sitwell, who helped to launch him as a writer. Speechless with gratitude, Welch watches intrigued as the legendary face has forkfuls of beetroot, tongue and potato stuffed into it. It is a graphic moment, and typical of the cold eye he casts on other people. 'I hear that Freddie has been killed in action,' he notes. 'He was always dirty and, one felt, faintly slippery all over.' Honesty of this calibre requires utter detachment, which is why Welch could never have written a novel. What are called his novels are really slices of journal – and that goes for I Left My Grandfather's House* (previously published only in a limited edition) which recounts a lonely hike through Sussex when he was eighteen.

The usual meetings with comradely naked males combine here with tart observation of fellow youth-hostellers, and with that zeal for rucksack and open road through which so many

*I Left my Grandfather's House by Denton Welch (Allison and Busby).

young men of the thirties expressed their vague social discontent. He did not write it till ten years after, by which time his spine had been broken, and it has the bright, unreal quality of life seen through a sickroom window. It takes you, as all his writing does, inside a personality which, even if you would not care to stay there long, is like nowhere else.

1984

East African alibis

Early on 24 January 1941 Josslyn Hay, Earl of Erroll, was discovered on the floor of his Buick some miles outside Nairobi with a bullet through his head. Sir Jock Delves Broughton, whose wife Erroll had seduced, stood trial for the murder, but was acquitted, and the crime remained unsolved. The police inquiries, though, took the lid off Kenya's colonial community, exposing a degree of dissipation among the aristocratic set which the British press found both deplorable and deliciously newsworthy. Most of the suspects had trouble establishing alibis because they were too drunk on the night of the shooting to remember where they were or whom they had slept with. That wealthy expatriates should be living it up like this, and getting themselves murdered, while Britain braved the blitz, was reckoned particularly bad form back home.

The headquarters of Kenyan debauchery, it emerged, was a feudal paradise dubbed 'Happy Valley' in the White Highlands, to which Lord Erroll had eloped with Lady Idina Gordon in 1924. It attracted a stream of well-born alcoholics, perverts, gigolos, crooks and drug-addicts, and their revels soon became legendary. The fun, as James Fox describes it in this rapt investigation of the affair, * does not sound exactly enthralling. At Erroll's parties the guests had to line up on arrival to watch Lady Idina having her bath – not, surely, the spectacle you'd most relish just before dinner. Later there was obligatory wife-swapping, organized by Idina, who kept a set of numbered keys and locked the fated couples in their bedrooms. An alternative diversion was burning down the houses of the Africans.

Erroll himself, one-time member of the British Union of Fascists, was, even by white Kenyan standards rather a stinker, though endowed, his friends insist with fabulous sexual charm. His innumerable women were all rich and married. He liked smashing up families and joking about the parental confusion

* *White Mischief* by James Fox (Jonathan Cape).

his liaisons occasioned. 'Come to Daddy', he once teasingly accosted a bewildered child in the Norfolk Hotel at Nairobi.

Children weren't encouraged in Happy Valley, since they interfered with the jollity. Erroll and Idina did produce a baby, but a glimpse of it dumped like shopping in the back of the Hispano-Suiza seems the only recorded sighting. When their partnership collapsed in a storm of recrimination and bad debts, Erroll found another married heiress to fleece, but his infidelities, and the rate at which he ran through her cash, drove her to despair. The local doctor came across her body one day, covered with heroin abscesses, in a house reeking of champagne and vomit – an aroma Happy Valley GPs must have become adept at identifying.

For viciousness, some of Erroll's neighbours ran him pretty close, as Mr Fox's researches have established. There was Jack Soames, arms smuggler and (like most of the male cast) old Etonian, described by his ex-wife as 'a sadist and voyeur of a very low degree' (not, one imagines, a snap judgement, since she had several high-degree ones to compare him with); and there was Lord Carbery, a pro-Nazi who specialized in cruelty to animals. He once dropped his wife's pet hen from an aeroplane to see if it would fly, and span a cat on a mechanical drill till its head split open. Apparently Carbery's mother spotted his propensity early on. One Christmas Day when he was four she begged him to be especially kind to animals to mark the festive season. Obediently Carbery went off and gave the cat the canaries to eat.

Among these sinister humanoids Broughton, the chief suspect, cuts rather a pathetic figure. An elderly man, he had only recently arrived in Kenya to escape the war, bringing a young wife whom Erroll dazzled and bedded within two months of her marriage. Broughton clearly craved affection, and found it hard to get, possibly because he was, in his friends' estimate, dishonest, charmless, morose, cowardly, cruel and impotent. The mystery of whether he killed Erroll still exerts, Mr Fox says, 'a strange power over all who come into contact with it'. If so, I must be a rare case of total immunity. What with the repulsiveness of almost everyone involved, and the tedium of the complex ballistics evidence, the question of who actually put a medium calibre bullet into the Earl's small calibre brain had become, I found, deeply unurgent well before the book's end.

That's not to say that Mr Fox's obsession proves arid – far

from it. He writes with marvellous flair about the African landscapes he travels across in his quest for clues. You soon realize that he is by far the most gifted person in his book, compellingly evocative in his choice of incidentals. He wanders around, disturbing the ghosts, under the jacaranda trees by Lake Naivasha, where Erroll once surveyed hippos and flamingos from his palatial home. He snuffs up the faded essences of colonialism among the chintz armchairs of Happy Valley's exclusive Muthaiga Club, and watches the midday light flaring off the leaves as bright as crystal. You follow him keenly in his discovery of a new world, and dread his plunging back into the grubby purlieus of the Erroll file.

His colleague in the early stages of his enquiry was Cyril Connolly who, with his mingled awe and hatred of rank, was drawn to the whiff of aristocratic corruption like a truffle-dog to truffles. Together they tracked down retired colonial civil servants in dim south-coast tea rooms – Hastings, St Leonards – and pumped them for disclosures over the buttered crumpets. In Mombasa Fox found Carbery's daughter Juanita, who told him as they lunched off parrot fish and quails how Broughton had confessed to her, the day after the murder, that he had shot Erroll.

The most bizarre survivor encountered, though, was an old-Harrovian ex-army officer whom Broughton had employed in insurance swindles. This man described how, acting on instructions, he broke into the Broughton mansions, cut several pictures from their frames, including two Romney portraits, took them to some waste ground, carved them up, and set light to them with petrol. ('You have no idea how *tough* canvas is. I had to chop and chop the beastly things.') This conversation took place in the Ritz, where their informant expressed outrage at the lack of basin-plugs in the washrooms. A concept of civilization which can accommodate itself to demolishing artworks, but demands proper comfort in hotels, somehow typifies Happy Valley thinking.

Two years after the murder Broughton killed himself by injection. He was found in a hotel room with fourteen puncture marks on his body and an empty morphia bottle floating in the lavatory. Quite as expressive as that stark moral tableau are the photos Fox prints of Erroll and his set in their heyday. The gormless faces and grotesque clothes provide a useful antidote to the glamours of myth. Only the close-up of Erroll's head in profile on the mortuary slab, with blood caked around the bullet hole under his ear, has any innocence or gentleness about it – as if he had recovered in death some of the humanity he squandered in life.

1982

Drunk with lilies

As Sacheverell Sitwell muses upon a life full of beautiful things in this mazy pleasure-ground of a book, * a sense of inhumanity accrues. His enthusiasms – for Japanese gardens of raked sand and stones, for the puppet drama of Osaka, for Rococo abbeys – have an unpeopled feel. He is drawn towards Avercamp's villages, cut off by snow, in which the figures, as he observes, mostly have their backs turned, indicating the seclusion of their deaf-mute painter. He argues that El Greco, whom he greatly admires, used wooden dolls instead of models. Jewelled skeletons in Spanish convents appeal to him: so do tortures, executions, ballet dancers incinerated by gas flares, and messy suicides like that of the obscure Dutchman Matterig who dismembered himself on Ramsgate beach. When live humans engage his attention they tend to be grotesques – cripples, all-in wrestlers – and they quickly fade into artworks. A passing hydrocephaloid is pronounced 'as clear in outline as a Dürer drawing', and cabmen in his boyhood swung their arms to keep warm 'like the droshky drivers in *Petrouchka*'. The tropical flowering trees which prompt his lushest prose are envisaged as the material of exotic gardens in which millionaires could shut themselves away: 'a theme remote indeed from the exigencies of abortion, free false teeth and spectacles, and the like, which under Socialism malform our island fame.'

This dread of people governs Mr Sitwell's thought. He is appalled by the tourist boom – unreasonably, for a persistent writer of travel books. He believes that civilization will soon founder beneath recklessly multiplying Asian hordes, aided by bearded drop-outs from caravan sites. Divine intervention cannot be expected: God does not exist. 'God is in ourselves' – provided we do not reside in Asia or caravans. To stop the swarming we should cut down on medicine. Care of the sick and old is 'not paramount'. The balance of nature, as exempli-

For Want of the Golden City by Sacheverell Sitwell (Thames and Hudson).

fied by the clustering infant effigies on old tombs, would bring
back with it the 'settled art forms' which we so much need.
Humanity has got its priorities wrong, as can be seen from the
vast audience which the 'oafish World Football Cup' attracts,
and the millions squandered on Concorde (a fraction of the sum,
Mr Sitwell observes, would ensure the distribution of his own
recent poems, which eight publishers have refused). The
modern impulse to abolish inherited wealth is another 'sure
path to destruction'. Equality of opportunity will 'cancel all
human incentive'. This reverence for incentive, it should be
noted, does not induce Mr Sitwell to regard favourably those
who have fought their way up from poor backgrounds. Pop
singers in chauffeur-driven cars send him into frenzies of
disgust, as does the 'rat-like squealing' of their female fans.
They are part of the conspiracy to make the world commonplace
– like the Cinzano posters which disfigure the Appian Way,
where 10,000 followers of Spartacus once hung on crosses
helping to restore the balance of nature. Conspiracies nearer
home, he covertly grumbles, have 'cheated' him of the family
house in Tuscany where he and his wife hoped to live out the
remainder of their days. Perhaps those responsible have taken
to heart his advice on the care of the old.

The remarkable contrast that emerges from all this is between
the sympathy and understanding Mr Sitwell expends on artefacts, and his response to the society in which he lives. Once the
subject of contemporary life is broached, what exudes is a
stream of hatred and envy – long hair, abstract painting,
'perpetual strikes in every branch of industry', all rolled in ruin
together. Even his language becomes debased in these outbursts. The ormolu diction of the arty parts – 'absinthe-tinted
nenuphars or nelumbiums' – gives place to blurted cliche: 'We
are in the permissive society with no strings attached.' Art does
not send him back to life more keenly equipped. It remains an
orgy of goodies, like the gardens he plans where 'one could be
perfectly dazed and drunk with lilies.'

The disjunction of art from the world he inhabits, besides
coarsening his view of society, harms his art criticism because it
cuts it off from living issues. The questions he toys with are
perfectly fanciful. What if Delacroix had seen the Noh plays?
Would not Hiroshige have enjoyed the RAF show at Farnbo-
rough? Of Rembrandt's *Rat-Killer*, 'one falls to wondering who
was his mother, and who sewed his rat-skin cap for him.' At this

level, no train of thought needs pursuing with any sternness, and the book slides from one subject to the next in a half-awake way: from a yew-dark shrubbery in Northamptonshire to the azulejo'd façades of Lisbon to Uganda flame trees; fromTrollope to Della Robbia; from Russian ballet to Mexico. Wonderful images dart out of the flux: an octopus capering to his meal 'hand over hand, out of his cavern'; Kabuki actors scowling from a poster, their mouths distorted 'like a badly tied bootlace looping at one end'. Just occasionally, these images sharpen his attack on the contemporary world. The Royal Festival Hall, compared to the theatre of golden caryatids that he loves, looks 'like the vastly magnified interior of a typewriter'. But the final impression is of lax opulence, a giant menu of predigested paintings and pieces of music. On any subject except art the thinking immediately runs shallow and even with art, once he enters the twentieth century, blanket prejudices click into action. Modern artists who wish to think his judgements awry will be cheered by the story that, when Modigliani died, he was offered the entire contents of the painter's studio (some eighty works) for £100, and let the opportunity go by. Several Modigliani drawings in his possession were used as wrapping for his shoes.

1973

Messiahs and pigs

It cannot have escaped teachers of English literature that much of their time is spent unfitting their pupils for the lives they will eventually have to lead. Most twentieth-century authors, and in particular the greats like Yeats, Eliot and Lawrence, who regularly feature in A-level and undergraduate syllabuses, inculcate an attitude of contempt for ordinary, decent, bread-earning citizens, which must inevitably unsettle youngsters who are on the point of choosing a career, unless they are mercifully too dense to get the modernists' message at all. Yeats's admiration for aristocrats, beggars and terrorists, and his complementary distaste for thrifty nine-to-fivers who 'add the halfpence to the pence', must, like Eliot's identification of London office-workers with the occupants of Dante's hell, have persuaded many a young hopeful that it would be not merely tiring but downright uncultured to get a job of work. And Lawrence's detestation of gainful employment of any kind, especially anything associated with machinery, would, if taken seriously by school-leavers, kill off British industry within a generation, and have us all living at the subsistence-agricultural level.

Robert Currie's book* is not overtly concerned with these educational problems, and the writers he discusses do not happen to include the three I have mentioned, but his thesis, tersely and brilliantly argued, amounts to an explanation of the ideological development which has brought us to this pass, and which has ensured that the beliefs and assumptions current in literature should be diametrically opposed to those embraced in life.

He sees normality-scorning modernism as a direct descendant of romanticism, and finds the seed of romanticism in the concept of a golden age, variously located before the growth of cities, or before steam engines, or before capitalism, in which man allegedly enjoyed a more unified relationship with himself, with nature, and with his fellows. This unity, romantic theorists

Genius by Robert Currie (Chatto and Windus).

argue, has been destroyed by modern evils such as mass education and the division of labour, which tend respectively to unhealthy self-consciousness and the conversion of human beings into narrow functionaries. Thus, Schiller criticized the 'clockwork of the State', with its rigorous differentiation of offices and occupations, on the grounds that it fragmented the 'inward union of human nature', and Marx, taking up Schiller's analysis, claimed that the worker in capitalist society was a human machine. Like other romantics, Marx noted that workers who had had their inward union destroyed quickly learnt to enjoy it and became denizens of the 'passive animal world of philistinism'. Romanticism has always derived much of its satisfaction from this sense of the piggishness of the great mass of mankind. However, humanity must be rescued, and it needs the outstanding individual, the genius, the secular Messiah, to transcend normality and lead the 'alienated' many back to a state of oneness which they themselves will pretty certainly have ceased to wish for.

The writers in whom Mr Currie tracks down versions or offshoots of this theory are numerous and, as might be expected, mostly German. But he gives extended attention to five: E. T. A. Hoffmann, Kierkegaard, Wyndham Lewis, Kafka and Beckett. Hoffmann's inclusion will surprise those who think of him as a peddler of Gothicism and fairy tales. In fact, Mr Currie points out, he deeply influenced Kierkegaard, Marx and Dostoevsky, and, as musician and music critic, inspired, among others, Schumann, Wagner and Tchaikovsky. The golden age which Hoffmann fancied contemplating was a time before urban development when men possessed 'an immediate perception of all being'. Like Lawrence, he seems to have believed that this benefit was still enjoyed, to some degree, by gamekeepers. But he held that the majority of mankind had lost it as a result of the onset of enlightenment, with its attendant ills such as roads, schools and vaccination. It remained for the romantic genius to break free from the tame, philistine world either by some erotic outrage (incest was the one Hoffmann favoured, though other romantics recommended sadism), or by political domination.

Kierkegaard, likewise, looked for an 'extraordinary' individual, a genius, who would put an end to the corrupt era of liberalism and democracy, and would transcend humdrum constraints like marriage and morality. This 'special' person, he taught, would be a 'legitimate exception' to ethical norms: a sinner who was superior to the law-abiding. 'There resides infinitely more good', Kierkegaard explained, 'in the demonic than in the trivial man.' Readers of Eliot will recognize this sentiment as it recurs in his essay on Baudelaire: 'It is better, in a paradoxical way, to do evil than to do nothing: at least we exist.'

Hitler afforded the mid twentieth century an ideal opportunity for deciding whether it was really better to do evil than to do nothing, and, as early as 1931, Wyndham Lewis, Mr Currie's third exponent of romanticism, had seized on Hitler as an embodiment of romantic genius. Lewis predicted that Hitler's noble austerity would cleanse Berlin of its homosexuality, its Jewish underworld and its nigger dances, and would introduce a new order, heralded in the 'personal neatness' and 'clear blue eyes' of the young Nazis. For Lewis, like other romantics, believed that power had been transferred, at some regrettable juncture in history, from educated, vital individuals, such as himself, to the philistine masses, and he felt that the process could be reversed only by dictatorship, which he equated with 'rule by the most vigorous and intelligent'.

After Hitler, it might have been difficult, even for romantics, to find much appeal in the idea of a transcendent demonic genius. But, in fact, the transcendental element in romanticism had been largely dropped, Mr Currie demonstrates, as far back as Kierkegaard. Its final rejection is the distinctive contribution of modernism. For the modernist, the hope of soaring above alienated man to some integrated realm, or of attaining the 'paradise on earth' that Lenin held out as the end of revolutionary struggle, is quite illusory. The most that can be expected is that the romantic genius may break through to a clearer, and therefore more calamitous and depressing view of the human condition. Hence the hopeless worlds of Kafka and Beckett. Though not transcendental in the old sense, these authors retain the romantic scorn for the many, and for things like work, love and acquisitiveness, from which normal people gain satisfaction. Kafka's Gregor Samsa, because he devotes himself assiduously to his job, turns into an insect. Another romantic feature both writers cling to is esotericism. The philistine multitude is warned off by an elaborate rampart of obscurity, so that the conscientious schoolboy or undergraduate has to work at the texts for a considerable time before he discovers that he is the sort of person they are insulting.

Though scrupulously objective in his critical analyses, Mr Currie is at no pains to conceal his impatience with the whole ideology of romantic genius. The lesson of history seems to him decisively against it. For, on the one hand, its exaltation of the one over the many has been shown to lead to totalitarianism and atrocity; and, on the other, modern man has patently opted for contented philistinism, despite romantic exhortations to something higher. Besides, when the higher something is, as in modernism, merely a gloomier view of our lot, it seems hardly worth striving for.

Perhaps literature might turn its attention, Mr Currie suggests, to discovering whether any justification can be offered for philistinism, since there is every reason to suppose that philistines will persist and that we ourselves will continue to be numbered among them. Might not culture do better without genius? What we need, arguably, is an art that will serve to sustain, rather than decry, our society, however 'alienating' that may appear to geniuses. Indeed such an art would recognize that 'alienation', if it denotes the growth of man's reflective faculties and of specialized roles, is imperative unless life is to be devoid of both interest and fulfilment.

The impetus of Mr Currie's argument is hard to withstand. His main fault, it seems to me, is that he fails to take account of a persistent tendency in romanticism – English romanticism, anyway – that runs directly counter to the one he stresses, in that it prizes multiplicity rather than unity, and seeks not transcendence but imaginative sympathy. Coleridge, after all, praised Shakespeare, a standard romantic example of genius, for being 'myriad-minded', not single-minded; and Keats's poetic ideal of 'negative capability' implies a dispersal of the self into the multiplicity of creatures and objects perceived, rather than transcendental oneness. Still, acknowledgement of this other tradition would not affect Mr Currie's conclusions about the tradition he traces. His remains one of those rare books that indelibly re-maps a section of one's intellectual landscape.

1974

Queenie Leavis and the Common Pursuit

It is now just half a century since the publication of Q. D. Leavis's *Fiction and the Reading Public*,* so it seems an opportune moment to take a fresh look at that celebrated work. M. B. Kinch, in his recent memoir of Mrs Leavis, says that its 'classic status' is generally acknowledged, and William Walsh refers to it, in his book on F. R. Leavis, as a 'penetrating study', 'firmly embedded in history', which shows Mrs Leavis's 'gift for social analysis'. These seem to me very surprising claims. But they are worth investigating not only in themselves, but also because they bear on the question of Mrs Leavis's influence upon her husband, and the extent to which she was responsible for works normally attributed to him. This is a subject which Mrs Leavis herself raised after Leavis's death. She was, she told Professor Boris Ford, a major but unacknowledged collaborator in a number of her husband's books. Professor Ford, writing to *The Times*, cites a letter he received from Mrs Leavis not long before she died, in which, he reports, she speaks 'surprisingly and quite feelingly' of how 'staggered' she was when she realized she was not to be credited as co-author of Leavis's *Culture and Environment*. She complains, too, that she was 'pushed out of *The Great Tradition*' which, she asserts, 'was my undertaking, and great parts of which, besides all the first chapter and all the footnotes, I wrote personally'. It has often been noted that when Leavis married in 1929 he had not published anything except a few reviews. His wife, we are now given to understand, not only stimulated him and gave him direction, but also personally undertook work published in his name.

Their co-operation has usually been acclaimed as a happy arrangement: the rich convergence of two fine minds. Professor Walsh tells us that the relationship was 'as creative as that of William and Dorothy Wordsworth'. But doubting voices can be heard, especially if one consults former colleagues and pupils of

*Fiction and the Reading Public by Q. D. Leavis (Chatto and Windus).

the Leavises. Some of this testimony must no doubt be discounted on grounds of hostility. However it is, I have found,
remarkably consistent. It is agreed that Mrs Leavis was the
dominant partner, and that her influence was, to a degree,
regrettable. She was much fiercer than Leavis, and unforgiving.
After quarrels with colleagues, he would be prepared to make it
up, but she would say 'We are not talking to them – don't you
remember?' She saw herself as a protecting influence, saving
Leavis from himself, and turning him into a monument. The
archetypal Jewish matriarch, she would send her man out to do
battle with the world, yet know that he would always remain
weaker than her, and need her strength. 'She scared most of us
"men" at Downing in my time,' writes an ex-pupil of Leavis's,
now a distinguished author. 'FRL I found kind-hearted, ready to
temper the wind to the shorn lamb. Less so her . . . I think that
Q was responsible for a lot of suffering and embitterment: if you
like, for keeping F more than up to the mark – well beyond it.'

These, as I say, are the views you meet with if you inquire
among those who knew the Leavises. They received a degree of
public corroboration recently in an article by Professor Muriel
Bradbrook published in the *Cambridge Review* and entitled 'Q.
D. Leavis: the Dynamics of Rejection'. Professor Bradbrook
presents Mrs Leavis, whom she knew from undergraduate days,
as a caustic and resentful figure, her trauma being her rejection
by her orthodox Jewish family when she married a gentile. It
was believed in Girton that the family read the burial service for
her. Mrs Leavis's hostile temperament made her, as Professor
Bradbrook sees it, eager to feel victimized and cast out. She
forced Leavis to break off longstanding friendships with Cambridge colleagues, and took upon herself the task of isolating
and directing him. To this end she was capable of deliberate
offensiveness. Professor Bradbrook reports that when Basil
Willey, for example, received a food parcel from the USA shortly
after the war and, remembering that the Leavises had a young
family, took it round and left it for them, he later found it
dumped on his own doorstep with the words 'We don't need
your charity'. When the Leavises moved to Bulstrode Gardens
the child from next door called round to bid them welcome and
offer help – only to have the door shut in her face by Queenie
who told her, 'We have our friends. We don't need any more.'

Professor Bradbrook's article contains more of the same kind
of thing – but why, it may be asked, rake up all this? Are not

these old scandals best forgotten? Do they not, in any case, belong to private life rather than to literary criticism? One answer is that, in Leavis's doctrine, it's the way life is lived that justifies the study of literature. Upon the discerning appreciation of art and literature by the gifted few, he tells us, 'the possibilities of fine living' at any time depend. This being so it seems proper to ask what fine living, as the Leavises practised it, involved.

But there is another and more important consideration. If, as it is claimed, Mrs Leavis's thinking decisively influenced her husband's criticism, then her social code and psychology can't be ignored, for they too must have had their influence on the scope and direction of his cultural activity. And if, as those close to the couple seem to agree, her power over his social life was in some ways damaging, then her intellectual effect may also have been damaging, and in comparable ways. I want to look at *Fiction and the Reading Public*, a work written at an early and formative stage of their relationship, to see if we can judge what that effect was.

The thesis of *Fiction and the Reading Public* is that the cultural situation in England has woefully deteriorated since the eighteenth century. A feature of the decline, we are told, is that the reading public has split. Real literature is now written by the few for the few, and is beyond the understanding of the great mass of readers, who remain half-educated. This state of affairs, Mrs Leavis believes, is new. In the past, she claims, 'no sharp dichotomy exists or can be made between the works of fiction which cultivated persons have found admirable, and those which have amused the uncultured'. The destruction of this unified culture can be ascribed largely to the coming of industrialism which, Mrs Leavis explains, put an end to the comeliness of the peasant life, and deprived the ordinary worker of 'the delight that a really interesting and varied round of duties gave'. The worker reads now, as he never needed to before, simply to stave off the boredom that modern life has introduced, or to seek escape in fantasy. The evil has been exacerbated and fed by the new phenomenon of the best seller. Mrs Leavis sent out questionnaires, while preparing her thesis, to a number of best selling novelists, asking how they viewed their work. She incorporates some of their replies into her argument. It is this, it seems, which has earned her book its reputation for advanced sociological method. Another destructive influence on culture in

Mrs Leavis's eyes has been the popular newspaper, especially as developed by Lord Northcliffe. By debasing the reading matter and stunting the vocabulary of the average man, tabloid journalism has effectively put literature, as Mrs Leavis understands it, out of his reach.

The first thing we should ask about this thesis is how accurate it is historically – for it is as an interpretation of history that it stands or falls. Is it true, as Mrs Leavis alleges, that pre-industrial England had a unified reading public, all enjoying the same books? Inevitably a preliminary question is what proportion of the population could read at all. Modern historians have found the degree and spread of literacy in earlier ages extremely difficult to calculate. But at least we can be sure that the assumption that most of the population could and would read books in the sixteenth and seventeenth centuries is unhistorical. A recent estimate by David Cressy in *Literacy and the Social Order* puts the national illiteracy rate in the mid-seventeenth century at 70 per cent, and since Cressy takes as his criterion of literacy merely the ability to write one's name, his results may in fact be too optimistic. Mrs Leavis's picture of cultured and uncultivated persons happily absorbed in the same works of fiction leaves the problem of illiteracy out of account altogether. She seems not to recognize the need for its investigation. This is enough to deprive her work of any real historical weight.

It may be objected that modern inquiries into the history of illiteracy were not available to her. She did not, in fact, make use of other and equally important historical evidence that was to hand. Only three years after her book appeared Cornell University Press published a work by the American scholar Louis B. Wright called *Middle-Class Culture in Elizabethan England*. This was a genuinely pioneering work, not superseded even today, and based on an extensive knowledge of the backwaters of Elizabethan publishing, into which Mrs Leavis shows no signs of having dipped. What Wright demonstrates is that our printed culture developed a new stratum in the latter half of the sixteenth century, catering for a new, unlearned, unsophisticated, and – to an unprecedented degree – female readership. The literature supplied comprised handbooks to social improvement, lessons in diligence and domestic relations, introductions to foreign languages and science, as well as stories for amusement and edification. Wright's accumulation of evidence contrasts strikingly with Mrs Leavis's unsupported assertions. He establishes once and for all that the concept of a unified reading public, prior to the advent of industry, is an illusion.

In the interests of her thesis Mrs Leavis seems too to have misread the few works of Elizabethan and seventeenth-century literature which she did consult. We can see this from her treatment of Deloney and Bunyan. Thomas Deloney was an Elizabethan novelist catering for artisan readers, and telling stories about clothiers, shoemakers, and other manufacturers. Mrs Leavis refers to him when arguing that the Elizabethans, unlike the degraded modern mass audience, did not need escapism in their fiction. They did not suffer, she says, from 'poverty of emotional life', requiring fantasy to nourish it. Accordingly we find, in Deloney, no 'day–dream, but a sturdy acceptance of things as they are'. As a critical comment on Deloney this is entirely misleading. His novels are, in fact, full of fantasy and wish-fulfilment, designed to show how noble and distinguished English cloth-workers and artisans have traditionally been. In *Jack of Newbury*, for example, the prodigiously successful and fictitious broadcloth weaver John Winchcomb, who is the novel's hero, banquets King Henry VIII in his own house and exchanges pleasantries with him.

Her reading of Bunyan is also untrustworthy. Again, her purpose is to praise the past at the expense of the present, and to this end she argues that we find in Bunyan 'no sharp black or white, vice or virtue, and no cheap system of rewards and punishments' such as evolves in later popular novelists. 'Nothing', she asserts, 'happens to the villains of his books in the way of poetic justice', they are merely 'left to themselves for ever'. To support this reading of Bunyan she instances his novel *The Life and Death of Mr Badman* in which Mr Badman, despite his evil career, dies, Mrs Leavis points out, 'as peacefully as a Christian', and she commends Bunyan for this 'deliberate sacrifice of an obvious lesson'. These remarks are, one can only say, astonishing. To claim that Bunyan, with his severe doctrine of evangelical Calvinism, makes no sharp distinction between vice and virtue is nothing short of mysterious. As for nothing happening to the villains of his novels – what actually happens to them, of course, is that they burn in hell for all eternity, and Bunyan makes this perfectly clear. Mrs Leavis's choice of the death of Mr Badman as an example is unfortunate for her case, for Badman's quiet death is a sign that he is irretrievably damned. God has blinded his eyes and hardened his heart so that he has no inkling of his impending fate, and cannot repent. Lest we should miss this, Bunyan brings in his character Mr Wiseman to give a full explanation of Badman's death immediately afterwards. The manner in which Badman died, says Wiseman, is 'an incontrovertible proof of his damnation'. God often deals so with the damned: they are 'kept from seeing what they are, and whither they are going, till they plunge down among the flames'. The main criticism to be made then of *Fiction and the Reading Public* is that it lacks a realistic historical dimension. It is a historical daydream, a sample of the escapism it condemns. Professor Walsh's reverent appraisal of it as 'firmly embedded in history' cannot survive examination.

If we are to believe that Mrs Leavis importantly influenced her husband's criticism, then the historical unreliability of *Fiction and the Reading Public* takes on an added significance. For F. R. Leavis's criticism, like hers, drew on a powerful historical myth concerning the break-up of the old organic community, and this myth took the place of any more accurate historical investigation. Leavis came to scorn historical 'background' as part of the scholarly irrelevance which stood between the critic and a genuine encounter with the text. He relied on his convictions, and on exposure of himself to the text's nuances. His essay on Bunyan in *The Common Pursuit* is disrespectful about Jack Lindsay's *John Bunyan: Maker of Myths*, though Lindsay offers a more detailed and useful account of Bunyan's historical situation than Leavis was capable of. Given Mrs Leavis's misreading of Bunyan, it seems probable that we have here a pointer to the disadvantages that could accrue from her co-operation. In so far as her influence on him confirmed him in his substitution of myth for history, it was not enlightening.

Nor did the influence that I am postulating concern only attitudes to history. A major characteristic of *Fiction and the Reading Public* is its arrogance. Peremptory certitude in expression combines with contempt for the majority and its tastes. Mrs Leavis refers to celebrated authors in a spirit of scathing superiority. Dickens, we are told, was emotionally 'not only uneducated but also immature'. Like Sir Walter Scott, he 'wrote in general very ill'. The critical reader 'winces', Mrs Leavis says, at the 'vulgarity and puerility' he meets with in Dickens, Thackeray, Kingsley and Meredith. This supercilious, bullying rhetoric was to become a potent part of the Leavis spell. What is most worrying about it is that Mrs Leavis does not seem to see the need to justify her opinions. It is the voice of a cultural dictator – and in that sense recognizably and ominously a voice of the thirties. She never suspects that her views might be relative or determined by class and education. She assumes that the literary works she prefers are simply superior, and to support this she shows that they possess the qualities she likes. The argument is circular. The daunting and intricate social, psychological and metaphyscal implications, which an investigator must face if he is to try to unravel the motives that underlie our literary value judgements, Mrs Leavis simply leaves out of account.

Now this, too, is close to Leavis's own procedure. It has often been remarked that what his criticism most glaringly lacks is any lucid statement of its central doctrines. It is full of innu-endos and unstated assumptions, the debatable nature of which Leavis does not seem prepared to recognize. In the March 1937 number of *Scrutiny* Dr Rene Wellek pointed this out, and asked for some clarification. 'I could wish', Wellek writes to Leavis, 'that you had stated your assumptions more explicitly and defended them more systematically'. Wellek goes on to abstract what he takes to be the main assumptions of Leavis's criticism, and he concludes with a plea that Leavis should acknowledge them for what they are, namely, arbitrary and subjective preferences. Wellek does not in fact dissent much from Leavis's opinions. All he asks, he says, is that he should defend them 'more abstractly', and become 'more conscious that large ethical, philosophical, and of course ultimately also aesthetic *choices* are involved'. But Leavis did not comply. He continued to write as if his aesthetic choices were absolutes. He refused to supply his work with the theoretical substructure Wellek required, and, more regrettably, he declined to discuss the interesting question of what such a substructure could actually elucidate. In all this the influence of his wife must, if we are to judge from the tone and demeanour of *Fiction and the Reading Public*, have been strongly supportive, confirming Leavis in his prejudices and obscuring the fact that they were, indeed, prejudices.

There is some evidence that in the very earliest part of his career, before his wife's influence over him had become deci-sive, Leavis was more open to fruitful doubt, and more prepared to concede the subjective status of aesthetic judgement. In his first publication, an essay on T. S. Eliot in the 1929 *Cambridge*

Review, he discussed the critic's need to achieve objectivity, and added, 'Actually, of course, this cannot be done, and there is no one demonstrably right judgement'. That admission is refreshingly out of key with the tenor of Leavis's later criticism, and it seems probable that his wife was at least partly responsible for the change.

A last point to be made about *Fiction and the Reading Public* is its surprising neglect of any involvement with the reading public. We have seen Professor Walsh praising its 'social analysis', but that, in any but the most cursory sense, is what it conspicuously lacks. Mrs Leavis did send out her questionnaires to authors, but her ideas about readers are not derived from any corresponding sampling or survey. There is no realistic enquiry into the conditions of life and leisure, into the mental and emotional habits, of the mass audience upon which she pronounces with such confidence. So far as we can see, she never, in the course of her investigations, spoke to a member of the reading public. The only trace of this kind of enquiry is her mention of a survey conducted by the *Sunday Dispatch* among its readers to find what modern books they thought would be read in a generation's time. This could scarcely be classed as a dependable sociological tool, and anyway Mrs Leavis discounts its findings when it suits her. Several *Dispatch* readers named Joyce's *Ulysses*, but Mrs Leavis put this down to the factitious fame censorship had conferred on the book, rather than to genuine critical insight. She advises us, towards the end of *Fiction and the Reading Public*, that if we wish to see what a mind warped by bestsellers is like, we shall find an 'invaluable reference point' in the Gerty MacDowell episode in *Ulysses*. Discussing Gerty's opinions, Mrs Leavis treats her, quite naively, as if she were a real person, and comments, 'Such a life is not only crude, impoverished, and narrow, it is dangerous.' It is, she declares, because such minds as Gerty's are among us that society is not 'efficiently equipped for the business of living'. This is certainly a remarkable procedure for a critic so opposed to escapism and to the substitution of literature for life. It is hardly what we should expect, either, when we take into account Mrs Leavis's constant warnings that literature ought to shock and disturb us, rather than merely confirming our prejudices. Finding that the fictional Gerty MacDowell accords gratifyingly with her own ideas about the mass audience, Mrs Leavis awards her the status of reality, and preaches about the danger to society Gerty represents – forgetting that Gerty is only a figment of a cultured imagination: an imagination, that is, representing the same educated minority as she belongs to herself.

Leavis's views on the mass audience are just as confident as his wife's, and based so far as we can tell on as little first-hand enquiry. His pamphlet *Mass Civilization and Minority Culture* came out in 1930, at the time when Mrs Leavis was engaged on the doctoral thesis that was to become *Fiction and the Reading Public*. Leavis's pamphlet obviously owes much to his wife's ideas, and draws on the same rather out-of-the-way sources, such as Miss Ethel Mannin's inane publicity for the Book Guild. It has the same disparagement of Northcliffe: even the same quotation from Hamilton Fyfe's biography. In other words, it is evidently the first fruits of the Leavises' collaboration, though Mrs Leavis went, as usual, unacknowledged. This means that Leavis's failure in the pamphlet to subject the concept of the mass to any analytic scrutiny, and his tendency to regard it as a dark, apocalyptic portent, are other aspects of his thought – or, rather, his failure of thought – that we can arguably attribute to his wife's influence.

What I have been trying to do is to raise doubts and questions. The evidence, I agree, is fragmentary at best. It all happened a long time ago. We can never know the full truth about *one* other mind, let alone two, and the interaction between them. The merits of Mrs Leavis's later criticism – the essays, for example, on Jane Austen, on Mrs Oliphant, on *Wuthering Heights* – have been amply recognised, and it is certainly no part of my purpose to dispute them here. Even *Fiction and the Reading Public* has its own kind of eloquence and excitement, helping us to understand the animus, and the antagonism towards common humanity, that lay behind the historical movement of the twenties and thirties which we now call Modernism. The fact remains that, as an argument, *Fiction and the Reading Public* has large, simple and demonstrable shortcomings. If we can accept them as indicative of the kind of pull that Mrs Leavis exerted over her husband's critical thought and manner at the outset of his career, when he was formulating his creed, then we shall, I think, be less ready to celebrate as entirely auspicious the close and lifelong collaboration which the Leavises, in their dedication of *Dickens the Novelist* to each other, congratulate themselves upon. It seems possible, even probable, that her dominating influence, while no doubt helping to ensure his eminence as a critic, was also responsible for what must now be seen as major flaws in his whole critical enterprise.

1982

Richard Aldington's septic psyche

'People seem to think you are both grumpy and cantankerous,' Lawrence Durrell plaintively reports, writing to Richard Aldington in 1959. After reading these letters,* people will be absolutely sure of it. Aldington comes across as a man so charged with venom that it would be risky to let him out of doors lest he blight the crops. He releases a deluge of detraction upon his fellow mortals – the 'Boches', the 'Yids', the RCs, the 'worthless wogs', and, of coure, the 'fucking English', among whose crimes a failure to appreciate Aldington's genius bulks, one gathers, pretty large. His hates are so widespread, ranging from Jesus Christ to income tax, that it's difficult to find any unifying key. But a rightish tinge is generally discernible. Fascist governments are, he pronounces, a 'damn sight better than the proletarian anarchy they replace', and their ideals compare favourably with 'the New Shithouse, and all that gang of cryptos'.

The breezy argot in which Aldington recounts his doings has a curiously familiar ring: 'The one-way streets here are a proper bugger' (this, on a health-trip to Zurich) 'but the medicos were amiable and struck me as very up to snuff'. Who else writes like that? After a while it dawns on you that the tone and intellectual level are uncannily close to those of John Wells's Denis Thatcher, though Aldington is, as it were, Denis with a septic psyche.

As the recipient of this rancid flow Durrell behaves with exemplary tact, shored up, one supposes, by his diplomatic training. Aldington – the one-time associate of D. H. Lawrence, Pound, Yeats, Aldous Huxley and other interwar notables – had long been a literary hero of his, and he began the correspondence when he discovered they were living near each other in the south of France. It lasted until Aldington's death in 1962, growing more ticklish as the publication of *The Alexandria Quartet* brought the younger man worldwide fame, while the elder fumed in obscurity. Durrell pumps counsel and flattery in

Literary Lifelines: The Richard Aldington – Lawrence Durrell Correspondence ed. Ian S. MacNiven and Harry T. Moore (Faber)

Aldington's direction, trying to coax his wounded giant back into the limelight and reproving his more illiberal seizures. At last, only weeks before his death, Aldington gets his share of longed-for glory when he is invited, ironically enough, to Moscow and fêted on his seventieth birthday by the USSR Writers' Union.

The central mystery in the volume, which the editors leave remarkably unprobed, relates to the reception of Aldington's debunking biography of T. E. Lawrence, published in 1955. It was this book, according to Aldington, that effectively dished him with the British Establishment, who could not bear the exposure of 'their favourite little sod' and conspired, in revenge, to ruin Aldington's fortunes. He alleges that Churchill, as PM, sent Liddell Hart, equipped with signed letters on Downing Street paper, to 'bully' Collins out of publishing the biography, and that, when this failed, the letters were shown to 'every editor in Fleet Street' so as to coerce British critics and journalists into vilifying him.

Professors MacNiven and Moore, two American scholars, accept this account of English literary life quite unreservedly, so far as one can tell, and add in their introduction that 'a virtually complete boycott by critics and publishers alike' removed Aldington's books from booksellers' displays, while 'highly placed Home Office officials, apparently including the Prime Minister', exerted pressure to ensure that Aldington's works went out of print in Britain. The editors produce no evidence at all to substantiate this scandalous saga – though they find time to clarify terms like 'lbw' and 'TUC' – so we're left in the dark as to the extent of its truth. Durrell sounds doubtful about it ('If, as you say, there is a boycott . . . '), and Aldington himself hardly inspires confidence as a witness. At one point he changes tack, declaring that the 'campaign' against him did not after all start with the Lawrence biography, but much earlier:

> I have *never* had a good press, and the same people who insulted me over that filthy little lying bugger – the Mortimers, the Nicolsons and all the rest of them – have attacked every book since *Death of a Hero*, always saying how dull and obscene and inferior my books are.

As it stands that sounds paranoid rather than persuasive, and the editors, as usual, abstain from any helpful documentation.

The literary side of the correspondence offers little in the way of subtlety. There is some chortling over 'bloody Henrietta James', 'Graham Greene-Grocer and Twaddling Eliot'. Aldington insists that the truly great poet of the century is Roy Campbell, and fondly recalls 'old Roy's' jokes about Jews. Auden and other 'pansy cowards' are, it's agreed, not poets at all but 'cunning phoneys'. In this atmosphere you'd not expect useful perception to thrive: nor does it. Reading the volumes of *The Alexandria Quartet'* as they come out, Aldington bellows appreciatively, and ventures the occasional critical insight – 'What a bloody fool Balthazar is – needs his arse kicked'. He does, though, spot a technical fault in *Mountolive*, pointing out that Balthazar is said to check his opponent's queen. In reply Durrell confesses that he's wholly ignorant of chess: 'it is like double entry book-keeping, I've never been able to understand it at all'. With his confident invocations of modern physics and his reference to the *Quartet* as a 'relativity-poem', Durrell can give the impression that he's the sort of sage for whom Einstein is bedtime reading, so it's reassuring to know that he's in reality baffled by a board game.

That aside, Durrell's letters throw little light on the *Quartet*, though written concurrently. The exotic cruelties that bespatter the novels – the aborted foetus in the sink, the hatpin driven into Toto's brain, the girls flogged to death – seem far removed from this kindly cove, putting himself out to cheer up an old deadbeat. Perhaps we should remember Durrell's own caveat that cruelty in a writer is simply the way a sentimentalist disguises his weakness. The swaggering expatriate sexuality of the *Quartet* – the complaint, for example, that in England 'almost all the really delicious things you can do to a woman are criminal offences' – likewise bears little relation to the Durrell we meet here, who apparently occupies his leisure hours with nothing bolder than chopping wood and drystone walling.

Where the letters do score is in humanity. The travel-brochure romanticism of the *Quartet* has no room for anything as ordinary as a human being. Aldington presents a new kind of challenge. His humanity hangs open like a clown's trousers – his pettiness, his rancour, his memories of the First World War which he uses as bids for sympathy. And Durrell meets this mundane awfulness with respect and something that sounds close to love – closer, indeed, than you'll find in the *Quartet*.

1981

Friends of promise

Cyril Connolly fell in love with Noel Blakiston when they were boys at Eton. Noel was an athletic lad, two years Cyril's junior, and (as the photo chosen for the frontispiece shows) much prettier. After going up to Balliol in 1922, Cyril pursued him with letters,* postcards and cables, sometimes at the rate of two a day, trying to fix up continental holidays, a few of which came off, and a *ménage à deux* in rural Devon, which didn't. The wooing continued while Connolly was in Jamaica with a tutoring job (Blakiston meantime had gone up to Magdalene, Cambridge), and eventually fizzled out at the end of the twenties when Blakiston got engaged. Connolly's rather unappealing assurances that he will 'pay all our fares, etc.' on the proposed jaunts suggest that he made the running, but whether he ever bedded his boyfriend isn't clear. He thanks him for 'contributing to the most sustained ecstasy of my life' on a trip to Sicily, but in the rarefied atmosphere of the letters that might well signify something more soulful than buggery. Or, on the other hand, might not. Mr Blakiston himself offers no guidance on such points. He admits to cutting sections out of Connolly's letters, and never tells us about the ones he sent in reply. His footnotes restrict themselves to identifying famous school-chums, and giving the dates of their CBEs and knighthoods.In his preface he explains that he feels pretty rotten about 'the vulgarity, the profanation of letting the laity in on such a privacy' at all, so presumably his unhelpfulness as an editor represents a last rag of modesty which he was unwilling to cast away.

Still, the letters reveal a lot about young Connolly, and amply merit publication. Eton, as *Enemies of Promise* concedes, bewitched and retarded him and his companions. After that festering, miniscule world of rewards and fairies, nothing else seemed real. University was an anticlimax. Politics, the General

*A Romantic Friendship: The Letters of Cyril Connolly to Noel Blakiston (Constable).

Strike, and Connolly's spell as a special constable, scarcely earn a mention. Instead we find Noel being adjured to recall little incidents of Eton life – 'Lower tea room, college fives, staying out, rears' – and send them along for Cyril's delectation, while Cyril despatches memories of 'gas mantles plopping in evening chapel, and looking at you through my fingers in the sevenfold Amen'. As late as 1927 he's still having dreams about being made second keeper of College Squash.

This regressive tendency was probably reinforced by his ill-success at Oxford, where he got a third in History – 'I find myself constantly hampered', he complained during Schools, 'by ignorance of the set books'. But things were bad at home, too. Stacked empties mounted in the parental house at Deepcut, Surrey, and Connolly *père* staggered around with their erstwhile contents inside him, revolting his son by his incoherence and the noises his stomach made. From such trials the adolescent's mind fled to the elegancies of the Greek Anthology, and to exotic Edens which Noel and he might share:

> What about a tower at Montril? by the sea and in an African huerta of steaming fruit trees with a view down the hill to the blue fields of cane which smell sweet at night and back to the snows of the Sierra Nevada from whence cool breezes blow?

He associated Noel with sunsets and idealism – 'Blossom by blossom the spring begins, thanks to you'. The notion of marriage to a girl seemed 'altogether disgusting' by comparison. Women were 'less beautiful and less intelligent than men', the friends agreed, besides being 'ungainly' and bestially ignorant. When Cyril allowed himself to take a girl out to lunch, it was only because her shingled hair reminded him of boys he'd loved at school.

Homosexuality and unworldiness went together. Blakiston seems to have been rather a prig, and Connolly curried favour by sending news of his own self-denial and high thinking. 'One must take a strong line about property – at any rate one's own, and decrease what one has, let alone not get any more.' When the affair ended, his natural greed and zest came bounding into the open. The last few letters are jubilant with marriage plans. He has found an American girl, Jean Bakewell, whose mother's house in Baltimore has 'more bathrooms than bedrooms and more cars than people'. Together they are trying to screw £2,000 a year out of her family. They aim to have a le Corbusier house in Torquay with a *pelota* court on the roof, and maybe a villa in Madeira where they can grow tropical fruits. Meanwhile they will swan around Europe and the Mediterranean and play with their pet animals. They buy some ferrets and two white mice, and stage a 'gladiatorial show'. The first mouse is satisfactorily slaughtered, but the other escapes, hides, and later gives birth to some young. One day Cyril finds it killing its offspring, so he and Jean, as punishment, place it in a stove pipe and put a ferret in at each end: 'there the ferrets pulled it practically in two'. Throughout this entertainment Connolly seems to have remained perfectly assured of his own superior refinement. 'I hope to God', he remarks in the same letter, 'Jean and I will be rich, simply to avoid contact with those millions of disgusting human beings.' Later he bought Jean a lemur, but it turned out to be 'just a machine for shitting and peeing', so they returned it to the shop. Presumably it was too big to feed to the ferrets. All told, it's a trifle surprising that Connolly, when he looked back at his early married life through mists of self-pity and idyllicism in *The Unquiet Grave*, should have chosen ferrets and lemurs to symbolize 'the innocent paradise' and 'the beauty of the healthy libido'.

Quite apart from enlightening one about Connolly, the letters are enticingly evocative of the places he visited, from Tangier to Fez to the slums of Oxford viewed from a canoe on the canal – 'very beautiful and Venetian with furnaces and railway engines and May and Lilac and rickety overhanging houses'. The side of Oxford he knew was, of course, the pampered academic one, with its gilded youths hopping in and out of their flannel bags and chauffeured motors. Almost everyone was from public school. The only non-public-school undergraduate we hear of gets thrown into the river and tied to a lamppost by some 'quiet and intellectual Trinity men', apparently with Connolly's complete approval, to pay him out for his 'vulgarity'. Celebrities on the edge of the Connolly circle include Maurice Bowra, Anthony Powell and Kenneth Clark ('a crashing bore').

One rather stunning fact that emerges from the letters is the extent to which the young Connolly was ignorant of English literature. As a King's Scholar at Eton he had enjoyed what would normally be reckoned the best education that England could afford. Yet several years after leaving Eton we find him announcing that he has just read *King Lear* for the first time (but hasn't yet got round to *Othello*), has just read *Wuthering Heights* ('a most shattering book and upsets one's ideas of Victorians very much'), has just read *Mansfield Park* ('so far I have always eschewed Jane Austen'), has just read *Jude the Obscure* (but finds Hardy's poetry 'rather cheap'), has read 'hardly any' Dickens and no Sterne, and has never before looked at 'The Deserted Village' or *Hyperion*. 'Do try *Paradise Lost*', he urges Blakiston, with the air of one recommending a curiosity recently stumbled on, and he assures his friend that 'Shakespeare could never have written "from morn he fell, from noon to dewie Eve/A summer's day"'. This confidence about what Shakespeare couldn't have written comes, we may note, about a twelvemonth before Connolly actually cast his eye over *King Lear*. And of course Milton didn't write Connolly's excerpt anyway. That Mr Blakiston can print the horrible misquotation without comment suggests that he has not, even yet, taken Connolly's advice.

In a way, though, the young Connolly's neglect of these classic English texts was characteristic, and mayn't have been the fault of his school. He always had a horror of being ordinary, and felt daunted by the well-trodden paths to success. The writers he likes quoting, both in these letters and in *The Unquiet Grave*, are mostly exotic or obscure – Du Bellay, Greek epigrammatists, Chamfort, Chuang Tsu, Pascal, Sainte-Beuve. This wasn't so much the result of pretentiousness as of a craving for the *outré* which came from the same part of his nature as the elaborate plans for foreign travel that fill his letters to Noel Blakiston. Like his yearning to hide himself away somewhere with this seemingly rather commonplace youth, the offbeat reading formed part of a larger escapism – the 'urge towards loneliness, isolation and obscurity' which he was later to diagnose as the Palinurus complex.

1975

A long season in hell

Imagine the kind of corrective treatment that might be meted out to a squad of recalcitrant polar bears by an orang-utan with an unusually vicious sense of humour, and you will have some glimmering of what human beings undergo in the course of Eugenia Ginzburg's memoirs.* A teacher and journalist, the mother of two small sons, and the wife of a Party offical in Kazan, she was arrested in 1937 during Stalin's purges on an absurd charge of 'terrorism', and sent to a forced labour camp in Siberia.

As she left the courtroom, protesting her innocence, her guard agreed laconically that she couldn't be guilty, otherwise she would not have got as little as ten years: the guilty were shot. At the camp she joined the tree-felling unit. The women were marched to work at 5.00 a.m. through the frozen forest, and at the day's end each was expected to have 4 cubic metres of timber cut and trimmed. Eugenia seldom managed more than a fifth of this quota, and as the bread ration was proportionate to the timber cut, she was soon starving. Failure to fulfil the norm was regarded as sabotage and punished by overnight confinement in an icy cell without so much as a bucket for sanitation.

As often during her years in the Arctic Auschwitz, she cheated death on this occasion by pure chance. A doctor who knew her relations in Leningrad arrived to conduct a medical inspection and wangled her a job as nurse in the camp children's home. That was in 1940, and the first volume of her memoirs, *Into the Whirlwind*, ended there. Circulated in the USSR through the secret channels of *samizdat* it leaked out to the West and became a best seller. *Within the Whirlwind* completes the story of what became, in the end, eighteen years' detention. It contains scenes from which the mind cowers in disbelief, and which are only readable at all because of the unemotional, matter-of-fact tone she has forced herself to adopt.

*Within the Whirlwind by Eugenia Ginzburg, translated by Ian Boland (Collins Harvill).

We enter a universe of death, peopled by rotting carcasses which walk upright and reveal themselves, on enquiry, as the Russian intelligentsia of the thirties – teachers, research workers, civil engineers, even ballet dancers – now black-toothed scarecrows, livid with boils and ulcers from malnutrition, their minds frenziedly occupied with the problems of the minute daily bread ration. Should you eat it all at once, on issue, in which case how will you stagger to work next day? Or should you save half for morning, in which case you will not sleep: the morsel of bread will torment you through your straw pillow all night? The dying solemnly bequeathed that evening's ration to favoured friends, and the corpse is propped up in the back row at roll call, to make sure the issue is forthcoming.

In the children's home the babies, who are the result of snatched camp romances, often between guards and prisoners, lie quietly dying of hunger, their faces wrinkled and wise, like the very old. Later Eugenia is transferred to a prison poultry farm, where even the chickens die of starvation, dropping dully from their perches at night. Her boss teaches her to spot them as they totter, and quickly chop off their heads, so that the birds can qualify for human consumption.

But it is as medical assistant at the area central hospital that she meets death most multitudinously. The place is packed with young boys, victims of slave labour at the Burkhala gold mines, all dying, with fearful speed, of TB. 'Later I tried to work out how many had died in my arms . . . It came to something like a thousand.'

For Eugenia, all these assignments counted as light duties. Less light intervened, as when she was marched, in her thin town shoes and dress, across 75 km of ice-bound waste to the Izvestkovaya punishment centre, and there left to starve, receiving no bread ration at all because she could not fulfil the production norm at the lime quarries. Yet she refused to die, and after Stalin's death was released and rehabilitated. She married a Catholic German doctor whom she met in the camps (her own husband, arrested too in the thirties, she believed dead) and they adopted a little girl from the camp kindergarten, now an actress at the Leningrad Comedy Theatre.

Eugenia's elder son, Alyosha, had been sent to a home for the children of political prisoners, and died of starvation during the war. The news of that was her bitterest agony. But her younger son, Vasya, survived and, on her release, was reunited with his mother. She had not seen him since he was a toddler and, stumbling confusedly towards the husky teenager who came to greet her, she found the images of her two sons merging, for an instant, into one:

> 'Alyosha, my darling,' I said in a whisper, almost involuntarily. Suddenly I heard a deep muffled voice: 'No, Mamma, I'm not Alyosha, I'm Vasya.'
> And then in a rapid whisper into my ear:
> 'Don't cry in front of them.'

Contempt for 'them' helps to keep Eugenia alive throughout – and 'them' includes not only the subhuman criminal riff-raff in the camps, who are encouraged to victimize the political prisoners, but also the legions of semi-literate bureaucrats, the peasant boys dressed up as camp commandants, and the high party officials with their vulgar wives drenched in White Lilac perfume. She is unashamedly an intellectual, and refuses to pretend that the cultured and sensitive are not superior to the ignorant, the brutish and the dull. Her ancestors, she proudly records, were people who would go without soup so long as they could raise learned children. In an England that has grown ashamed of education, and thinks it immoral to sacrifice anything for it, this makes heartening reading. At night in the camps Eugenia and her friends would recite to each other poems they knew by heart – Akhmatova, Pasternak, Mandelstam. Poetry, observes Heinrich Böll in his introduction, revealed itself in these extremes as one of life's basic necessities.

What words could be adequate to commend such a book? Its spiritual insight, and its cast of simpletons, saints and psychopaths, recall Dostoevsky. But to praise it simply as literature degrades it. The obvious comparison is with *The Gulag Archipelago*. *Within the Whirlwind* lacks Solzhenitsyn's historical and geographical sweep, his fathomless substrata of personal tragedies. He is the Dante of the Soviet inferno: Eugenia Ginzburg's, a voice from a single circle of hell. But as Solzhenitsyn says, to taste the sea all you need is one gulp. It's a taste few readers of this astonishing testimony will forget.

1981

The disintegration of Sartre

This *Farewell to Sartre** is avowedly a labour of love, which just goes to show that love has strange ways of expressing itself. It opens with an account of Sartre's drooling senility (not recommended for older readers). Then come lengthy taped exchanges in which Sartre, blind and sick, is quizzed on multiple topics, ranging from his schooldays to his dislike of tomatoes. Since Simone de Beauvoir lived with him for fifty years she must, unless she was unusually inattentive, have known the answers to most of these queries already. The reader gets a strong sense of make-believe, or at best of disguised therapy, with the brisk and terrifying de Beauvoir prodding the luckless sage into enunciation so as to occupy his mind and keep him off the bottle.

The replies she elicits suggest that Sartre's famed political leftism was essentially a personality disorder, rooted in hatred of himself, and by extension of his family and class. As a boy he was obsessed by the idea that he was ugly – a suspicion his playmates unanimously corroborated. He had a squint and a puny physique, and on one nightmare occasion a small girl he was in love with ridiculed him publicly for these flaws. Since then, he avows, he has always assumed that people who catch sight of him will automatically be hostile. Even in youth, physical exercise gave him no pleasure. He was afraid of getting tired or falling over, and it brought him out in boils.

To compensate, he invented an 'imaginary body', which was that of of a powerful warrior killing columns of enemies. He dreamed of shooting blacks and yellow men, and snatching girls from blazing houses, and these reveries did not cease with childhood but lasted all his life. At secondary school he joined a 'violent and brutal' gang which terrorized wealthier students. As a weedy young schoolmaster, he was drawn to the boxers and athletes among his colleagues and relished their talk. 'What I liked were stories about men's lives with sex and fighting in

Adieux: A Farewell to Sartre by Simone de Beauvoir, translated by Patrick O'Brian (André Deutsch with Weidenfeld and Nicolson).

them.' Given these tastes it was almost inevitable that Sartre should come to idolize a mythical 'proletariat', which he imagines in terms of physical and sexual potency. He talks of 'the untamed, deep thrust' of proletarian justice, and admires violent revolutionaries who, he claims, are 'immediately ethical'.

He loathes the bourgeoisie because membership of it has cut him off from 'the people'. Not that he has any practical experience of this class: indeed, he stresses that 'the people' do not yet exist in France. Presumably they will evolve at some point in the revolutionary process. Meanwhile his mystical populism provides a handy pretext for despising those people who do happen to be alive – such as readers of his books. The realization that he writes for a contemptible bourgeois public, not for proletarians, 'deeply troubles' him.

The orgins of this class prejudice, as of much else in Sartre, were personal and childish. As he relates in *Words*, his father died when he was two, and his adored mother remarried. He detested his stepfather, a philistine scientist who had no respect for Sartre's budding literary talents but who, as head of a La Rochelle shipyard, was impregnably rich and successful. Sartre resented the cash handouts he was obliged to accept from this interloper, so he started stealing from his mother's handbag – the classic recourse of the unloved child. He needed the money to buy popularity with his schoolfellows, treating them to pastries and cinema tickets. When the thefts came to light, he was sent away to school in Paris. So the bourgeoisie, in the person of his stepfather, had robbed him of his mother, besides forcing him into crime, and he never forgave it. He became a writer and intellectual to avenge himself on his mother's seducer. 'My stepfather was perpetually the person I wrote against. The fact of writing put me above him.'

Putting himself above others has occupied Sartre a good deal. Though he would not have cared to admit it, he was an exemplary product of bourgeois competitive individualism. His grandparents, who brought him up, told him he was a 'little prince', and that the masses were semi-human. He came to appreciate his own genius early on: 'I talked to my friends as a genius talks to his friends.' It did not matter that schoolmasters gave him lowish grades: in his 'deep subjective reality' he remained, he knew, a superman. With the publication of *Nausea* his apotheosis was complete: 'At that point I was immortal, and I was assured of my immortality'.

It eventually dawns on Mme de Beauvior that the superlatives Sartre sprinkles on himself combine rather oddly with his vaunted belief in human equality, and she takes him up on the point. Why, she enquires, did he scorn his fellow students at the Sorbonne? That, Sartre explains, was because they were not quite human, and never would be. Most people are like that. They do not want to have 'real' human qualities. They choose to be stupid, even though with 'a slight change of their attitude' they could be quite like Sartre. So human beings, he concludes, are potentially equal, but really a lot of them are 'swine'. Bourgeois swine, of course.

Sartre's insecurity and self-esteem affected, as his replies show, every corner of his life. He refused the Nobel Prize, and other awards, to assert his aristocratic elevation: 'I've thought myself above any honours that could be offered'. He dreaded being dependent: even asking the way in the street filled him with horror. He gave huge tips, so as to keep a distance between himself and the common ruck. Men repelled him, since they represented a threat: 'I find the adult male deeply disgusting.' He liked making love to women because it put him at an advantage, but he dared not let the pleasure be reciprocal. There was always 'a touch of sadism' in his love, for 'the other person yielded, and I did not'.

For someone so crippled by bodily inhibitions, the natural world was a minefield. Anything suggestive of fecundity gave him the shivers. At the seaside, while others relaxed on the sand, he would perch frigidly on a block of stone. He shrank from touching soft or moist surfaces, which reminded him of bodily secretions. Fruit was 'too natural': he preferred clean, man-made eatables, like cakes. His demand that intellectuals should 'integrate with the masses' seems even more unreal than it would otherwise, coming from a man who could not bear to face an orange.

His fastidiousness must have made his body's disintegration peculiarly hideous for him. Mme de Beauvior spares us, and herself, nothing: the dribble on his shirt, the food spilt over his shoes, the wet patches on chairs, the soiled pyjamas at night. Towards the end he was piped up to a plastic bag of urine which he trailed round the ward when she visited. Terrible bedsores developed and when, just after his death, she wished briefly to lie beside him, a nurse stopped her. 'Take care: the gangrene.' Sartre endured his illness with calm indifference – the same rational detachment that made him so dauntlessly honest about his life and personality. Only his blindness prompted agonized cries. That apart, he accepted degradation, and refused to give up hope. 'Obviously it's bearable only if you think it's temporary,' he said. It was, of course.

1984

What exactly do you mean?

The belief that writers ought to have ideas still lingers. In academic circles, particularly, there is a strong feeling that any author worth his salt will possess a philosophy, ideally one of roughly thesis length. This seems unfair. No one considers it part of the duty of musicians or painters to provide useful tips about human nature or the meaning of the universe. Why should a poet or novelist be saddled with such concerns, simply because his artistic medium is words? In the new volume of *Paris Review Interviews** a refreshingly large number of the writers interviewed protest that they have nothing whatever of general import to say. 'We have no message at all' (Borges); 'no idea about philosophical positions and world views' (George Seferis); 'no moral aim' (Anthony Burgess). John Updike puts the point with, as usual, the maximum elegance:

> Everything is infinitely fine, and any opinion is somehow coarser than the texture of the real thing. I find it hard to have opinions . . . I think of my books not as sermons or directives in a war of ideas but as objects, with different shapes and textures and the mysteriousness of anything that exists.

Of course, if asking writers for opinions is truly futile, then so are *Paris Review Interviews*. Sensing this, perhaps, several of the authors in this batch were reluctant, at first, to co-operate, and Steinbeck managed to die before an interview could be arranged. (His contribution has been cobbled together from old letters.)

Understandably, what the writers are least keen to be asked is what their works 'mean' – as if what they actually write were so much cryptographic flummery easily bypassable by a little plain speaking. Isak Dinesen voices the general exasperation on this count: 'I intend everything as it's stated. It would be terrible if the explanation of the work were outside the work itself.' For

Writers at Work: The Paris Review Interviews ed. George Plimpton (Secker and Warburg).

people who teach and write about literature, on the other hand, it would be terrible if it were not. Self-explanatory artefacts would put many of them out of business. Hence, maybe, the tendency among critics (observable in Wilfred Sheed's simpering preface to this volume) to treat writers as lovable weirdies who don't appreciate the real significance of what they're about.

The writers, for their part, seem to regard the critics with disdain or apathy – 'curious sucker fish', Steinbeck calls them; and John Berryman tells a story about a girl graduate writing a thesis on his debt to Hebrew elegiac metre, a subject about which he is in fact totally ignorant. The horror of a girl squandering youth and energy on such a project seems to escape Berryman entirely. 'It's a harmless industry,' he comments. 'It gets people degrees.'

Anyone who takes the study of literature seriously is bound to find such cynicism depressing, especially, somehow, when it comes from a drink-sodden wreck like Berryman who, in common with other writers in the volume, could hardly be said to be an advertisement for the life-enhancing effects of art. Kerouac, gabbling on with the fluency of a jammed beer-tap about his contempt for 'all-that-crap craft business' and his determination to 'take no shit from nobody', is probably, from this viewpoint, the most repellent specimen on display. Under the joint influence of booze, and of some little white pills which the interviewers take along for Kerouac and themselves to munch, his interview gradually disintegrates into addled chaos. No doubt it's meant to come across as a riot of liberated fun – an expression, as Kerouac himself puts it, of 'the ecstatic tom-foolery of the age'. But why one should suppress one's instinctive disgust at such a performance isn't, to me, apparent.

Anne Sexton also strikes one as an interviewee it would have been worth going a long way round to avoid. Quite apart from the inevitable moans about having to cook and change nappies, her solemn and unswerving self-concern is soon wearying. Her discovery of her 'creative depths', her long and variegated history of mental illness, her 'courage' and 'daring' in writing about it, her relationship with Maxine Kumin ('part superego, part sister, as well as pal of my desk'), are all chronicled with remorseless garrulity. Apparently a psychiatrist once told her she had a 'leaky ego', and you can see the aptness of his diagnosis. The tone of her monologue wobbles between winsome affectation ('I not only have lived, but loved, that some-

time miracle') and pseudo-male brashness, as in her advice to
Maxine on the art of the novel – 'I told her "Fuck structure and
grab your characters by the time balls".' Besides being mud-
dling, that seems a desperately impoverished utterance for
someone whose craft is supposed to be words. That Anne
Sexton later killed herself hardly makes one happier, of course,
about finding her interview so awful, or about her satisfactoriness as a human being.

It's a relief to turn from these derelicts to Borges – blind,
cheerful, a model of courtesy, sanely and articulately aware of
the inner violence which his (and anyone's) culture both subli-
mates and fosters. He meets daily, he explains, with a little
group of students in his room at the Biblioteca Nacional, to
translate *Beowulf* or Norse sagas. He relates the appeal these
savage narratives have for him to his fascination, when he was a
youth in the slums, with a particularly murderous kind of knife
used in street fights. Typically it was the knife's name *(el vaivén:*
the come and go) that gripped him: 'you see the flash, the
sudden flash'. His passion for verbal expressiveness has taken
him into corners of English literature unrummaged even by
most specialists. The versatile Bishop Wilkins (1614–72) is an
especial favourite. 'He created a beautiful word, a word that's a
poem in itself, full of hopelessness, sadness and despair: the
word *neverness* . . . I don't think it's ever been used.'

The interview which works best as entertainment is Robert
Graves's, partly because he had the luck to be allocated the two
most gormless interviewers, partly because he enjoys loosing,
out of the blue, statements that sound both authoritative and
wholly bogus – as, for instance, 'The leading atomic scientist in
Australia agreed with me the other day that time does not really
exist', or, 'They find now that if a snail eats another snail it gets
that second snail's memory.' Reeling from conversation-
stoppers of this calibre, the men from the *Paris Review* either
change the subject quickly to something neutral ('How many
books have you published?') or, more venturesomely, rise to the
bait – 'Did you really mean that? That God had a wife?' – only to
be pelted with further lumps of miscellaneous erudition.

The Auden interview also has its moments. 'I don't see how
any civilized person can watch TV, far less own a set' is a
judgement to be cherished (as, for that matter, is Nabokov's
comment, in his interview, on 'the pretentious nonsense of Mr
Pound, that total fake'). And Auden's comfy lingo ('peeve',

'dotty', 'not my cup of tea') brings him back almost as vividly as does the fissured visage in Hockney's drawing. On women he is, as usual, perceptive: 'No woman ever wrote nonsense verse. Women are realists: I think if men knew what women said to each other about them, the human race would die out.' No doubt his homosexuality helped to give him this understanding and fear. Christopher Isherwood, who also figures in the volume, observes how precious homosexuality is to a writer, since it allows him to see everything from an abnormal angle.

Auden's hopelessness about the arts is, nowadays, less abnormal: 'The arts can do nothing. The social and political history of Europe would be what it has been if Dante, Shakespeare, Michelangelo, Mozart, et al., had never lived.' Even if that's true (and it's a dictum that takes its confidence from the knowledge that the matter can't be demonstrated either way), Shakespeare and the rest have undeniably made the social and political history easier to put up with. Besides, since Auden holds that the poet's one political duty is to set an example of the correct use of his mother tongue (because when language deteriorates, force takes over), he must believe that the arts *could* have a political effect, whether or not they have yet.

Most of the writers interviewed are old, so there is plentiful reminiscence. Conrad Aiken recalls his wild drinking bouts with Eliot, on one of which, towards the end of his life, Eliot got so paralytic that he couldn't uncross his ankles and had to be lifted into the taxi by Valerie. 'A splendid occasion,' Aiken chuckles. Less splendid, of course, in sober print. Perhaps, after all, the best story is Isherwood's about Stravinsky. They once drove out to the Sequoia forest, and Stravinsky, a tiny figure, stood for a long while gazing up at a giant Sequoia. Then, turning to Isherwood, he said: 'That's serious.' It's more than can always be said for writers, or interviews.

1977

Books, raw and cooked

Structuralism is not a subject that grips the ordinary reader much. Its articles of faith are likely to strike him as a mixture of the self-evident and the impossible. Thus the proposition, solemnly repeated by structuralists, that language is a system of signs (or 'signifiers') seems to him too obvious for remark. Who ever imagined otherwise? On the other hand, the ideas floated by the wilder type of structuralist – that literary texts ought to mean anything we require them to, or that authors do not create their works but are created by them – pretty clearly call for a spell of sedation and devoted nursing.

David Lodge acknowledges that much structuralist theory defies common sense, and he picks it over cautiously. He has no use for the Marxist branch, sometimes called 'poststructuralism,' which seeks to show that literary works are simply mediations of ideologies ('All literature is propaganda,' in Orwell's phrase). As a novelist Lodge likes to maintain contact with his public, whereas the aim of poststructuralist discourse (e.g., in Derrida) is he suspects, 'the mystification and intimidation of the reader'. All this naturally puts one on Lodge's side, and his title *Working with Structuralism* * has a making-the-best-of-it ring, rather like 'Surviving with Sciatica'. It's meant to convey, he explains, 'working alongside structuralism: recognizing its existence as a fact of intellectual life'.

Still, the claims he makes for the bits of structuralism he decides to work with seem rather excessive. To exemplify the 'long-neglected riches' of the Russian Formalists, he cites Schklovsky's concept of 'defamiliarization', according to which, he tells us, the purpose of all art is to defamiliarize things which have become dulled for us, through habit. A sound notion: but weren't the Russian Formalists a little behindhand? What about Shelley: 'Poetry lifts the veil from the hidden beauty of the world, and makes familiar objects as if they were not familiar'?

Working with Structuralism: Essays and Reviews on 19th and 20th century Literature by David Lodge (Routledge and Kegan Paul).

Or, going back another half-century, what about Johnson pick-ing *The Rape of the Lock* as a highpoint of literary art because in it 'familiar things are made new'? As an instance of the 'huge intellectual advances' achieved by structuralism, defamiliari-zation doesn't seem the happiest choice.

Perhaps, though, the new theories will look better when applied to an actual text. To show their practical powers Lodge takes Hemingway's story 'Cat in the Rain' and brings to bear on it 'the whole battery of modern formalism and structuralism'. In the story a bored young American staying with her husband at an Italian hotel sees a cat outside in the rain, but when she goes to rescue it it has disappeared. The hotel staff evince concern at her disappointment, and at the story's end a maid appears in the couple's room bearing a big tortoise-shell cat ' for the Signora'. The question is, of course, is it the same cat? If it is, then the gross animal reality is presumably meant to make the woman's sentimental yearnings look rather absurd. If it's not, we learn something about the lack of understanding between the hard-headed Italians and their spoiled guests.

Lodge, having got the story in his sights, bombards it with massed structuralism, picking out the narrative 'indices', 'nuc-lei' and 'catalysers', and reducing the whole thing to a 'thematic four-term homology'. When the smoke has cleared, he tells us that we can't be sure whether it was the same cat or not. True, we knew that already, but now we're surer we can't be sure. We have 'a confirmation of the story's indeterminacy.'

Well, you can't have everything. Maybe structuralism may be more use when it comes to evaluation. To prove it in this role ·Lodge goes to work on *Hard Times*. Critics, he points out, have differed over the value of Dickens's novel because they can't agree whether it gives a fair account of nineteenth-century industrial society. But, Lodge urges, if we apply a little struc-turalism the difficulty vanishes. For we find that the book borrows its methods from popular theatre and pantomime, so we are able to appreciate that Dickens, by this 'brilliantly imaginative stroke', has freed himself from the need to be accurate about capitalism, trades unions, and the other topicali-ties he handles.

But has he? Isn't it precisely the point of those who attack the book that melodrama and broad comedy provide a falsifying and irresponsible vehicle for the social concerns Dickens raises? Merely spotting the debt to popular theatre (which requires, in any case, no structuralist acumen) is the beginning not the end of the argument.

At this stage you begin to feel that if these are the fruits of working with structuralism it might be an idea to try working without it. Happily the same thought strikes Lodge. His essays progressively abandon their structuralist flourishes and grow sharper by consequence. A masterly piece on Hardy's *The Woodlanders* detects in it two opposed versions of the natural world. There is the stress on murderous evolutionary struggle, with the very trees throttling one another. But beside this raw Darwinism Hardy places evocations of ancient Greek pastoral elegy – the lament for a dead shepherd (in this case, Giles Winterborne) whom the woods and meadow flowers tenderly mourn. The book's strength, Lodge argues, stems from the delicate balance Hardy holds between these conflicting value-systems.

And to persuade us that the echoes of Greek elegy aren't chance, he notes that Theocritus featured on Hardy's 1887 reading list, and that a translation of the 'Lament for Bion' appeared in *Macmillan's Magazine*, where *The Woodlanders* was serialized, while Hardy was writing the last chapters. This, of course, is just the sort of biographical check-up which structuralists scorn, so it's good to have its efficacy demonstrated. The two essays on Evelyn Waugh, where Lodge focuses on the venomous and destructive side of Waugh's psyche (admittedly, a largish target) have a similar force.

Ultimately all the essays circle round this problem of the relation between art and life. Lodge's own novels adopt the classic realist mode, denounced by structuralists because its logical, cause-and-effect world is false, as Lodge concedes, to 'the chaotic nature of subjective experience'. But then, you can't be true to that sort of experience without becoming chaotic, subjective, and unread except by a few structuralists. Interest in this quandary draws Lodge, as a critic, to kinds of writing which stretch reality to, or past, its limits – the 'New Journalism', proclaimed by Tom Wolfe, which garbs itself in the colours of fiction, but outbids fiction by being fact; or Ted Hughes's *Crow* which, Lodge suggests, transposes grave biblical questions into the techniques of a Tom-and-Jerry cartoon. He's provoking and engrossing on both topics – as, indeed, on all he touches, even structuralism.

1981

Love and the laureate of death

In England, Hilaire Belloc once noted, the mention of poetry will disperse a crowd faster than a fire hose. English poets, if they want an audience, have to find ways of neutralizing this native distaste, and Sir John Betjeman's solution has been to masquerade as a sad clown – a lovable, woebegone Peter Pan, keening over the nursery teas and teddy bears of his lost Elysium. It has proved wildly successful. Betjeman's cachet is by now that of a cherished public monument. It would be only mildly surprising to hear that he had been acquired by the National Trust. No other living poet can muster anything approaching his readership: the *Collected Poems* have sold close on a million copies.

And quite right too. For beneath the clown's mask can be descried traits that have, in the past, signalled major poets: the howling gulfs of implacable emotion, the rigorous technical mastery, the lonely uncompromising vision. With Betjeman, appearances are always deceptive. The affable bumbler seethes with hate inside: it escapes, now and then, in acrid spurts – 'Come, friendly bombs, and fall on Slough', for example, or the joyous paean at the scene of a car crash where 'the first-class brains of a senior civil servant' lie scattered on the road.

Deceptive, too, is the air of misty nostalgia the poems give off. No poet is in fact more precise, as Philip Larkin, an eager disciple, has insisted. Betjeman's poetic realm brims with exact locations like a street directory, its actuality certified by swarms of brand names and architectural data. Alone among the poets of his generation, Betjeman has catalogued our real suburban world in which housewives queue at MacFisheries and Elaine, in well-cut Windsmoor, daintily alights at Ruislip Gardens. Nor (it's another of his enriching complications) does his rapture over such mundane epiphanies prevent him from looking forward with satisfaction to the day when humankind will wipe itself out, and leave the globe to the starfish and the hawthorn.

Bevis Hillier unearthed the thirty-odd items in *Uncollected*

*Poems** while at work on the poet's papers for the official biography. They include, among some duds, poems no sensible reader will miss. The best of them touch on dying, that undying Betjeman bugbear. Whatever his relations with contemporary life, he is unchallengeably the laureate of contemporary death, and has traced, in poem after poem, its horribly normal advance from the preliminary twinge ('First there was putting hot-water bottles to it') to the fatal X-ray photographs and the hospital bed, conveniently placed for you to hear your relatives, in the car park below, making off cheerily to tea and telly.

Unlike most poets, Betjeman has added terrors to death, presenting moments so real that they become part of your own premonitions. This is true, for instance, of 'Devonshire St., W.I.', arguably his best poem, where the doomed patient steps aghast from the consulting room into a newly alien world:

No hope. And the iron nob of this palisade
So cold to the touch, is luckier now than he.

Uncollected Poems contains nothing as haunting as that, but there is a plaintive monologue spoken by a retired postal clerk ('since the wife died the house seems lonely-like') which catches the triteness of grief with cruel accuracy, and there are two poems about hell. In one the poet, walking along King's Road, senses the underground furnace that gapes for him; in the other, his old teddy bear Archibald, perched over his bed, warns 'They'll burn you on the Judgement Day'.

Betjeman and hell have always been a problem. What, you wonder, has he done to make him so sure he'll go there? True, there are several rather enigmatic poems about betraying a girl and leading a double life (a new one, 'Guilt', appears here); but even supposing these were autobiographical, such a lapse could hardly merit eternal combustion. Or could it? Maybe the Hillier biography will shed some light. Betjeman's hellfire God has puzzlingly little in common with the gracious deity portrayed in other poems ('Christmas', say), and the intellectual difficulties of a belief in hell are never faced. A doubter might point out that a God who put his enemies in hell would have to be more vicious than almost any human being: even Hitler, even Stalin, even Vlad the Impaler would surely, if consulted,

Uncollected Poems by John Betjeman (John Murray).

set some term to their victims' agonies – and if they would not we should scarcely love and worship them for it.

Of course, no Christian's terror of hell will be diminished by rational argument, least of all Betjeman's. His brain is poised on an extremely sensitive ejector seat, and at the merest mention of religion it vanishes with a melodious whizz. Its loss doesn't matter much in the long run, because his poetry always draws on emotion rather than reason for its strength. His basic conviction that the world ought ideally to be organized for the preservation of thatched cottages and old railway lines is not conspicuously reasonable, though it appeals to something stubbornly regressive in many thinking people.

His social views, in the satirical poems, depend likewise on irrational loathing – of businessmen, oilmen, admen, and planners of every sort. Only a simpleton could subscribe to the blanket vilification of such callings that Betjeman urges on us, or could believe, as he seems to, that there are bureaucrats at large eager to cover England with workers' flats and fields of soya beans. Betjeman substitutes these wild fantasies for rational thought because rational thought has demonstrably done nothing to stop the erosion of the England he loves, and because only the extravagance of unreason can match his disgust at the atrocities we surround ourselves with – caravan sites, providing instant slums at every beauty spot, and lamps like concrete gallows bathing the roads in yellow vomit.

His belief in hell, and the shuddering anticipation of being tortured there himself, can be seen as facets of Betjeman's masochism. He gets delicious shivers, as the poems abundantly testify, from the idea of prostrating himself before muscular, sporty girls who whack things – Miss J. Hunter Dunn with her warm-handled tennis racket, or Pam who swipes the rhododendrons ('Lucky the rhododendrons'). Betjeman's punitive God is, in one respect, an apotheosis of these beefy lovelies – a deity in drag, as it were, equipped with the divine equivalents of jodhpurs and riding whip. We should not laugh: or rather we should admire Betjeman for letting us laugh. Part of his stature comes (to quote Larkin again) from his being prepared to release feelings that we are ashamed of and so ridicule.

Besides, the wish to feel hurt is ultimately what prompts Betjeman's most poignant and beautiful lyrics. When he mourns for the enormous hayfields of Perivale, or the lovertrod lanes that once rambled round Tooting Bec, he is deliberately stimulating grief, as any poet must who aims to touch the buried springs of tenderness in us. 'Man is in love and love's what vanishes. What more is there to say?' asks Yeats, unanswerably. But poets, by making us feel for what vanishes, can ensure that it does not quite vanish. Betjeman has done this for a whole array of loved things: for steam and gaslight and sunset-gilded Surrey pines and the hassocky smell of churches – for, in fact, the special world that he has saved and made his own.

1983

A star looks down

Games are our beginnings. When Dirk Bogarde was little his father used to make him and his sister play observation games. How many pots and pans were there in the shop window? How many jugs with pink roses? In the Underground, memorize the faces and feet. Who had the bunion, the toe-caps, the brogues?

It was the groundwork of Dirk's career. He built a library in his brain of clothes, nervous tics, facial expressions which allowed him to turn into other people. Shoes, he came to realize, were the key to character. From them develop the walk, the stance, the sag or spread of the shoulders, the breathing. Like most of his insights, it's not something you'll learn from the academic studies of drama.

Bogarde's eye for crucial odds and ends makes him an irresistible writer. His war experiences, with which this second volume of memoirs starts,* come back in bursts of searing detail: a soldier in a kilt, lying in the cow-parsley beyond the D-Day beaches, the *Daily Mirror* stuck to his blown-away face; Belsen, and the starved girl who ran along holding his hand, her breasts swinging like empty pockets; the mass grave in the wood outside Soltau where tent-pegs, driven in, sank into slime.

In Germany he watched the freed slave-labourers beginning their revenge: a band of shaven-headed women tipping a grand piano out of an upstairs window into a magnolia – everything exploding in splintered keys and white blossom, while the ashen-faced owners, with two small children, stood mute beside him. Then there was the Far East – Calcutta, Java, Malaya; the air alight with parrots and flowering trees; the pith helmets bobbing on the water outside Bombay, like jellyfish, as the troopships sailed for England.

There are no heroics. As an Air Photographic Interpreter (observation again) he largely escaped combat – or so, modestly, he makes out. Back home he scrambled for a toehold in a

Snakes and Ladders by Dirk Bogarde (Chatto and Windus).

London bulging with out-of-work actors. The Rank organisation told him he had the wrong sort of neck, and his head was too small for the camera. When he'd sent the press into raptures with a stage appearance in a little theatre off Notting Hill Gate, Rank agreed to overlook these blemishes and gave him a contract. *Doctor in the House* and its progeny made him a star, adored for his simple personality and raised eyebrow. In public, his flies had to be sewn up to protect him from his more ardent admirers, and when he appeared on stage, screams, moans and chants of 'We love you, Dirk' echoed through the auditorium. At a matinee in Cardiff the Scene Dock doors caved in, releasing a horde of policemen and young women into the cast. After that he stuck to films.

'Pretty vile, really,' observed his sensible sister, and he agreed; but the rewards were hardly negligible. The Oxo tin in which he'd stored his first professional earnings gave way to a succession of picture-book mansions, rolling acres, aviaries of tropical birds and similar palliatives. Glittering house-parties occupied the weekends, and Santa Claus took to leaving gold and jewels from Cartier's or Tiffany's in the Christmas stockings.

Luckily for the ordinary reader, it all sounds faintly repellent. The film industry, we're left in no doubt, accommodates a highish proportion of sharks and stinkers and they stare out from these pages as vivid as nettle-rash. The financial backers are all over-tailored apes, with tiny Neanderthal brains buried deep behind their cigars. The celebrities prance and preen themselves: Noel Coward waspish and bossy; Visconti, with his palaces and his boot-licking entourage, boasting that he's a Communist. Even the nice people have an unreliable sort of vivacity, like bottles of fizzy drink – gushing all over you one minute, and flat and sour the next. Of course, there are exceptions. Kay Kendall and Judy Garland both emerge glowing – though the idea of a close friendship with Judy Garland loses some of its glamour when you learn that it entailed her phoning you from New York at four in the morning several times a week to tell you that she was afraid of the dark.

In 1959 he went to Hollywood. From the moment of stepping off the plane – to be greeted by a football-bosomed majorette with a smile 'like a silent scream' – his impressions are uproariously hostile. The place unrolls itelf in a cavalcade of mind-crunching vulgarity, reaching its bedraggled apogee in the cage of live, pink-dyed, rhinestone-antlered reindeer which provides the centrepiece for the local Yuletide fun. Americans have never taken to Bogarde or his films, apparently, and he repays their dislike with zest, depicting as their most prominent national traits a taste for sharp practice and a moronic numbness to nuance.

The closing chapters have a melancholy air. Ashamed of his popular success, he turned to serious films and his English audiences fled in horror. Fans who went to see him in *The Doctor's Dilemma*, believing it to be yet another 'Doctor' frolic, were naturally aghast. His new policy, he explains, was to 'disturb' rather than entertain and, like many artists with this smug aim, he curiously expected people to sit still and tolerate disturbance rather than go elsewhere. To make matters worse, a new kind of idol, less shy and sporting, had arrived: Brando, Presley, James Dean. Feeling neglected, he packed up and left England for good. As luck would have it, the gathering gloom was just the right training for his next and greatest part – von Aschenbach in Visconti's *Death in Venice*. Tired, defeated, wistfully pursuing an elusive ideal, he could, in a sense, play himself.

Not that the gloom is exactly impenetrable. He survives, resilient and disdainful, in a highly enviable Provençal farm with twelve acres of vine and jasmine fields and four hundred ancient olive trees to shut out the squalid world. His prospects as a writer look rosy. His first volume of autobiography, *A Postillion Struck by Lightning*, was a triumph: so is this. Quite apart from his startling visual gifts, he has gained, from years of acting and script writing, an infallible ear. Every dialogue, every voice, rings true. The book fairly yammers with life; and when you look up from the pages you're surprised to find how quiet it has gone.

1978

Admissible evidence

You seldom come across hatred as virulent as John Osborne's for his mother. Her defects furnish the *leitmotiv* of this autobiography,* gloweringly returned to whenever Osborne's other grievances cease to absorb him for a moment. Quite what the old lady did to merit such odium remains unclear. She had a hard life, scrubbing floors in a Foundling Hospital at the age of twelve, and later attaining modest renown as a barmaid. She could juggle with bottles, and pour four glasses of beer at once, and these skills enabled her to provide cash handouts and meals at Joe Lyons for her graceless son who, in early manhood, showed little talent for gainful employment.

True she was, according to Osborne, boring, querulous, and keen on nagging him in public, but these are traditional motherly qualities which most children learn to tolerate. He also claims that she lacked any capacity for joy – a strange charge, coming from him, since the world view projected in these pages is about as joyous as an attack of shingles. His one moment of pure delight came during the blitz when a near-miss rocked the Osborne home, bringing down the ceilings. His mother, seated on the lavatory at the time, hobbled out stunned and blackened, her bloomers still dangling round her knees. Osborne collapsed in mirth.

By contrast a saintly radiance encircles the memory of his father – an artistic, gentle failure, who worked as an advertising copywriter until TB forced him to give it up. He acquired on retirement an imitation-oak clock and £20, which he blued on a family holiday at Margate. Then the National Advertising Benevolent Society sent him to Ventnor to die, which he did quite quickly – though not before parents and son had celebrated a last painful Christmas together. Osborne, aged eleven, interpreted his mother's short temper at this crisis as callousness,

A Better Class of Person: An Autobiography, 1929–1956 by John Osborne (Faber).

and has never, one suspects, forgiven either her or the world for his bereavement.

The back streets off the Fulham Palace Road were the Osborne home ground, an area of crippled trees and brick terraces, harbouring an extensive collection of uncles, aunts and grand-parents who are pinned out here with scathing care. There was grandma Osborne with her mean spirit and loose dentures, 'terminally lazy' grandpa Osborne, given to coming downstairs in his combs, and the 'whey-faced wormy little bankteller' Uncle John.

Marginally less distasteful were his mother's family – her-niated grandpa Grove, known as the smartest publican in London back in the days of hansom cabs and cigars, who was the model for Billy Rice in *The Entertainer*, and gaunt grandma Grove, a head cleaner at Woolworths. A morose, abusive bunch, they were nevertheless all dedicated to keeping up appearances, and would have been shocked to discover that they were nurturing a ruthless little video-recorder among the lace mats and aspidistras.

When Osborne was seven the family moved out along the Waterloo–Effingham line into the raw Surrey suburbs, settling at Stoneleigh. He found the district charmless, though nearby Nonsuch park gave scope for Robin Hood games and sexual experiments with a local Maid Marian. His delicate health kept him away from school most of the time. He was subject to fainting fits, chronic bedwetting and acne, and contracted rheumatic fever which confined him for several months to a wheelchair and a draconian convalescent home in Dorset. On the rare occasions when he did enter the school playground, the other boys instantly recognized him as a cissy, and beat him up.

He did make one friend, though , a boy called Micky Wall whose parents ran a Ford saloon and enjoyed a slightly more spacious life-style than the average, which appealed to young Osborne's acute class-consciousness. There were seaside pic-nics, with Tizer and salmon sandwiches, and the two boys developed bookish tastes together – Stevenson, Kipling, Poe and Shaw's prefaces. They also spent an idyllic autumn gorging plums in the Walls's orchard and watching the Battle of Britain being fought overhead.

Having seen Osborne senior into his grave, the National Advertising Benevolent Society now generously sent the son to a small Devon boarding school, St Michael's. Those who admin-

ister such charities probably do not expect gratitude, and will
certainly find none here. Osborne, we learn, quickly identified
the place as a specious imitation of the high-class establishment
he should by rights have been sent to. The headmaster, he
complained, looked like a solicitor's clerk. Still, he learnt a lot at
St Michael's, progressing from almost total ignorance to School
Cert. standard. Excerpts from the school magazine which he
reprints show that he also gained proficiency in cricket and
boxing. He put this to use before he left by punching the
headmaster in the mouth and knocking him backwwards over
two tables – the man's offence being that he had switched off a
radio Osborne was listening to.

Armed with his School Cert. he entered journalism, joining
Gas World where his job was to scan the daily press for stories
with a gas interest. These were the days of National Service, but
after a look at his medical record the army decided that it would
have absolutely no use for him even in an emergency, so he
drifted, via the Gaycroft School of Music and Dancing, North
Cheam, to amateur dramatics and rep. Meanwhile he had
become engaged to a girl whom he jilted with what he admits
was 'callous indecency', though he comforted himself with the
thought that her father was 'the kind of man I knew my father
would have despised'.

The dole, dishwashing, and Christmas work with the GPO
eked out his meagre rewards as an actor. On tour he found
snugness and occasional sex in a succession of theatrical digs
with stuffed fox terriers in the front parlours, and collarless
husbands poring over racing papers in the back kitchens. He
liked it, but since he seldom hid his opinion of his professional
colleagues his spells of employment were brief.

For a time he ran his own company, subsisting on evaporated
milk and boiled nettles. Then, in rep at Bridgwater, he fell in
love with and married Pamela Lane, to the dismay of her parents
who (like Alison's in *Look Back in Anger*) hired private detectives
to investigate him. Osborne charitably points out that Mr and
Mrs Lane, despite this resemblance, belonged to a lower class
than Alison's family, had Somerset accents and were in trade.
The story ends (for now) with Pamela going off to Switzerland
with a virile dentist, and Osborne pouring his wounded feelings into *Look Back*.

These memoirs, like the play, are best when openly offensive.
Occasionally a sad, lofty tone creeps in, which ill becomes him.

It is absurd for him to wag his head over people who delight in others' discomfort, when he also tells us how at a London party he inserted a used condom into a sandwich and handed it to a much-hated actress, revelling in her appalled grimace. The mixed-up sexual feelings such an episode suggest are presumably, like his colourful malevolence, to be credited in some obscure way to his mother's effect on him. Since that malevolence revitalized the English stage, perhaps we should all spare her a little grateful applause. She will need something to cheer her up if she reads this book.

1981

The blackboard jumble

Edward Blishen's marathon memoirs began in 1955 with *Roaring Boys*, and additional volumes of self-exposure have been appearing regularly ever since. By rights, this shameless bid to make a living out of his life should have foundered long ago, for nothing especially momentous has ever happened to Blishen, or to the assorted kinsfolk he chronicles. That, though, is rather his point. The Blishen mission is to show that the commonplace is marvellous if you see it imaginatively enough, and in this new book, as usual, he rambles among his memories so beguilingly that your only worry is lest he should stop.

His big chance of observing the commonplace occurred back in the fifties when he taught for six years in a deadbeat North London secondary modern, tactfully disguised in his account as 'Stonehill Street'. It had a spine-chilling delinquency record, but Blishen is the sort of teacher who, dropped into *Paradise Lost*, would instantly recognize Satan as pathetically misunderstood (dreadful home background; autocratic father), and by the exertion of gentle cultural uplift would soon have the Prince of Darkness doing a paper-round and delighting in classroom readings of *Goblin Market*. That, roughly, was Blishen's effect on the Stonehill Street mafia. But his success did not reconcile him to the system. He continued to regard secondary moderns as a dirty trick played by society on its failures, and *Roaring Boys*, which put across this view, enjoyed considerable vogue among educationalists in the debate which gave birth to comprehensives.

*Donkey Work** restarts the story there. Alarmed to find himself an expert, without quite knowing what he's expert at, Blishen is taken up by the pedagogic establishment and flown out to give seminars in Canada and East Germany. The Canadians are genially vague about their guest's identity. Chairmen introduce him variously as the editor and TV critic of the *New Statesman* and, more cagily, as 'the author of many thoughts upon many

*Donkey Work by Edward Blishen (Hamish Hamilton).

themes'. The East Germans conduct all discussion on a high
theoretical plane, thus keeping safely out of touch with both
Blishen and reality. Back home, the new university of 'Ribches-
ter' (i.e. York, according to *Who's Who in Education)* makes him a
part-time lecturer. To the unprejudiced reader the place sounds
like hell on earth, with young academics rabbiting on about
D'Annunzio and Kierkegaard every mealtime, and a gruffly
impish Professor of Education ('Maurice') who pesters his
visitors about what books they've read, while burning their
breakfast toast.

Any normal person would want to wire Maurice up to this
obsolete toaster and pass several hundred volts through him.
Blishen, though, is charmed by the whole performance – which
makes one wonder, not for the first time, whether a little venom
would not improve his make-up. 'You've got a good word to say
for everybody,' his father once snapped, 'It drives me up the
wall.' Ironically his father is the one figure for whom good
words, in the Blishen archive, are very thinly spread.

A neat-minded philistine of gleaming respectability, the elder
Blishen's sole ambition was to climb from the lowest rank of the
civil service to the next one up. He spent his leisure patrolling
his immaculate rectangle of garden, and tearing off boughs from
his neighbours' shrubs if they fractionally infringed his air-
space. His retirement to a bungaloid strip of the south coast was
marred by the monstrous conduct of the seagulls which, he
believed, deliberately held in their massive excretions until they
were flying over his roof.

To a man of these sensibilities it was naturally devastating to
discover that he had begotten a mild-mannered highbrow like
Blishen, who refused to secure a decent office job and requested
– of all things – to go to university. It was the classic grammar-
school scholarship-boy set up – struggling, envious father;
terrified, obstinate son – and it swept the polite suburban
Blishens into screaming rages. This crisis, written up in *Sorry
Dad,* is still Blishen's best thing: the beady-eyed malice with
which he notes down his father's gaffes and vulgarities has
never been matched in intensity since – as if he used up a whole
lifetime's bile at one go.

But despite dad's absence *Donkey Work* has its own rich crop
of eccentrics – normal folk, all of them, except that they're caught
under Blishen's mischievously accurate lens. It's odd that the
teaching profession hasn't taken concerted action to silence him

before now, seeing that he portrays them so persistently as a set of lovable loonies.

Few of the educators he introduced into *A Nest of Teachers* seemed safe to be let out alone, and in this instalment we have the maidenly Miss Butcher, headmistress of the girls school adjoining Stonehill Street, who simply cannot fathom why the boys spend so much time peering over the fence at her girls. 'Do they wish to help pump up our footballs?' Equally unnerving is the male colleague, worried about the rarity with which he and his wife manage sexual relations, who keeps bursting into Blishen's classroom for a frank bout of comparative statistics.

In the art of generating embarrassment, though, these two are amateurs compared with Mrs Hoffnung, a majestic Austrian lady who conducts Blishen round the Metropolitan Museum of Art during a stopover in New York. Unluckily Blishen discovers, when he wishes to relieve himself, that the lavatories are situated on the far side of the entrance turnstiles, and Mrs Hoffnung takes up his case in ringing tones with the surprised attendants. 'He wants to go to the toilet. Can you not understand? Is it difficult to understand?' Half-blinded with shame Blishen plunges through the turnstile, grabs the nearest door handle, and finds himself in a broom closet. From the foyer, now filling with interested onlookers, Mrs Hoffnung continues to bellow helpfully. 'He is from London! He thinks it is a toilet!'

Hearing with awful clarity what people say has always been a Blishen strength, picked up during his apprenticeship as a reporter on a local newspaper (just as well he never got to university). He remembers in 1940 covering the funeral of a child killed in an air raid, and overhearing, incredulously, the dull priest remark beforehand 'I'm afraid the mother's going to be a nuisance'. Talk, in Blishen's hi-fi renderings of it, is dense with these traps and giveaways – dense, too, with unmeant comedy. If we really listened to what we say, he makes you feel, we'd never open our mouths.

His own style, though it seems as easeful as snoring, is a virtuoso creation, conveying his carefully unsystematized relations with reality. He zooms into his new landscape with poetic excitement – the St Lawrence, craggy with splintered ice; Vancouver, huddling eggshell-frail under its mountains. But he doesn't need the exotic to set him off. An outbreak of dry rot in the house; an experimental pipe of herbal tobacco – these, by the time he has finished with them, acquire positively operatic grandeur. Understanding people, he argues, is impossible: any person at any moment is the repository of thousands of pieces of trivial information. Only the writer who gives these their due can lift the veil from the mundane complexities that we all are. He works at it, here, as enjoyably as ever. Anyone lucky enough to have all Blishen still to read should lose no time starting.

1983

The flash of lightning

Do not read this book in public.* You will risk severe internal injuries from trying to suppress your laughter. What's worse, you can't put it down once started. Its addictive powers stun all normal, decent resistance within seconds. Australia, in Clive James's childhood memories, resembles an animated cartoon feature impacted with a disaster movie. Natural and unnatural hazards abound. Snakes of demonic temperament garrison the countryside, and venomous spiders zoom out of the ground, fitted with long-range fuel tanks and warheads.

Young James grew up in Jannali, a Sydney outpost of shacks, building lots and railway line, with non-stop sun and exotic flora turning every back yard into a Technicolor shellburst. Dad was a POW with the Japs. That left Mum and Aunt Dora – a giant lady who would hurtle through space at moments of crisis, corsets creaking like guy ropes, to snatch the infant James from peril. There was also grandpa, a senile agglomeration of smells and speech-impediments, whom one occasionally stumbled over in dark corners.

James comes across as the kind of child it would have been advisable to live in an entirely different part of the town from. He wasn't exactly a delinquent, but he had the same effect on his surroundings. Go-cart races, under his management, ended with treasured front gardens scythed flat and ambulances queueing to remove the wounded. Jumping off moving trains, another favourite sport, progressed through thresholds of daring, until a friend jumped off one which didn't happen to be stopping at the station at all and broke every bone in his body except his left femur. Building sites offered less costly fun: joyful hours were spent reducing tiles and porcelain lavatory bowls to their constituent molecules.

As an ardent patron of the local Odeon, James strove to model himself on screen heroes. In a cloak and mask run up by his patient mum he took to flitting through the streets at night,

Unreliable Memoirs by Clive James (Jonathan Cape).

designating himself the Flash of Lightning, until the cloak snagged on a fence he was climbing over and almost strangled its mythic wearer. Accidents seemed to follow him around, even when he was not directly responsible. A chemistry teacher, showing James's class how careful you must be when handling potassium, managed to ignite the school's entire supply, and was collected by another of the hard-worked ambulance crews.

Miraculously, no one actually died as a result of James's adventures, but it was a near thing. Employed as a bus conductor during a long vac from Sydney university, he unwittingly closed the automatic doors around the neck of an old lady who was about to step aboard. Her head and hat, decorated with wax fruits, remained inside, while the lower part of her person, still clutching two shopping baskets, contrived to keep pace with the accelerating vehicle, until her fellow passengers released her.

James's growth to sexual maturity is narrated with a frankness that would make the Cerne Abbas giant seem coy. Much of his boyhood was spent worrying about the size of his 'tonk' (as he disarmingly dubs it), and there was a nightmare moment at summer camp when he almost sliced it off whilst failing to clear a barbed-wire fence. Happily it survived and prospered, accompanying him actively through college and national service.

Behind all the brashness lay a tragedy. By a cruel trick of fate, James's father, having survived the Jap prison camp, died in an air crash on his way to rejoin his family at the war's end. The sight of his mother's agony scarred him, James believes, for life. He turned himself into a small-time hoodlum and class clown as a refuge from the abyss of despair he had glimpsed. Not that he credits himself with any extravagant filial sympathies. His account of his reactions is candid and unsparing, and he recalls with perfect accuracy the callousness with which youth arms itself against adult grief. His mother gets into the narrative only marginally, but her portrait is the more realistic for being almost hidden by the son's ego.

Cagily, James warns us that his book is a disguised novel – a figment got up to sound like truth. But that is all memories can ever amount to. Factual or not, it glows like life, and, despite the jokes, love suffuses everything – the marbles and cigarette cards and Saturday afternoon films; the candy bars which exploded over your tongue like honeyed shrapnel; the beach dryads wearing T-shirts and a dab of zinc cream on their noses. Even the grasshoppers, ticking away in the trees, glint like jewels from a lost paradise. His exuberance with words seems as natural as sun-tan, and makes you want to up sticks and head for NSW right away.

This is easily his best book to date – which is saying a lot. As a literary critic he often dazzles, but has the bad habit of dropping names like a punctured encyclopaedia (to compensate, maybe, for his unlettered youth). Here no smog of learning screens you from the full glare of the Jamesian imagination. Not to be missed.

1980

Death and the benefits of ignorance

About death, we're all in the dark. The one certainty is that those who pronounce upon it don't know what they're talking about. This makes it a special treat for the imagination, and in D. J. Enright's anthology it's the range of the imagining – the endless, death-defying marathon of make-believe – that impresses. Take afterlives. For Buddhists of the first century AD, heaven was a sort of lido where bathers found that the water rose exactly as high as they wished – to ankles, knees, hips or ears. Good Muslims, the Koran teaches, will sit hereafter on soft couches with dark-eyed virgins, 'as chaste as the sheltered eggs of ostriches'.

Christians, of course, look forward to what George Orwell once impiously described as choir practice in a jeweller's shop. But refinements on this basic formula abound. William King, Archbishop of Dublin, considered that observing the torments of the damned might be 'productive of some real happiness in heaven'. Others, like the poet Edward Young, have hoped to join the great minds of antiquity in an airborne discussion group.

Any, or all, of these may come true, or not. But read in bulk they're bizarre, and equally so are the things people have pictured death as – a river, a door, a horseman or, in the view of one American student quizzed by psychologists, a dark-suited stranger with a goatee – 'quiet and kind of scary: Death does not say much but it's almost impossible to outsmart him.' Almost?

We lend death these disguises because they make it distinct and familiar enough to contemplate. The word 'death' itself is a ruse of this sort – one of the battalion of abstract nouns we tidy up the universe with. 'There is no death,' cries Malroux clear-sightedly, 'There is only me, me, who is going to die.' Even that verb 'die' is ridiculously and optimistically active, given what it stands for. Dying is not something you do: it does for you. You'd need not language but a hole in language to express it.

*The Oxford Book of Death,** on the other hand, is solid

*The Oxford Book of Death ed. D. J. Enright (OUP).

language from start to finish, and that is why it is less harrowing, and less deathly, than you might fear. Once death has become a word, language can make it vanish like a conjuror's rabbit. 'Death', Wittgenstein announces decisively, 'is not an event in life. Death is not lived through.' For the logically minded that must be a great comfort. Dying, though, does have to be lived through, even by philosophers, and that is its main drawback. 'I'm not afraid to die', explains Woody Allen, 'I just don't want to be there when it happens.'

The bright side of death is canvassed by several of Enright's spokesmen. Life wouldn't be the same without it. 'It is our knowledge that we have to die which makes us human,' points out Alexander Smith. Work, art, science, humour and romantic love have all been invented in response to this inkling of impending cancellation, which the more backward animals lack. So, one must add, have other distinctively human benefits like war, torture and genocide, which enable people to feel a little less mortal by ensuring that others feel a lot more so.

Quite apart from these civilizing influences, death, its apologists argue, lets you out of something which no one would seriously want to persist in for ever. 'Whoever has lived long enough to find out what life is', muses Mark Twain, 'knows how deep a debt of gratitude we owe to Adam. He brought death into the world.' That sounds clever, but isn't. For it is precisely the presence of death, with its attendant fears and griefs, that makes us glad life isn't endless. If death hadn't been introduced, we shouldn't need it.

Still, as things stand Twain is right. Everyone wearies of life sooner or later, and if the human body came equipped with a simple 'off' switch none of us, surely, would have survived adolescence. It's the palaver suicide entails that keeps us from embarking on it. According to Erasmus, God deliberately made death horrible because He realized that if it weren't people would be killing themselves all over the place. Enright, whose introductions to the different departments of death add much wisdom to his book, suggests that it's our sense of the ridiculous, our dislike for melodrama, that deters us from self-slaughter. How, we ask, can we take ourselves so seriously?

Whether we do away with ourselves or not, there are the dead to dispose of – a pressing need, seeing how obscenely changed even the most loved flesh suddenly becomes. Sir Thomas Browne declared that the thought of death filled him with shame, not fear, since it would turn him, in an instant, into something his wife and children shunned. The resources surveyed in Jessica Mitford's *The American Way of Death* might have eased his mind. Tinted with Nature-Glo, 'the ultimate in cosmetic embalming', and with a choice of more than sixty colour-matched shades for his casket-lining, Sir Thomas could have done his folks credit. Alternatively they could have deep-frozen him to await a cure for death – a *naïveté* which it has taken the most advanced nation in world history to dream up. By comparison the sacred custom, among the Melanesians of New Guinea, of ritually eating their dead, seems healthy and realistic.

Statistics of mortality being what they are, one or two readers who started this review have probably passed on by now. But for those still here, Enright offers various alleviations. Leopardi, for example, tells us that death is not really painful, because in the final stages nature dulls the areas of sensation. Personally I'd prefer assurance on that point from someone with firsthand experience, though I quite see it's difficult to arrange.

In the sections of his book that might prove unbearable, like that on 'Children and Death', Enright mercifully soft pedals. The files of any children's ward could yield materials more desolating than anything here. But one of death's few redeeming features is that children understand it even less than we do – a fact confirmed by Freud's rather shocked story about a nine-year-old at the Natural History Museum who piped up 'I'm so fond of you, Mummy: when you die I'll have you stuffed.'

The 'Last Words' section also provides relief. It's strange, when you consider the terminal agonies surrounding them, how comic these utterances seem. Hegel, for instance, who expired with the words, 'Only one man ever understood me . . . and he didn't understand me', can surely not have intended to amuse. Our laughter, like the elation felt after funerals, shows us closing ranks against the dead out of relief at our own survival.

English culture in the last thirty years would be a lot poorer without Enright. A champion of ordinary existence against the whimsies of the over-educated, he might seem the natural choice for the Oxford Book of Life, not Death. But they come to the same in the end, and the only flaw in this bracingly cosmopolitan anthology, ranging from ancient China to *Dr Who*, is the omission of anything by himself. His 'On the Death of a Child' is the only twentieth-century poem which can vie, in tenderness and control, with Ben Jonson's elegy for his son. Despite this lack, his book is a tonic, as well as a wholesome draught of mortality, and should be widely popular – for death, as he says, if not the in thing is decidedly the coming thing.

1983

The sport of a mad master

Your first thought on finishing this magisterial biography of Robert Lowell is, What a Skunk.* Your second is that allowances must be made. Lowell was, after all, mad much of the time, so can't be held responsible, and in his saner spells friends often seem to have found him charming. For all that, the testimony which Hamilton busily and, it seems, quite benignly piles up spreads over Lowell's reputation like an attack of mange. He will never look the same again. You start disliking him quite early on. Thuggish, thick and narcissistic, he terrorized smaller boys at school and stole from them, earning the nickname 'Cal', which was short for both Caliban and Caligula – the emperor whose 'disgusting traits', an ex-classmate confided to Hamilton, Lowell's most resembled.

At Harvard he combined contempt for the mass of students with dismal academic showing. Noted for brute strength, he would pretend to be a bear, and used this jape to humiliate victims. Once he held Allen Tate out of a second-floor window while reciting Tate's poetry in his special bear voice – which must, admittedly, have been quite funny if you weren't Tate. Not all his violence was gamesome. When his father wrote reproving him for his conduct with a girlfriend, Lowell rushed to the family home and struck him down. During a bout of drunken driving, he rammed a wall, smashing the nose of his wife-to-be Jean Stafford. It took a series of painful operations to repair it: then Lowell punched her and smashed it again.

These lapses did not prevent him taking a sanctimonious line on public occasions. His graduation day address emphasized that aristocrats like himself and his audience must maintain a 'superior way of life', and guard against the incursions of Philistines and Goths. For someone with this keen sense of his natural election, the Catholic Church had potent charms. Once converted, Lowell's tyranny over his wife became a sacred duty. She was subjected to Mass each morning, Benediction each

*Robert Lowell: A Biography by Ian Hamilton (Faber).

evening, and two rosaries a day. Newspapers and sexual relations were banned.

Jean, whose success as a novelist enabled her to buy a house for Lowell to live in, recalls having to clean up after he and his poetic pals had staggered to bed, 'sodden, but not too far gone to lose their conceit'. Though he counted on her for these domestic chores, he despised her for being plebeian enough to do them, and ended the marriage after five years with 'calm, olympian brutality'.

At the same time he threw over the Catholic Church, announcing that it had 'served its purpose'; but he retained some traits of the religious fanatic. Fiercely anti-Communist, he had supported the Franco side in Spain, and in 1949 on the eve of the McCarthy era he took part in an ugly piece of witch-hunting at Yaddo writers' colony, where a woman organizer, whose hospitality he had often enjoyed, came under suspicion, quite falsely, of harbouring a Soviet agent. Lowell demanded that she be fired, and warned the Yaddo curators that, if they disobeyed him, he would stir up his 'influential friends in the world of culture'. Luckily this bullying failed, and several authors signed a petition deploring the threat to civil liberties Lowell represented. But Lowell remained convinced of God's approval, and proclaimed that his attempt at victimization had been rewarded by 'an incredible outpouring of grace'.

The outpouring proved too copious. Lowell was found running round the streets of Bloomington, Indiana, crying out against devils and homosexuals, and it took four policemen to get him into a straitjacket. On his release from hospital, the writer Elizabeth Hardwick took him in and married him, because he had no place to go. 'How happy we'll be together, writing the world's masterpieces', he burbled with his usual modesty. During the next sixteen years he had nine breakdowns, and it became a nightmare to Elizabeth, since it always fell to her to call the police and have him committed, both for her own safety and for that of their child.

The attacks followed a habitual pattern. Lowell would grow manic, 'talking like a machine gun, with blazing eyes', and fall tempestuously in love. Once it was with Jackie Kennedy, once with an air hostess whom he tried to remove from the plane so that they could start a new life together in South America. In this phase he would put on outrageous acts – climbing naked on equestrian statues; standing up at the opera and conducting.

Simple-minded fans adored these capers, thinking it was how a real poet ought to carry on. Then would come the punch-ups, the padded cells, the electric shock treatment. On recovery, he tended to ditch his used girlfriends abruptly. A Latvian dancer, whom he had introduced all round as his future wife, received his adieu in the shape of an instruction from his solicitors to quit the flat he had rented for her within two days.

This high-handedness went with his sense of patrician rank. He loved studying his distinguished ancestry, and was fascinated by other supermen. He would extol Hitler, and refer humorously to his extermination of the Jews. The need to put down the negroes was another conversational enthusiasm. Given these tastes, the attention of the British upper crust naturally flattered him. The young Earl of Gowrie got a job as Lowell's assistant at Harvard, and was pleased to find that his employer made 'the same sort of jokes as my mates at Oxford and Eton'.

At All Souls for a visiting fellowship Lowell, now fifty-three, met the Guinness heiress Lady Caroline Blackwood, and romance blossomed. Elizabeth, who had given up her teaching post to join her husband in England, found herself and their daughter quietly abandoned. Her reactions make painful reading: 'My utter contempt for both of you for the misery you have brought to two people who had never hurt you knows no bounds.' Worse, she discovered that Lowell planned to publish excerpts from her frantic letters, telegrams and phone calls in a series of poems about the break-up. Even staunch friends expressed shock at this degree of cruelty, and when the poems appeared they were understandably seen by feminist critics as a display of aggrandized and merciless masculinity.

The harm Lowell's personality did to his poetry is clear. Its irresponsible obscurity, and its tedious preoccupation with his family and personal history, reflect his self-absorption. Hamilton quotes damaging criticism of these aspects from other commentators, and adds some of his own. He does not, it's true, produce anything that makes you feel Lowell's poetry deserved the admiring attention it got twenty years ago. But that would need a different book, and one probably now unwritable. The book he does give us combines tough intelligence, tireless research, and a proper respect for the suffering it probes. The documentation – unpublished letters, interviews – is massive. Lowell's renowned public stands – his conscientious objection in the Second World War, his protest over Vietnam – lose their heroic simplicity and are seen for the first time in the context of his private morass. It is a remarkable addition to the annals of literature.

1983

Larkin: poet of deprivation

In one of the reviews and interviews collected here* Larkin
condemns Pound, Picasso and modernist art generally for being
'in contradiction of human life as we know it'. The normal
reader, coming upon this, feels like cheering at the spectacle of
sanity creeping back into critical discourse. But as he works
through the rest of the volume the suspicion steals over him that
Larkin's own resemblance to human life as we know it is not
very close. His attitude to most accredited sources of pleasure
would make Scrooge seem unduly frolicsome. Marriage, the
company of other people, the environment ('I don't really notice
where I live'), children ('selfish, noisy, cruel, vulgar little
brutes'), books ('I don't read much'), theatre and foreign travel
are surveyed with uniform distaste. He concedes, in a rare
upsurge of zest, that he wouldn't mind seeing China if he could
come back the same day. But this apart, he gives a convincing
impression of having had his life-support system inadvertently
unplugged.

This nullness, though it makes him rather an unzippy interviewee, lies near the heart of his power as a poet. Like his hero
in *Jill* he understands 'how appallingly little life is'. His acceptance of futility, and the glum wit with which he faces it, make
him a spokesman for our age, which has to find a way of
surviving in the aftermath of belief and hope. Larkin is a
modern stoic, today's Seneca. It's absurd to bemoan the fewness
of his poems. If he were more prolific, it would falsify everything he stands for. Sterility is his element. 'Deprivation for me',
he volunteers, 'is what daffodils were for Wordsworth' – which
is true, except that Larkin on deprivation is better than Wordsworth on daffodils.

Here and there in the book you get glimpses of what has
shaped his belligerently negative personality. He was at Oxford
during the war when clothes rationing, food rationing and

*Required Writing: Miscellaneous Pieces 1955–1982 by Philip Larkin
(Faber).

conscription had put an end to the pansy falderols of the thirties. Empty coal scuttles, closed restaurants – the austerity of the place entered his soul and came to seem right and good. He remembers the shock, on a post-war visit to Oxford, of seeing an undergraduate with shoulder-length curls and a skyblue cloak, and realizing that the foolery was starting again.

The roots of his diminished expectations go back beyond Oxford, though. At school he felt an outsider, mocked and shy. He stammered so badly that at railway ticket offices he had to hand in scraps of paper stating his destination, instead of trying to speak. He was acutely short-sighted, though no one realized it, so classes were a matter of sitting in foggy dread, waiting for questions to be sprung on him. After a while the masters left him pityingly alone. Most of the character-traits that toughen Larkin's writing could be traced either to this early taste of ostracism, or to a nostalgia for wartime drabness, which many of his generation share.

Unlike many modern poets, he does not think that being unintelligible is a vital qualification for the job. Having known dumbness, he values communication. He hates show-offs, bohemians, and anyone who associates being an artist with spouting foreign languages, committing adultery and shirking the washing up. He questions the sacred modernist assumption that any person who can produce a medical certificate of recent insanity should automatically rank, as a writer, above those who cannot.

He sides with the common man, who pays good money for a book and expects to be entertained in return. His application of the pleasure principle in real life makes refreshing reading. He recalls the relief he felt when he first realized you could walk out of a theatre. It was at a performance of *The Playboy of the Western World*, and when the bell rang at the end of the interval he thought 'Am I enjoying myself? No, I've never watched such stupid balls.' So he had another drink and walked out into the evening sunshine.

These standards make him suspicious of Arts Council subsidies, National Assistance, and anything else that protects the irresponsible and the work-shy. His vision of a typical university English course is of droves of supine youngsters signing on each autumn to unriddle nonsense which no writer would dare produce if there weren't a captive audience being given grants to wade through it.

He announces rather primly that his own education 'was at no time a charge on public or other funds'. Presumably his solitude as a lad helped to harden these ideas of self-reliance. On the other hand, as university librarian he draws his income from public funds, so he does not seem ideally placed to champion a strict market economy. His politics, he admits, are instinctive, not reasoned. He identifies the Right with thrift and hard work; the Left with idleness, greed and treason. 'I adore Mrs Thatcher.'

Much of this is leg-pull, one hopes. He likes to tease. The *Paris Review* interviewer, evidently a severely cultural type, asks his view of Jorge Luis Borges. 'Who is Jorge Luis Borges?' returns Larkin equably. No doubt it was in a similarly jestful spirit that he included here a long address delivered at the Standing Conference of National and University Librarians, an item so slumberously dull that it is punctuated, in the reader's imagination, by soft thuds as the less hardy custodians nod off and slump to the carpet.

A puzzle is why Larkin decided to omit from the book his most engaging piece of autobiography, published in an ephemeral magazine called *Umbrella* in 1959. There he recalled his childhood in Coventry more cheerfully than he seems to now – the Eldorado box-tricycle selling lime-green and strawberry-pink ices; the walk to school past a line of munching, nose-bagged station horses; the elaborate games played with Famous Cricketers cigarette cards, where the star was Bradman 'enclosed in a legend that grew bigger daily like a gigantic indestructible crystal'.

He talks about his friends, including Jim, a boy from a slightly higher income bracket, who lived in a big house with a tennis court and a spare room for the Hornby layout. When you played there, Chelsea buns and Corona were brought up at eleven. He and Jim corresponded for ten years – 'real letters, that is, not dependent on time or place'. As usual in those days, girls remained an unknown species: he grew up 'to regard sexual recreation as a socially remote thing like baccarat or clog dancing'.

The whole piece is a gem, and its omission here woeful. Still, there are compensations – classic articles on Betjeman and Hardy; book reviews about Auden, Wilfred Owen, Edward Thomas and many others, written with Larkin's bracing mixture of punch and subtlety; plaudits for Ian Fleming, Barbara Pym, detective novels, jazz; personal anecdotes – Larkin whizzing down the fast lane of the M1 blinded by tears at Wordsworth's 'Immortality Ode' coming over the car radio. Simply because it's by Larkin, *Required Writing* is required reading for anyone who cares about contemporary literature – and, of course, for those supine droves who sign on each autumn.

1983

The joy of Heaney

'Remember everything and keep your head' a friendly ghost tells Seamus Heaney in *Station Island*.* In Ireland, where memory has traditionally entailed blood crying for vengeance, that is hard advice to follow. Heaney, a big gentle bear caught in the sectarian crossfire, must be almost equally sick by now of fellow Catholics chivvying him to write political verse, and bland English critics congratulating him on not taking sides. During the seventies his poetry gravitated towards deep, dark places – wells, peat bogs – where he could escape from the pack and become absorbed instead in the soft textures of decay that had haunted him since childhood.

He looked, in these depths, for himself. More than any other poet since Wordsworth he can make us understand that the outside world is not outside but what we are made of. Our feelings are echoes of the realities we touch and see. 'Nature', as Cézanne said, 'is on the inside.' And thought, on this reckoning, is a spindly offshoot thrown up by dense mulches of sensation which begin to gather in us at birth – or in the womb. 'We are earthworms of the earth', one of the new poems proposes, 'and all that has gone through us is what will be our trace.'

What goes through Heaney is as random as most life, but he weighs and sounds it to discover how it has helped to bring him about. A clutter of keepsakes in the poem-sequence 'Shelf Life' includes a granite chip from Joyce's Martello tower, 'jaggy, salty, punitive', which he recognizes as an opposite of himself. An old pewter plate, slithery, fogged-up, gives him an image of his own soul. His poems swoop, without warning, back along memory trails, and the reader must watch for these time-warps to forestall bafflement. 'Sheelagh na Gig' (a title which, like others of Heaney's, pointedly offers no help to the Brits) seems to be about the adult Heaney looking at a carved woman under some eaves, but suddenly lands us in a barn where the boy Heaney watches grain being poured from a sack's 'lapped and supple

Station Island by Seamus Heaney (Faber).

mouth' and notices, under the thatch, the dark entry of a bird's nest or rat hole. It is not just, we are meant to realize, that the carving reminds him of that childhood thrill. What he sees is fixed and limited by what he once saw. Reality is personal and cumulative.

It also consists of things rather than words. A poem about a long-dead child (a sister, one gathers, who died in infancy) centres on a seaside trinket, a grotto of glued shells, that she once owned. After her death it was stowed away in tissue paper, but to take it out and touch it – 'like touching birds' eggs' – was a surer arousal of her presence, and absence, than words could manage. Feeling and object were too closely knit for language to intrude, and words themselves, in Heaney's scheme, sink back into things at last. He imagines them drifting through the summer like pollen, settling in 'the uvulae of stones' and 'the soft lungs of hawthorn'.

Each object in Heaney's thickly sensuous world comes packed with all its past, like a memory. 'The Sandpit' takes the housing estate which his grandparents moved to when he was small, and disintegrates it into its constituent sand and gravel so as to watch it slowly grow again. Whatever happened around the houses as they were built – the workers' daydreams, the sound of river water – was tapped like a code into the walls with each chop of the bricklayer's trowel, or so Heaney would have us feel. Even a house brick, he wants to remind us, stands at the intersection of an immemorially complicated past and an inconceivably complicated future.

It is this insight, applied to people, that deters Heaney from the simplification of the intellect that political alignment requires. He will not swell the ranks. But he feels guilty at his own tameness, especially as he acknowledges the gut loyalties of an Ulster Catholic. The 'Station Island' sequence, the heart of this new book, is an act of self-accusation. Set on a pilgrimage site in Lough Derg, Co. Donegal, where Heaney wanders among the worshippers, it recounts a series of dream meetings with familiar ghosts. One, 'a bleeding, pale-faced boy, plastered in mud', is Heaney's cousin, Colum McCartney, who was shot through the head by Protestant terrorists while driving home one Sunday in Co. Armargh. Heaney commemorated McCartney in his last collection *Field Work*. But the ghost arraigns him for those gentle, unvengeful verses, and demands tribal solidarity.

He does not get it. For the last ghost, met in the car park, is that of James Joyce, brisk, cutting, who tells Heaney to get a hold of himself, stop wringing his hands, and forget about Irish national grudges: 'That subject people stuff is a cod's game/ infantile, like your peasant pilgrimage'. What Heaney, in Joyce's voice, commands himself to strike out for is loneliness and joy – not 'doing the decent thing' but probing along tangents beyond the expected.

Heaney's translation of the medieval Irish story *Sweeney Astray*† fits in more aptly here than you might suppose. A pagan king of Ulster who was turned into a bird for daring to strike a Christian priest, Sweeney can be taken, Heaney points out, as a figure of the displaced, guilty artist. His defiance of the cleric, for which he was doomed to flap around Ireland living off water- cress, is a version of the quarrel, close to Heaney, between the free creative imagination and the constraints of religious or political obligation.

Despite the fancied escape into a magic bird that Heaney organizes, *Station Island* is a worried book, and the richer for it. If any crumb of comfort can be gleaned from the communal agony of Northern Ireland, it is that Ireland's major living poet has not greeted the tragedy with rhetoric and commitment (always plentiful commodities) but with appropriately modern reactions of doubt, pain and self-distrust. The poems cling to objects and textures partly because they, unlike people, can be relied on not to denounce you or demand your allegiance. A piece of sandstone is commended for being 'reliably dense and bricky'; sloe gin (which gets a brief, glittering poem all to itself) is pronounced 'bitter and dependable'.

Writing for his children Heaney recommends education not in ideas but things. Through touch and sight the personality will find its depth. He walks with his daughter to a pump where a bird has nested, and watches her gently uncap it to see the single egg. It will be good to remember this, he tells her, when she has grown away and stands 'at the very centre of the empty city'. Why it will be good, he does not explain, or need to. His poetry does not argue, it makes itself felt. Nor does it deceive with hope. Flying a kite with his sons, he makes them take the string to feel 'the strumming, rooted, long-tailed pull of grief'

†*Sweeney Astray* by Seamus Heaney (Faber).

which they were born for. The outer world informs and creates the inner.

Heaney's large public is in luck. *Station Island* surpasses even what one might reasonably expect from this magnificently gifted poet.

1984

Bringing it all back home

One quality Craig Raine lacks is dignity. We should all be very glad about that. Though useful for politicians, patriots, and other ritualists, dignity in poets is apt to stun the imagination like *rigor mortis*. Raine, by contrast, unstiffens the contents of the known world so that they float free and couple in exultant, unheard-of metaphors. Like Whitman or Christopher Smart, he applauds the universe. The title poem of this dazzling new collection* is a hymn to Life or Nature – a nameless 'She' whose bounty the poet harvests and transmutes into language. It is all, thank goodness, a far cry from *The Waste Land*, and the indictment of earthly existence as foul and absurd, which has been a sacred tenet of Modernism from Eliot to Beckett.

Raine's undignified liking for life is a family gift, or so we gather from the hilarious and tender autobiographical essay which is one of the outstanding pleasures of this volume. His father, an unemployed ex-boxer turned spiritualist and faith healer, was a formidably indecorous figure, given to publicly cursing his foes – sometimes with fearful effect. A magistrate who deprived him of his publican's license for receiving stolen liquor lost his wife in a car crash within a week. Quite apart from this paranormal knack, Raine senior was a physiology lesson and horror film rolled into one. He had been blown up in a munitions factory during the war, a mishap which occasioned five major brain operations and left him with soft dents in the top of his skull which young Raine was allowed to finger. Slivers of bloody bone would occasionally exit from these holes. He also had epileptic fits, and whimpering trances during which he would seem to be trying to pick shreds of mangled flesh off his clothes – the remnants, his family presumed, of his colleagues in the munitions factory.

Despite these setbacks, Raine clearly adored his father, enraptured by his strength and by the lavish gouts of Dettol he slurped into his bathwater. Visiting him during his recurrent

Rich by Craig Raine (Faber).

spells in hospital, he would climb into his bed in shoes and raincoat to consume pots of malt extract which his father had lovingly hoarded. This sensuous education made up for the lack of more usual social advantages. The family lived in a damp prefab, and Raine's only book as a child was a cartoon version of Stevenson's *Kidnapped*, stitched together by his mother from the pages of a comic weekly.

Being excused literature throughout his formative years must have helped to generate Raine's poetic originality. But he has caught up on book-learning since. He worships James Joyce, and shares his respect for the uncensored stuff of experience, including those anatomical details such as chicken pox scars or the furrows left by underwear elastic, which elegant accounts of the human frame tend to gloss over. One poem here celebrates the simulated iron filings in a woman's shaved armpits and 'the harelip glistening' between her legs. Another poem, 'Arsehole', caused a flutter a year or two back when the *Observer* foolishly refused to publish it. In fact it is a graceful – almost flowery – attempt to create beauty where ugliness is normally seen. That seems a sound policy for poets nowadays. At a time when words like 'nuclear warhead' can be used in public without anyone apparently considering them obscene, it seems important to stress that the human body is decent and mentionable, all over, inside and out.

Another sphere of activity rather sniffed at by the high-minded which Raine redeems for poetry is ordinary family life – washing up, taking the kids for a walk. You get no hint from Raine, as you would certainly have done from any poet worth his salt a few years back, that such humdrum occupations are essentially inferior to reading Heidegger or brushing up your Celtic mythology.

What differentiates life from death, Raine brings us round to seeing, is in the last resort a mass of cherished incidentals – like the smell of fresh pencil sharpenings, or (in 'Widower', which commemorates a dead woman) the sight of a crumb of yolk caught in the hairs beside her smile as she pushed her breakfast tray away. In one of the most moving poems, 'The Man Who Invented Pain', the recital of the trivial becomes a valiant weapon against extinction. It tells the story of a soldier who was shot for releasing a basket of carrier pigeons. He spent the hours before his execution composing, for his parents' benefit, a year's supply of letters home, to be posted at regular intervals.

Raine's metaphors themselves are often miniature protests against stillness or deadness. He likes angular things which suggest, by their cramped posture, imminent movement. A lobster on a plate crouches like a wicket keeper; a deckchair waits 'poised like a cricket'. The world is about to spring, or split: a railway station presents itself as a 'terminus of zips'. Boundlessly inventive, Raine clicks his magic lantern and shows wildly divergent creatures hiding in the same object. One moment a grand piano is resting its head on its hand, listening to Mozart; the next, it has transformed into a shark – a 'grinning grand/with its dangerous fin'.

Like Picasso, from whom this book takes its epigraph, Raine pursues fugitive likenesses which do not normally occur, but would if the world were squashed or bent a little. John Donne was another poet who enjoyed this kind of spatial adventure. Raine sees a pack of luggage labels on his desk as a 'synopsis of leeks', trailing blanched roots. The image works only if you imagine flattened, geometrical leeks, which is what 'synopsis' invites you to do.

A poem about a servant girl who smashes her skull falling downstairs ends with a doctor turning the dead face to discover 'a phrenologist's head' – the newsprint from a paper, which someone has tidily slipped under the opened skull, has transferred itself, back to front, on to the brain. A moment's thought tells you it could not happen. In real death, a mess of blood, hair and bone would come between Raine and the inscribed white china head he wants to imagine. But he has persisted, for all that, in imagining it – adapting normality to suit his imperious vision.

This quest beyond the actual gives him an interest in people whose faculties have been massively disrupted, or have not yet developed. Two poems are about men who have had strokes, and are amazedly tottering back into the universe which we accept as normal. Another poem inspects the modifications to ordinary perception caused by extreme hunger; and 'Inca', the most haunting item in the book, is about a child – Raine's small daughter. Because she is ignorant, new to the world, and pre-literate, the idea that she inhabits the same time and space as us is, Raine sees, an illusion. Her perceptions are unguessable. Like every child, she is as lost and unreachable as an Inca.

On the strength of these exploratory poems, Raine might, I suppose, qualify as an 'experimental' writer – if that word had not become an infallible signal for feeble-witted, self-absorbed authorial gamesomeness. For prospective readers, what needs to be proclaimed is that Raine, far from being in that gruesome category, is enormously enjoyable, one of the three or four poets now writing in English whose every new book – every new poem – deserves to be awaited with eager impatience.

1984